The Harrowsmith

Perennial Garden

The Harrowsmith

Perennial Garden

Flowers for Three Seasons
Patrick Lima

Camden House

© Copyright 1987 by
Camden House Publishing

Canadian Cataloguing in Publication
Data

Lima, Patrick
   The Harrowsmith perennial garden

Includes index.
ISBN 0-920656-74-9

1. Perennials.   I. Title.

SB434.L45 1987 635.9'32 C87-094878-4

Library of Congress Catalogue Card
Number: 87-072625

Front Cover: *Iris reticulata*. Photograph
by Derek Fell

Back Cover: Pansies (*Viola* spp) in
foreground, with tulips, irises, chives and
budding peonies behind. Photograph by
John Scanlan

Trade distribution by
Firefly Books
3520 Pharmacy Avenue, Unit 1-C
Scarborough, Ontario
Canada M1W 2T8

Printed in Canada for
Camden House Publishing
(a division of Telemedia Publishing Inc.)
7 Queen Victoria Road
Camden East, Ontario
K0K 1J0

Designed by
Linda J. Menyes

Colour separations by
Herzig Somerville Limited
Toronto, Ontario

Printed and bound in Canada by
D.W. Friesen & Sons Ltd.
Altona, Manitoba

Printed on 80-lb. Friesen Matte

Dedicated to Nancy Lou and Palmer Patterson, with gratitude.

Certain perennials are so showy that the remainder of the garden is best designed around them. Daffodils and tulips, for instance, are the theme plants of spring, while lilies such as the pale yellow 'Dawn Star,' LEFT, become the focal points in July or August, months when most of the popular perennials have already ceased flowering. Although lilies have a reputation for being difficult to grow, they are in fact easy-care plants that bloom in a range of colours and conformations and can be easily propagated.

Contents

Among the northern perennials that bloom in April and May—a full five weeks on average—are polyanthus primroses, which are available in countless colours and variations in form. After a number of years, provided the original plant has been given the shady, moist conditions it requires, it can be divided easily into several of its kind. Division is a method of propagation that applies to many perennials and means that gardeners can fill large spaces inexpensively.

Introduction

Much of the rosy glow in the early-summer garden is provided by pinks, species of Dianthus *valued both for their neat mounds of silver or green foliage and for their extravagant crops of spice-scented flowers. About a dozen species of pinks have been grown at Larkwhistle, where the sweet, sandy soil suits the flowers well.*

In this, Patrick Lima's second book-length exploration of his labour of love known as Larkwhistle, he describes the Ontario garden's specialty, perennial flowers. From the time its first snowdrops and crocuses bloom in April, through the bursting of spectacular delphiniums and irises in early summer, until fall, with its sunny daisies and day lilies, Larkwhistle shines like a small, bright jewel on the green arm that is the Bruce Peninsula, a promontory that divides Lake Huron from Georgian Bay. The garden's colour and vitality are the result of neither site nor situation – this is a flat former hayfield where winter temperatures can plummet to minus 40 degrees – but of carefully chosen and situated plants, which present viewers (and there are many) with constantly changing pictures of amiable grace. *The Harrowsmith Illustrated Book of Herbs* (Camden House, 1985) outlined the ways in which Lima and his partner, John Scanlan, worked with various herbs – culinary, medicinal and simply historical – to produce a garden that was both beautiful and useful. This time, Lima expands his scope to cover the three seasons of work and wonder that are the lot of the perennial flower gardener.

A perennial is, of course, a flower that "lives from one season to the next, repeating each year the process of leafing out, flowering and seed-

they needed or missed. As Lima writes, "After cultivating both food and flowers organically for more than a decade, I feel that no crop, let alone a drift of summer colour, is worth coaxing with chemicals." The beauty of this particular garden, then, is not forced or temporary or exploitive. Larkwhistle is cared for as a living entity, whose soil and plants will continue to improve at least as long as Lima and Scanlan are its caretakers.

Rather than an encyclopaedia of all perennial flowers, this is a guide to only the most impressive of those that grow at Larkwhistle. The book is set up chronologically, from the earliest spring blossoms to the final blush of autumn. Because some flowers bloom briefly and others for quite a long time, however, overlaps occur. If it were not necessary to divide books into chapters, what one would see here would be a single narrative describing a flowing process of plant growth, bloom and fading until the ground freezes. The timing of this process is dependent upon climate. For readers in other areas, what Lima describes as the June garden may occur in May or even July, but the relative sequence will remain constant, daffodils almost always preceding peonies and so forth. Only small adjustments, garnered from a year's experience, will be needed to make the book's chronology fit one's particular circumstances.

"Gardening is a gentle art, a lively science," Lima muses. "The rhythmic physical work outdoors refreshes and strengthens the body and often calms the mind. When we touch the earth and involve ourselves cooperatively with nature's cycles, we reaffirm our link with the living planet that sustains us."

It is this attitude that has its manifestation in the glorious garden that is Larkwhistle. If both the author's creed and his knowledge — as dependent upon one another as a hand and trowel — are communicated to others by this book, there should soon be many gardens as fine as Larkwhistle, even if they are no larger than a single border, their creation no more complex than a single moment of inspiration.   — *Jennifer Bennett*

ing," as Lima writes in the first chapter. A few biennials, which can be treated much as perennials, are included too, but in either case, the flowers that rate top marks with Lima are those that are hardy enough to survive the winters and are also attractive, easy to tend and noninvasive. In addition, the plants cannot be overly susceptible to diseases, because Larkwhistle is tended organically. No chemical pesticides or fertilizers are used there, nor are

Larkwhistle in June presents pictures of gently harmonizing colours that characterize the Ontario garden from April to October. Tended organically, the garden is as easy on the environment as it is peaceful and beautiful: "When we touch the earth and involve ourselves cooperatively with nature's cycles, we reaffirm our link with the living planet that sustains us."

Seasons in the Sun

A consideration of perennial gardens

Each bed or border of perennial flowers brings its own gifts, with colours changing from day to day throughout the three seasons of a northern garden such as Larkwhistle. While a perennial is any plant that lives from one year to the next, perennials intended to keep a northern garden colourful must also be hardy, that is, capable of surviving cold winter temperatures.

Flower gardens are created for pleasure, pure and simple. And what pleasure Larkwhistle provides my partner and me! After more than a decade, an early-morning tour of our flowerbeds is still more of a certainty than breakfast is — and every bit as nourishing. Each bed or border brings its own gifts: fat bumblebees, brilliant butterflies, the sultry scent of trumpet lilies and the heady bouquet of peonies. Colours change from day to day, flower following flower as the days warm into summer, then cool toward autumn. Trilling red-wings, yodelling bobolinks and, of course, whistling meadowlarks sound the signals for changes of phase and bloom as Larkwhistle, this place of rest and revival, this garden I call home, makes its own stately way through yet another spring, summer and fall, the three glorious seasons of northern perennials.

Larkwhistle is devoted to perennials. Here, the moment the snow curtain lifts in March, the drama of a new season begins. At this early date, the maple trees in the woods across the way are holding their buds in check, lilac and honeysuckle shrubs stand stark and leafless against the pale sky, and the vegetable beds are bare. But in the flower garden, things are happening already. After a day or two of south winds and sunshine, tentative sparks of colour appear along border edges and there are signs of stirring everywhere. The flower garden is full of promise and potential. Imagination propels us through the coming months, conjuring up the colours and fragrances hidden in emerging shoots and winter-tousled mats. Soon, the impressive noses of crown imperials and the lesser snouts of other spring bulbs push through the cool earth and seem to sniff out the prospects of growing weather. Bleeding hearts, columbines and aconites begin to unfurl their foliage in a slow fan dance, while rough, hairy tufts of Oriental poppies stretch to catch the sun and many other garden dwellers respond, in their own way, to an irresistible urge to grow.

We have not planted a single thing this spring, but from the time the first snowdrop rings a silent signal, we can look forward to waves of flowers — just ripples at first — following each other over the half year, April to September, which we cherish as our growing season. Snowdrops and crocuses give way to daffodils and primroses. These exit a month later, as tulips, bleeding hearts and creeping phlox take the stage against a backdrop of perfumed lilacs. As June bows in, a rainbow of irises fills the garden, fat Oriental poppies pop their furry buds in small explosions of scarlet, and spicy pinks swarm along the border edges. Soon, peonies loll their opulent pink and crimson flowers onto a spread of silver artemisia, and tapered foxgloves spire up behind old-fashioned roses. Lilies that have been inching upward all these weeks finally hang out exotic Turk's-caps — vibrant orange, wine-dark or soft yellow — above a cloud of baby's-breath. It won't be long, then, before the tall mullein candles flicker among wands of rose loosestrife and yellow day lilies. Showy stonecrop keeps its corner of the garden presentable from the time its succulent silver rosettes emerge until heads of mauve-pink flowers, a rest-stop for passing butterflies, mellow to warm brown, in keeping with the autumn scene.

Perennial Pleasures

"When spring arrives," a friend responded after I asked her why she plants perennials, "three-quarters of my gardening work is already done. Many of the decisions about what goes where have been made. There's always something happening in a perennial bed: new plants flowering as others fade, a specially planned picture coming to life. It's exciting to watch the progress of perennials."

In the widest sense, a perennial is any plant that lives from one season to the next, repeating each year the process of leafing out, flowering and seeding. (In contrast, annuals such as marigolds and nasturtiums accomplish all they have to do in one season. Once they have matured and dispersed seeds, they die.) Perennial plants intended to keep a northern garden colourful from year to year

must also be hardy, that is, capable of surviving a full-blown northern winter. All of the plants discussed in this book, except for a few disappointments duly noted, have endured several winters in central Ontario, where temperatures can drop to minus 40 degrees for short periods. However, a heavy snow cover, the very best protection for plant roots, invariably insulates our ground. Readers in areas where winters are either cold and dry or unpredictable in temperature and precipitation may have a different tale to tell about some of the perennials that we find successful.

The dependable snow has encouraged us to fill our garden with plants that hibernate underground for part of the year. To "hardy" and "perennial," therefore, as descriptions of most of our plants, I must add "herbaceous," a term that defines a plant's stems and leaves as soft and sappy, unlike the hard, woody, more or less permanent framework of shrubs and trees. The foliage and stems of many herbaceous plants die back to ground level over winter, while the roots remain dormant but alive, to sprout a fresh sheaf of greenery and a new crop of flowers each season. But not all perennials retreat for the cold months; pinks, candytuft, creeping phlox, arabis and other brave mountain plants keep their leaves year-round. These are hardy evergreen, or "evergrey," herbaceous perennials. Throughout the text, when I use the word "perennial," the more exact term "hardy herbaceous perennial" is implied.

Hardy plants of one kind or another can bring colour and beauty to every corner of a garden, but success is more likely to attend gardeners who know their plants. In the chapters that follow, I will make the introductions. After that, guided tours through other gardens—especially at times when your own lacks colour—will always be instructive, as will strolls around botanical gardens and trips to local nurseries. Wherever you go, take note of plants that not only appeal to you but also appear to be thriving in an environment similar to your own.

The Environment

The first step, then, toward a thriving flower garden is an assessment of that environment. Take a look at your own situation, and indulge in flights of fancy tempered by a realistic appraisal of the site. Before you select plants, it is important to determine if their once-and-future home will suit them. Questions to ask are:
• How long does the sun shine here each day and for what part of the day? Sun-loving plants generally need about six hours of sunlight to thrive, but sunrise until noon or a midday spell of sunshine is more

There is always something to look forward to in a perennial garden. At Larkwhistle, FACING PAGE, *tulips give way to irises bordered by pansies, and soon after, peonies burst into bloom. These plants die back to ground level over winter, but a few, such as the hardy mountain plants white double arabis and pink creeping phlox,* ABOVE, *are evergreen or "evergrey" perennials that brave the winter above ground.*

productive of growth than, say, 3 p.m. until dusk. Is there more light in spring before nearby deciduous trees leaf out? If that is the case, the early spring-blooming bulbs and many native woodlanders can be planted generously. I find it counterproductive and ultimately frustrating to attempt ardent sun-lovers such as pinks or yarrows in dark shade or to inflict the noonday sun on shade-craving primulas.

• Do all the winds of heaven howl through the garden, or is it sheltered by evergreens or buildings? Wind can be buffered with fences or plantings, but an overly close environment in a humid climate can be a breeding ground for fungus. The free flow of air helps keep a garden healthy. However, while delphiniums may not mildew in a breezy garden, they will certainly need stakes. Gardeners aiming for low maintenance on a windy site might forgo delphiniums in favour of self-supporting loosestrife or monkshood.

• What is the earth like—acidic or sweet? Is the soil dense, sticky clay, coarse-textured, dryish sand, decent loam or a mixture of subsoil and rubble left by the construction crew? Of all the specifics of a site, the earth is the most amenable to improvement. There is relatively little one can do about climate, but any soil, no matter how inhospitable to plant growth at the start, responds to consistent generous treatment. (More about that in the next chapter.) An initial careful look at your garden space will make future garden tours more pleasant. No plant will please you for long if it looks as though it would rather be anywhere but in your garden.

With the garden site assessed, the pleasant task of searching out suitable plants begins. "What can I plant," a visitor once asked, "that will come up year after year, flower all summer and take care of itself?" Well, no single plant (that I know of) will do all of that, but a selection of perennials—as few as a dozen different kinds—chosen to succeed one another in bloom, and planted with some thought given to height, habit of growth and colour, fills the bill exactly for low maintenance, continuous flowering and relative

permanence. In the chapters to come, I will take readers through the flower gardener's year, phase by phase, from the flowers that bloom soon after the snow to those that bide their time until waning summer. Perennials can highlight any corner with bright blossoms and varied leaf shapes, shades and textures, but they reach their full pictorial potential when different kinds are grouped together in a bed or border.

Beds and Borders

A bed is a freestanding island of cultivated ground, usually surrounded by a grassy sea; you walk around a bed viewing it from all sides. A border, in contrast, is backed by a fence, shrubs, hedge, patio or wall and fronted by a path or lawn; you generally view it from one side only. Both arrangements have advantages and disadvantages. A bed of flowers is usually easier to tend and cultivate than a border. Even if a bed is 10 feet across at its widest point, much of the space will come within the gardener's reach from one side or the other, and a few stepping stones bring you even closer to the plants for staking, trimming and bouquet picking. A border, on the other hand, is automatically brought into focus by the wall or by other features of the landscape that define it.

In theory, a bed can be dug anywhere in the landscape, thus allowing a gardener to grow favourite flowers—irises, poppies and pinks, for instance—in a shaded yard's only sunny patch or primroses in the one shadowy corner of an open garden. In practice, however, a flower-decked island in a lawn-sea can look awkward and artificial unless it is thoughtfully positioned, proportioned and shaped in relation to the house or existing trees, evergreens or shrubs—"anchored," as a noted garden designer puts it. The outline of a bed may be arrow-straight or gracefully curving, depending upon the site and the lay of the land, but busy squiggles or a saw-toothed effect are better avoided.

Because borders are suggested by site parameters such as fences, hedges or driveways, they are easier

to site; but they demand certain considerations. If a border's backdrop blocks the sun, plants may grow lanky and weak-kneed. As well, a living background such as shrubs or a hedge can take much of the water and nutrients from nearby perennials, necessitating thorough and more frequent soil enrichment. Finally, given their one-sidedness, densely planted borders can be hard to get at—as I discovered. At Larkwhistle, many of the perennials are planted in 10-foot-wide borders backed by split-rail fencing and inspired by turn-of-the-century gardening books long on romance and short on practicality. Visitors often say (and we silently agree) that these borders are glorious, with plants layered in both time and space, the whole scene changing several times during the season. But tending such a planting becomes a game of wary tiptoeing, a delicate balancing act, a rather strange yoga routine: hold your breath, make a long stretch, cultivator in hand, to nip budding bindweed under back-of-

the-border delphiniums, pivot on the spot and make a grand leap from mid-border to path without squashing coral bells at the edge.

Borders need not be grand and inaccessible to be beautiful. In a newly planted, lattice-enclosed space at Larkwhistle — "the quiet garden," we call it — 5-foot-wide borders are a pleasure to tend and ample enough to accommodate three bands of perennials from front to back. Dianthus, mounding hardy geraniums, creeping savory, lady's mantle and lamb's ears tumble over the raised concrete edging. Yard-high bellflowers, obedient plants, Madonna lilies, white bleeding hearts, phlox and veronicas weave through the middle sections, while clumps of delphiniums, *Artemisia lactiflora* and snakeroot spire up in the background. Sweet autumn clematis drapes the lattice with dark green all summer and a flurry of vanilla-scented white stars in September. Even a prickly rugosa rose and a grey-leaved Russian olive tree find space. For the most part, spring bulbs are omitted here, and

this as much as the manageable size of the borders facilitates the work. From mid-June till fall, there are always flowers, never the lavish profusion (and occasional confusion) of the big borders but a pleasant, easygoing show.

While it is possible to squeeze two seasons of bloom into a quite narrow space — a 2½-foot border can grow dwarf spring flowers along the edge and a line of summer perennials behind — longer-blooming, if more complex, pictures are possible on a wider canvas. If a bed or border is from 5 to 10 feet wide, there is room for low plants to spill over the edges and drift back to meet others of medium height, weaving through the middle section, while tall plants congregate toward the back. Perennial gardening evolved as a more naturalistic, less studied alternative to strictly regimented annual bedding — a line of white alyssum, a line of blue lobelia, a line of red geraniums. Although some orderly souls may prefer precise, stepped bands of low, medium and tall perennials, is

Borders need not be grand and inaccessible to be beautiful. In "the quiet garden" at Larkwhistle, easily tended 5-foot-wide beds are planted with tall feathery Artemisia lactiflora, *white dianthus and good foliage perennials such as Siberian irises and ornamental grasses for a pleasant display from June until September.*

there any point in copying a summer bedding pattern with permanent plants? Instead, strive for what one old-time writer calls "a rolling contour – plains, foothills and mountains, if one may use so gigantic a simile – the highlands creeping out over the plains and the plains reaching back among the hills."

Garden Pictures

I assume that the perennial gardener's aim (or the gardener's perennial aim) is not simply to assemble an odds-and-ends collection of hardy plants and to plunk them any which way around the garden but rather to design and plan a space so that it will not only be full and flowery for as long as possible but will also appear fresh and luxuriant, if only leafy, during lapses in colour.

Given that few perennials flower for more than a month, and some of the most spectacular for a much shorter time, a gardener aiming for three seasons of bloom must select some species that fly their colours in spring; others, perhaps the majority, that bloom during the summer months; and a few that warm the garden during the frosty weeks of fall. At Larkwhistle, the beds and borders change face almost entirely every three weeks or so, as certain plants light up and others fade. This means that the garden presents a successive series of "living pictures," as Gertrude Jekyll, English garden artist extraordinaire of the last century, called them. Jekyll considered each area of the garden as an artistic composition in which all the elements, from ground covers to trees, should be in harmony. A garden, she wrote, "may be fashioned into a dream of beauty, a place of rest and refreshment of mind and body – a series of soul-satisfying pictures."

A fruitful approach to garden designing is to think in terms of seasons of bloom and pictorial associations, themes and accompaniments. During each bloom phase, certain plants stand out as obvious themes around which garden pictures are composed. Indeed, gardeners often refer to crocus or daffodil time, to tulip, lilac, iris, peony, lily or chrysanthemum time. But even these

garden divas shine brighter in company with other flowers, the supporting *corps de fleurs*, so to speak. Daffodils are lovelier above a floor of arabis or interplanted with Virginia bluebells or shadowy blue *Phlox divaricata*. Pink or yellow tulips are enhanced by mats of "moonlit blue" creeping phlox or seas of forget-me-nots. Simple pinks set off opulent peonies and irises, and lilies gleam through a mist of baby's-breath. All through the text, I pass along similar suggestions for pictorial perennial groupings for each flowering phase.

The Gardener's Art

A newly cleared bed or border, weed-free and raked fine and smooth, is a blank canvas awaiting the gardener's art. The colours of flowers in all their flashing brilliance or subtle shading are what garden artists work with. Plant form, habit and height – whether gracefully arching, low and mounding, tapering skyward or broadly bushy – also figure in the composition.

In designing a bed or border, consider the relative heights of adjacent plants. The 2-foot peach-leaved bellflower looks just fine in front of a yard-high peony but puny against a 7-foot delphinium. A plant's overall form or silhouette also figures in the picture. Broadly rounded or bushy perennials of medium height such as gas plants, false indigo, certain yarrows and artemisias, peonies, hardy geraniums, baby's-breath and day lilies are effective foregrounds for tall, slender hollyhocks, delphiniums, aconites, tiger lilies, snakeroots, *Artemisia lactiflora* and perennial sunflowers.

While this sort of mingling is the essence of perennial gardening, consider, too, that most species show their true colours more effectively if several of the same kind are grouped together. A single coral bell plant is pretty, but so dainty it may go unnoticed, whereas five or six clumps set a foot from one another create a misty breadth of pink or red. A lone *Salvia superba* looks a trifle weedy, but bring five together and the massed purple-violet spikes glow dark and brilliant. One foxglove, lily or iris is lost in the landscape, but a congregation of bell-hung spires, exotic trumpets or multicoloured fleurs-de-lis forms an arresting feature. In general, perennials that are slender in habit, and those with dainty flowers in particular, make a more impressive statement when massed. Gertrude Jekyll spoke of setting perennials, again several of one kind, in "drifts" of casually shaped groups – elongated ovals, kidney shapes – rather than three in a triangle, four in a square and so on. Her motives were practical as well as aesthetic. A drift of one kind, she says, "not only has a more pictorial effect, but a thin, long planting does not leave an unsightly empty space when the flowers are done and leaves have perhaps died down."

But not all plants need to be massed. Certain of them are fine as specimens, that is, single plants set in strategic places. Those that qualify as specimens may have opulent, showy blossoms or especially bold and long-lasting leaves, or they may be particularly bulky or wide-spreading so that one plant is a drift all on its own. Some perennials meet all three criteria. A dozen specimen plants, all described in later chapters, include peonies, tall yellow yarrows, hostas, gas plants, baby's-breath, anchusas, loosestrife, cushion euphorbias, Siberian irises, day lilies, false indigo and well-grown clumps of delphiniums, which punctuate the back of a border with violet or sky blue fountains.

Fill in the Blanks

Although it is entirely possible to design a perennial planting that shows some colour from spring until fall, that is not to say that the entire bed or border will be lit up, nonstop, from end to end the whole season through. Lulls in the fireworks are inevitable. Delphiniums, eremurus and globe thistles are routinely cut back when their flowers fade. Empty spots are left where spring bulbs, lovely in their day, have become mere masses of withered leaves. Gaps occur where Oriental poppies go underground for the summer.

"Many perennials . . . lose all pride in their appearance as soon as flowering is accomplished," says Louise Beebe Wilder in *Colour in My Garden* (1918). "They go to seed most untidily, quite lose their figures and make no effort at all to grow old with dignity and grace."

At Larkwhistle, we solve what Wilder calls the "problem of the bare places" in a few simple but effective ways. I pass them along in the hope that they will help beginners "past the disheartening stages when the blank spaces seem so much more numerous than the full and luxuriant ones."

Perhaps our best way to cover for tulips, daffodils, crown imperials and larger spring bulbs is to plant the bulbs in conjunction with later-rising but ultimately spreading perennials that will hide the fading bulb greenery with a screen of flowers and foliage. If the chosen perennials remain fresh and leafy the season through, so much the better; we have accomplished two crops of flowers in one spot and kept the place pleasantly furnished with foliage. Thus, at Larkwhistle, most of our peonies and day lilies have attendant groups of daffodils planted close by (but no bulbs within 10 inches of the perennial's crown). As the daffodils bloom, the peonies are just unfurling their spring crimson fans and the day lilies are showing their green spears, but later, the foliage of these peren-

For every phase, there are what could be called thematic perennials around which garden pictures are composed. At Larkwhistle, FACING PAGE, *April and early May bring lavish bouquets of daffodils that are set off by blue grape hyacinths and pink and lavender creeping phlox. Among the daffodils,* LEFT, *day lilies, peonies and silver artemisias emerge to hide the fading bulb foliage with a leafy canopy and to provide late colour in the same bed.*

nials will grow up and arch over to form a concealing umbrella. Similarly, tulips, narcissi and Spanish squills weave through groups of phlox, heleniums, yellow yarrows, hardy geraniums, false indigo and the summer daisies—robust perennials all well able to withstand the bulb competition. Pink tulips are particularly nice growing among clumps of succulent grey-leaved *Sedum spectabile*, the showy stonecrops, or half hidden among yarrow's silver, fernlike foliage. Pools of crocuses or blue grape hyacinths lap right up to emerging day lilies or late-rising loosestrife or hostas. Notice that bulbs are teamed with strong-growing summer perennials that can stay put for many years. Other perennials suited to masking bulb defection are meadow rue, ornamental grasses and, for small bulbs only, herbs such as hyssop, rue, southernwood and *Artemisia* 'Lambrook Silver.' Daffodils are especially appealing among delicate, unfurling fern fronds.

Any perennials that are cut back after flowering are best concealed behind a bushy foreground plant with long-lasting leaves. In fact, choosing a selection of plants just for their foliage is another way to mask empty spots. Flower gardeners, by definition, concentrate their efforts on a crop of colour, but perennial growers soon learn that many of their permanent plants have rather fleeting flowers—three weeks to a month is the average bloom time. And their leaves may be unappealing, spare or ephemeral. Over the years, I have come to appreciate any plant that maintains a steady show of foliage. Used generously, perennials with fine and lasting leaves go a long way toward keeping a flower garden fresh, full and luxuriant, especially if they are set conspicuously toward the front and midsections of a garden. Those not described elsewhere in the book include:

• Lamb's ear (*Stachys lanata*). Some of the whitest foliage in our garden grows from this velvety plant, whose wands of small, rose-purple flowers grow several feet tall in June.

• Lady's mantle (*Alchemilla mollis*). This foot-tall ground cover with handsome, broad, pleated blue-green leaves does best in shady ground, although it will thrive in sun in a cool garden.

• Thyme (*Thymus* spp). Thymes in many varieties may hug the ground, grow into small mounds of wiry branches or become upright shrubs as tall as 15 inches. Small-leaved, fragrant plants, they are ideal ground covers in dry, sunny places.

• Sedum (*Sedum* spp). The creeping species of sedum bloom in shades from pink to red or yellow and are best in sunny, dry gardens.

• Meadow rue (*Thalictrum delavayi*) has fine branching stems and tiny lilac flowers with golden stamens.

• Ornamental grasses are sold in many species, from the popular perennial gardener's garters (*Phalaris arundinacea picta*) to annuals that need replanting each spring.

• Ferns of several varieties do best in shady, moist soil.

Among good foliage plants described elsewhere in this book are several for sunny border edges: coral bells, candytuft, creeping phlox, silver dianthus and grey-leaved snow-in-summer. Winding through the middle of the Larkwhistle borders are peonies, gas plants, Siberian irises, hardy geraniums, obedient plants, silver artemisias and yarrows, woolly mulleins, elegant columbines and several species of perennial cornflowers. *Centaurea dealbata rosea* grows especially lovely leaves. Behind these, aconites, false indigo, he-leniums and the more restrained hardy sunflowers form a persistently leafy backdrop. All create a stable verdant or silver-grey setting for the fleeting flowers that grow in sunny spots. For shady places, there are snakeroots, day lilies, the rush-leaved Siberian irises, loosestrife, whose leaves turn reddish in fall, and hostas, for elegant, persistent leaves. A garden that grows its share of fine foliage plants appears fresh and full the season through, even during inevitable declines in colour.

Living Colour

And yet, when all is said and done, colour is a flower garden's reason for being. If I were content with green, I'd plant a lawn and be done with it. But I'm not. I hunger for colour. I am especially partial to blue, white and yellow flowers in combination. During the early years of gardening at Larkwhistle, a spring trio of yellow and white crocuses interplanted with blue glory-of-the-snow was so simple to do and so satisfying to look at that I was encouraged to colour-scheme an iris bed. I scoured McMillan's iris catalogue for cultivars I thought would work well together and one July day set out rhizomes that promised a picture shading from cream to clear yellow, soft blue to indigo. White *Dianthus arenarius* would tumble over the edge next to blue-spiked veronica. Further along went a carpet of golden-leaved thyme. Taking a suggestion from an old book, I tucked feathery tufts of blue and white perennial flax (*Linum perenne*) among the irises. Some clumps of Iceland poppies, pretty *Artemisia* 'Lambrook Silver' and fragrant yellow "lemon lilies" salvaged from the former farm garden went in where space allowed.

At the same time, my partner John was planting an iris bed with flowers ranging from dusky violet through shades of lavender to pink. Rose-toned dianthus, pink coral bells and grey and white cerastium ribboned the edge, and a few purple and white lupins provided vertical accents. The next June, there was a smattering of bloom as the plants clumped up, but the following summer, when

Colour is the flower garden's reason
for being, but contrasts in plant form
and texture add considerable interest.
For instance, an edging of tufted pinks
and a mounding of hardy geraniums,
FACING PAGE, provide a foil for the
upright growth of lilies. Borders
planted with generous groups of good
foliage perennials such as reedy
Siberian irises, LEFT, remain fresh
and full-looking even during the
inevitable declines in colour.

the irises and others reached a climax of colour, I thought I had never seen anything lovelier. And I knew that colour scheming was worth the effort.

Almost the essence of pictorial gardening, colour planning simply entails juxtaposing two or three perennials (and perhaps some annuals) that share a bloom phase and whose combined colours appeal to the garden-maker. Some gardeners have very definite colour tastes—no magenta, no mustard-yellow or orange, lots of pink and blue—and their plantings are apt to have a focus from the start. But other gardeners are not in the habit of considering colour beyond "I like it bright and lots of it" and may not know how to approach colour planning.

One of the gardening columns of Vita Sackville-West, co-creator of England's famous Sissinghurst garden during the early 1900s, tells how she chose companion plants by plucking flowers and strolling around the garden holding them up to other plants or "sticking them into the ground and then standing back to observe the harmony." By so doing, she could observe the combined effect before she committed herself to a planting. Good plan. Sometimes I'll pick, say, a spray of yellow leopard's bane (*Doronicum* spp), a brilliant but hard-to-place spring daisy, and hold it next to different tulips or creeping phlox blooming at the same time, or I'll wander around with a branch of loosestrife until I find a pleasant complement—dusky blue monkshood or purple day lilies. The result of such a strategy for Sackville-West was the creation of beautiful beds and garden "rooms" with limited colour schemes—an all-white garden, for instance, as well as one that focused on blues, another on harmonizing reds.

There are no hard-and-fast rules of colour combining. Although each phase brings many perennials to bloom, I encourage a novice gardener or anyone essaying a new bed or border to settle on several site-suitable plants for each phase—early spring, late spring, June, midsummer, late summer/fall—and to use these as the primary colours in a composition. Early pictures are easy to arrange; the soft yellow, white, blue and lavender that appear soon after the snow melts create a limited and naturally harmonious palette. But later, as tulips appear and throughout the summer months, a bit of colour planning can make the difference between an appealing, artistic garden and one that may be, as Jekyll put it, "jarring and displeasing."

It is easiest to define colours as warm or cool. Warm tones have a dash (or more) of yellow, while cool colours lean toward blue. As a rule, the two colour categories are kept apart at Larkwhistle, but colours within one group or the other are often put together. Scarlet, for instance, is a warm or yellowish red that works with orange and creamy yellow. Crimson is a cool or bluish red that becomes purple with the addition of more blue. Thus crimson or mauve (a cool pink) phlox combine with slate-blue or deep violet monkshood. On the other hand, dianthus have cool or bluish shades of pink that appear muddy or dull next to warm pink or salmon-toned Oriental poppies or coral bells.

Shades of the same colour are sure to appear unified. I am partial to white, creamy yellow, lemon and deeper golden yellow. For a broader spectrum, orange, salmon or a touch of scarlet can be used as sparks or highlights with the yellow. But a patch of scarlet sweet William lapping against an equal mass of bold yellow marguerites or yarrows strikes me as too hot for beauty. As any painter knows, proportion – the relative amount of one colour to another – is important. As Louise B. Wilder notes in *Colour in My Garden*, "A single scarlet poppy will kindle into life a whole sea of dim blue campanulas, whereas an equal mass of scarlet would so outshine the fainter hue as to make it appear poor and dull."

The reference to scarlet and lavender points out that sometimes, bringing together both warm and cool colours results in a rich and vibrant picture, a "harmony of contrast." As I mentioned, a bed of blue-toned and yellow-toned irises that I planted is beautiful. And orange or apricot day lilies are almost mouthwatering in front of dark violet delphiniums, while purple salvia 'East Friesland' makes a brave show with tall yellow yarrows. Orange

tulips behind lavender-blue creeping phlox are striking but entirely pleasant contrasts that lack the raw disparity of, say, deep yellow tulips and strong pink creeping phlox.

One writer, on the other hand, theorizes that "all colours go well together in a garden if only they are thoroughly mixed up." This may have been the same person who coined the phrase "a riot of colour," but who wants a riot in the garden? Life is nervous enough.

I find that colour harmony – an easy blending of one hue with the next – is easier to live with (if not always easier to manage) than sharply contrasting tints. For me, a successful planting depends as much on what combinations are avoided as it does on the colours I choose. That is why I keep orange tiger lilies out of sight of magenta phlox but team both with dusky blue aconites. Red bergamot never shares a bed with mustard-yellow yarrow, but in separate places, both shine behind a neutral cloud of baby's-breath or a foreground of fluffy white Shasta daisies. Scarlet, yellow and orange are strictly taboo in a corner of Larkwhistle given over to pink and crimson peonies, coral bells, blue violas, lavender alliums and rose-coloured foxgloves. In another part of the garden, pink, mauve and magenta flowers never crop up in a day lily border coloured in broad swaths of sunset shades – yellow,

Almost the essence of pictorial gardening, colour planning simply entails grouping several perennials that share a bloom phase and whose combined colours appeal to the gardener. At Larkwhistle, John Scanlan's rosy border, FACING PAGE, *presents a consistent scheme of pink, crimson, blue, lavender and white throughout the season. Other borders have colour schemes that alter as the seasons progress. All of the June flowers,* LEFT, *such as irises, pinks, pyrethrums, coral bells, snow-in-summer and the rest, are hidden in the same borders shown on pages 18 and 19.*

23

apricot, flame — with cool lavender contrast supplied by clumps of balloon flowers.

Fortunately, there are a few colours that, to my eye, are so easy-going and noncombative that they not only get along with any other hue but also help to draw otherwise conflicting elements into harmony. Green, of course, is the universal neutral among plants. Soft creamy yellow or pale lemon, a shade worn by some tulips, many bearded irises, mulleins, certain meadow rues and the lovely 'Moonshine' yarrow, subdues the most brilliant magenta and lives amicably even with belligerent scarlet. Clear sky blue, a colour rare enough but displayed beautifully by delphiniums, fits in anywhere. As well, dusky lavender-blue — found typically in bellflowers, balloon flowers, aconites, globe thistles, many irises, dwarf catnip and, of course, lavender — is a gentle, melting colour and one that many people seem to overlook. And "deep purple flowers," as one old-time writer noted, "are of significant value to the creator of garden pictures.

Their character is almost of shadow, and shadow is as important in the garden as upon the canvas to define the quality of light and to give variety and interest to the composition." The same observant gardener also wrote that "yellow, orange and scarlet flowers show to greatest advantage in full sunshine. In shadow, they seem to lose much of their flash and vigour; while the reverse is true of lavender, violet and blue flowers. These in shadow assume a piercing distinctness, while in sunshine, much of their colour seems to be scattered among the sunbeams and their outlines blurred."

Grey foliage, too, or the misty grey-white bloom of baby's-breath serves a neutral, peacemaking role among more flagrant flowers. The jury is still out on coldly white flowers. One expert reckons that the stark white worn by candytuft or Shasta daisies simply separates neighbouring colours into distinctly contrasting blocks, especially if white is "dotted about the garden"; others recommend white to bridge opposing colours.

Certainly, white used with a broad brush, especially against a background of dark evergreens, has dignity and repose. Our "quiet garden" is planted entirely with white flowers in a green and silver setting; the atmosphere is peaceful, the place a calm and quiet retreat where a tired gardener can take his rest, sit at the edge of the little reflecting pool and trail a blistered hand in the cool water where a white lotus-flower grows.

In planning all aspects of garden design, including colour, I find a garden notebook essential. Once or twice during each stage of bloom, my partner and I go around the garden and jot down changes we would like to make that fall or the next spring. The "picture book" is filled with brief reminders to, for example, move a clump of yellow intermediate irises next to blue perennial cornflowers for early June colour after the tulips are over or to divide dark purple aconite in three pieces to go behind pink bee balm.

Perhaps it is true, then, that gardening is the art of observation, as someone once said. Some of the changes we recommend in the garden notebook may never happen, and others may not work out just as planned, but in the process of observing what we like and don't like but wish for, we take time to study the garden closely, exercise our creative senses and delight in some of nature's most beautiful and gracious expressions. At these times, nature is our teacher, and the plants themselves show us how to both appreciate and express beauty. That is, after all, what a flower garden is all about.

Or, as John Ruskin wrote, "We cannot fathom the mystery of a single flower, nor is it intended that we should; but that the pursuit of science should constantly be betrayed by the love of beauty and accuracy of knowledge by tenderness of emotion." Gardening is a gentle art, a lively science. The rhythmic work outdoors refreshes and strengthens the body and often calms the mind. When we touch the earth and involve ourselves cooperatively with nature's cycles, we reaffirm our link with the living planet that sustains us.

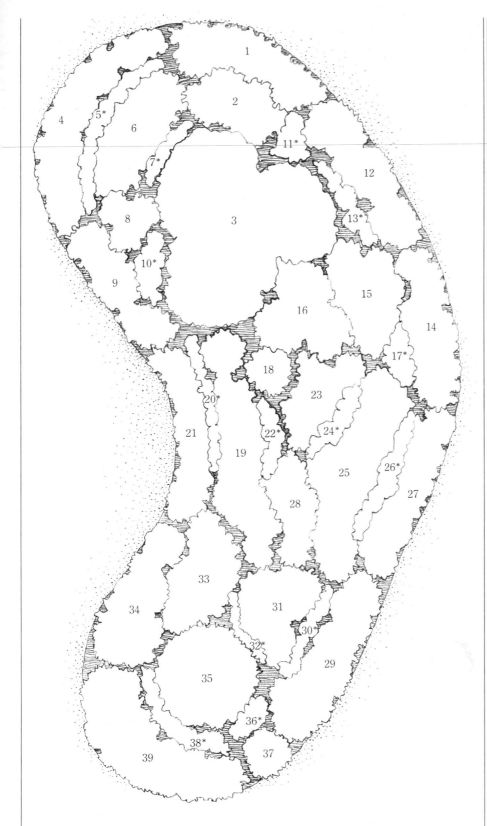

Perennials for a dry, sunny site

This island bed, which is 25 feet from end to end, could be planted in an exposed part of the lawn or surrounded by a patio. All of the plants marked with an asterisk* are spring-flowering bulbs that grow up through neighbouring plants.

1 *Dianthus allwoodii*
2 Bearded irises
3 Three peonies 'Mrs. Livingston Ferrand'
4 Sedum
5* Crocuses
6 *Anthemis tinctoria*
7* Daffodils
8 Bearded irises
9 *Saponaria ocymoides*
10* *Tulipa kaufmanniana* and glory-of-the-snow
11* Darwin tulips
12 *Gypsophila repens*
13* Glory-of-the-snow
14 *Dianthus allwoodii*
15 Bearded irises
16 *Verbascum bombyciferum*
17* Tulips
18 Baby's-breath
19 *Yarrow* 'Moonshine'
20* Crocuses
21 Variegated lemon thyme
22* Daffodils
23 *Papaver orientale*
24* Daffodils
25 *Salvia superba*
26* Siberian scilla
27 Artemisia 'Silver Mound'
28 *Eryngium planum*
29 *Nepeta mussinii*
30* Crocuses
31 *Yucca filamentosa*
32* Daffodils
33 Bearded irises
34 *Dianthus deltoides*
35 Peony 'Kansas Crimson'
36* Snowdrops
37 *Asclepias tuberosa*
38* Lily-flowered tulips
39 *Euphorbia epithymoides*

The single peony 'Dainty' shows how white flowers planted in drifts, FACING PAGE, *can draw conflicting colours into harmony.*

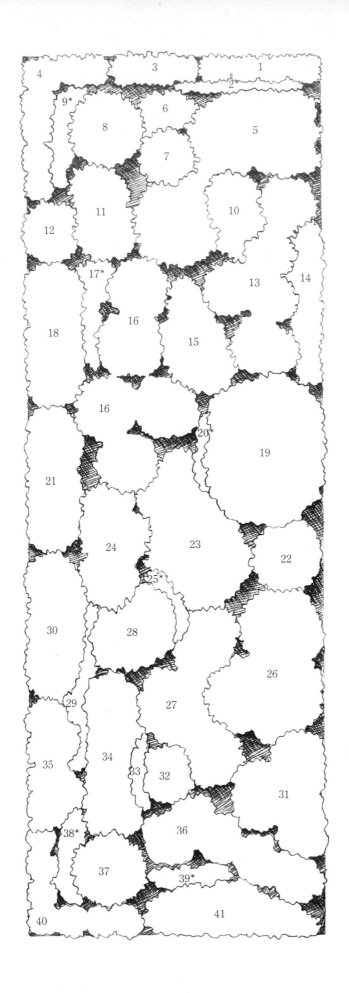

Section of a Larkwhistle Border

This border section is 30 feet long and 10 feet wide, making it spectacular but difficult to tend when a certain amount of stepping in the border becomes necessary. The colour theme here is blue and pink, with touches of red and white and, later in the season, a shift into yellows. The plants marked with an asterisk* are spring-flowering bulbs that grow up through the neighbouring plants.

1   Double arabis
2* Crocuses
3   *Nepeta mussinii*
4   *Dianthus arenarius*
5   Day lily 'Hyperion' and narcissus
6   Lily
7   Baby's-breath
8   Peony 'Sea Shell'
9* Small spring bulbs
10 Lily 'Wanda'
11 *Pyrethrum roseum*
12 Candytuft
13 *Phlox paniculata* and narcissus
14 *Fritillaria imperialis*
15 *Eryngium alpinum*
16 *Sedum spectabile*
17* Tulips (pink)
18 *Phlox subulata* (lavender)
19 Flowering crab
20* Narcissus
21 Lavender 'Hidcote Blue'
22 Clematis 'Pink Chiffon'
23 *Aconitum napellus* 'Bicolor'
24 Yarrow 'Moonshine'
25* Narcissus
26 Delphinium 'Summer Skies'
27 *Helenium autumnale*
28 Lily
29* Crocuses
30 *Stachys lanata*
31 Hollyhocks, single pink
32 Baby's-breath
33* Narcissus
34 *Papaver orientale*
35 *Heuchera sanguinea* (pink)
36 Siberian iris 'Orville Fay'
37 Peony 'Crinkled White'
38* *Scilla campanulata*
39* Tulips (white)
40 *Dianthus caesius*
41 *Phlox subulata* (pink)

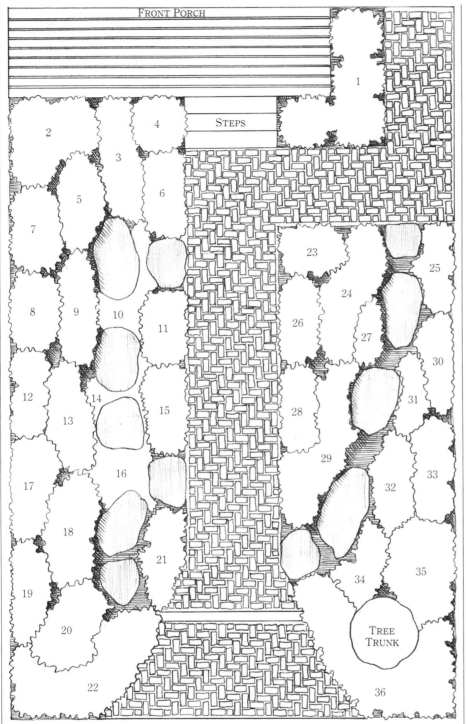

City Garden (Front Yard)

This front yard is 25 feet wide and 40 feet long and includes a porch and a pathway that leads down to the street.

1   Peonies or day lilies, underplanted with grape hyacinths
2   Forsythia underplanted with *Scilla sibirica*
3   Leopard's bane underplanted with daffodils
4   Peony
5   Lily
6   Candytuft
7   *Dicentra spectabilis*
8   *Phlox paniculata*
9   Dwarf day lily
10   Corsican mint
11   Coral bells underplanted with crocuses
12   Lily
13   Columbines underplanted with tulips
14   *Campanula muralis*
15   *Campanula carpatica* underplanted with crocuses
16   *Viola odorata*
17   Siberian irises
18   Dwarf day lilies underplanted with tulips
19   Purple loosestrife underplanted with daffodils
20   *Thalictrum aquilegifolium*
21   Polyanthus primrose
22   Hosta 'Medio-variegata' underplanted on both sides with *Scilla sibirica,* snowdrops, glory-of-the-snow
23   *Hosta sieboldiana* 'Elegans'
24   *Geranium sanguineum* underplanted with tulips
25   *Phlox stolonifera* or *P. divaricata*
26   *Campanula carpatica* underplanted with crocuses
27   *Campanula persicifolia*
28   Coral bells underplanted with crocuses
29   Polyanthus primrose
30   Monkshood or delphinium
31   Lily
32   Dwarf day lily underplanted with tulips
33   Coneflower
34   *Campanula persicifolia*
35   *Polemonium caeruleum*
36   Hosta 'Medio-variegata'

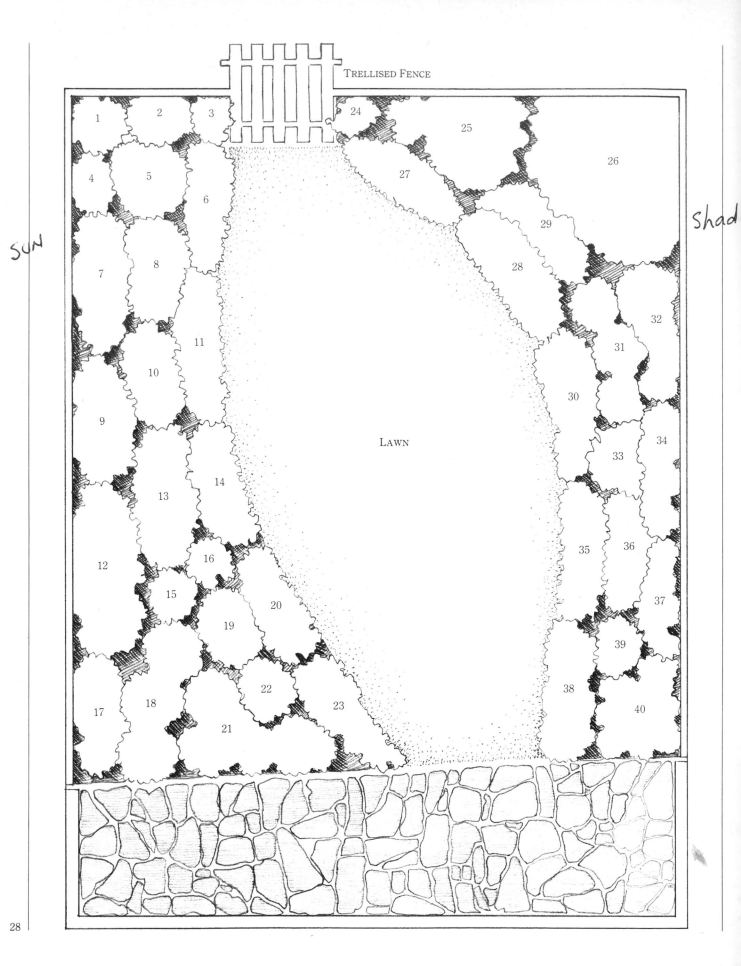

TRELLISED FENCE

SUN

Shad

LAWN

City Garden (Backyard)

This backyard is assumed to be 25 feet by 40 feet. At the top of the diagram, beyond the fence, is a vegetable and herb garden 6 feet by 25 feet in size. The left side of the perennial flower garden is in sun; the right side, in shade. The house is at the bottom of the diagram, beyond the patio.

1   Delphinium
2   Day lily – colour A
3   *Clematis* × *jackmanii*
4   Rose 'Mrs. Anthony Waterer'
5   Peony
6   *Dianthus allwoodii*
7   *Helenium autumnale*
8   *Centaurea montana*
9   *Lilium tigrinum*
10 Bearded iris
11 Veronica
12 Single hollyhocks
13 Yarrow 'Coronation Gold'
14 *Campanula carpatica*
15 Baby's-breath
16 *Papaver orientale*
17 Rugosa rose 'Jens Munk'
18 *Phlox paniculata*
19 Day lily – colour B
20 *Hosta plantaginea*
21 *Sedum spectabile*
22 Bearded iris
23 Coral bells (pink)
24 Rose 'New Dawn'
25 *Cornus alba* 'Elegantissima'
26 Crab apple 'Royalty'
27 Tradescantia (blue)
28 Astilbe or polyanthus
    primrose
29 Siberian iris
30 *Geranium sanguineum*
31 *Polemonium caeruleum*
32 Sweet cicely
33 *Dicentra spectabilis*
34 Purple loosestrife 'Morden
    Pink'
35 *Viola cornuta*
36 *Thalictrum aquilegifolium*
37 *Aconitum napellus* 'Bicolor'
38 Hosta 'Frances Williams'
39 Columbine
40 *Cimicifuga racemosa*

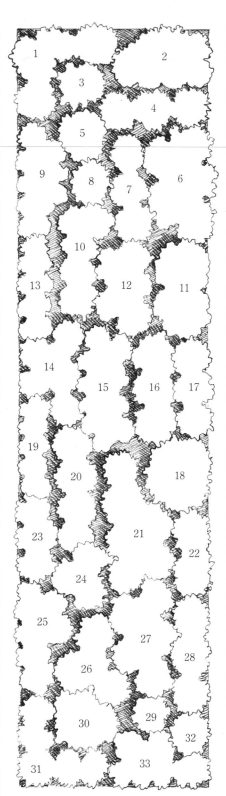

Low-Maintenance Border

This perennial flower border grows at Camp Allsaw, a children's summer camp that is attended only during the summer months. It needs to be brightly coloured, easy to care for and, as the camp teaches orgainc gardening methods, relatively pest-free. It is 40 feet long by 10 feet wide.

1   Hosta (Cultivar A)
2   Bleeding heart 'Luxuriant'
3   Lily
4   Day lily (Cultivar A)
5   *Gypsophila repens*
6   *Aconitum napellus* 'Bicolor'
7   *Helenium autumnale*
8   Day lily (Cultivar B)
9   Coral bells
10 Yarrow 'Moonshine'
11 Rugosa rose 'Jens Munk'
12 *Monarda didyma*
13 Bellflower 'Blue Clips'
14 Salvia 'East Friesland'
15 Lily (white)
16 Purple loosestrife
17 *Artemisia lactiflora*
18 Rugosa rose 'Jens Munk'
19 Shasta daisy, double
20 Yarrow 'Gold Plate'
21 Phlox (white)
22 Perennial sunflower
23 Tradescantia
24 Bergamot (pink)
25 *Heuchera sanguinea*
26 *Sedum spectabile*
27 Purple loosestrife
28 *Aconitum napellus*
29 Day lily 'Hyperion'
30 Lily
31 Hosta (Cultivar B)
32 Day lily (Cultivar C)
33 *Heuchera sanguinea*

Earth Tones

Soil care, seeding and garden routines

With the most basic equipment—flats, flowerpots, blended soil and a few packets of seeds—it is possible to raise a batch of young perennials at a fraction of the cost of nursery plants. Seed can also open the doors to unusual flowers seldom available on nursery benches.

"Labour is the house that love dwells in," says a Russian proverb. Like any loving link, that between gardener and garden requires care and maintenance. First, land must be cleared and plants sown or set in place. Thereafter, every garden, even one stocked with only the most self-sufficient perennials, needs routine attention: weeding, watering and, as a foundation for all, the creation and sustenance of good soil.

Whether a flower garden takes shape from a detailed paper plan or evolves in a more spontaneous fashion, its beauty ultimately depends on plants that are robust, healthy and obviously thriving, plants that have been chosen to suit the garden site and then are set in good-hearted ground. It has been said that any soil that grows a decent crop of potatoes or cabbages will grow perennials well. This does not minimize the fertility that perennials need but rather emphasizes that most are hungry, husky plants which, in order to reach their full potential, must sink their roots into the same sort of nourishing earth that produces bushels of edible roots and greens. The fact that perennials stay in one place for years is a further inducement to provide them with fertility from the start.

But even before that, sod breaking might be in order, unless a gardener decides to cultivate perennials in an established vegetable garden – not a bad idea, considering that the land there is already cleared and probably well enriched. Clearing land by hand is a gardener's most difficult task, but it is also work that, if done thoroughly, need be done only once. By

contrast, extracting quack grass and choking bindweed from the crowns of one's precious perennials is an ongoing and (probably) a losing battle; every scrap of root left in a perennial bed will come back.

"Skim off the turf," one gardening book blithely instructs as the first step toward making a garden – as if turf were akin to cream floating on milk. At Larkwhistle, on the other hand, the recipe for converting a strip of lawn or a corner of a field into a new flowerbed goes something more like this:

First, we delineate the space by marking off straight-edged borders with stakes and string or curving outlines with a length of garden hose wiggled about until it describes the desired graceful sweep. Then, we slice along the defined edge with a sharp, flat-edged spade and slice the enclosed turf into a grid of chunks somewhat smaller than a foot square. These will have to be lifted, so they should be kept as small as can be easily managed. Using a spading fork, we pry loose a chunk of sod, flip it earth-side up and whack away at the roots with the fork tines to loosen as much of the precious topsoil as possible. Then we spear the chunk of sod, lift it and shake out the topsoil; sandy soil falls away more readily than sticky clay. On clay soil, try to time sod breaking so that the ground is at its most crumbly, not sodden in early spring or baked to an unyielding crust in the heat of summer.

Gradually – an hour a day of sod skimming is a workout – the area is completely cleared. Good quality sods may be used to create a new lawn area – water them as soon as they are positioned – or the sods can be piled by themselves upside down in an out-of-the-way place to compost. A tarpaulin over the pile discourages the grass from sprouting. Twitch-grass roots or perennial weeds soon infest a regular compost pile. When the space is stripped of sod, we rake the earth to catch stray roots, rocks and rubbish. If the area can be left fallow for several weeks, any elusive roots will sprout, and a bit of spot digging should catch the last of the troublemakers.

Clearing land is the surest way to acquaint oneself with the tilth and

texture of a garden's soil, which may range from pure sand (coarse-textured, open, warm and dry) to pure clay (fine-textured, cool, gummy when wet, brick-hard when dry and fit only for ceramics). Thankfully, most gardeners begin with something in between, with any luck, loam – a balanced, evenly textured blend of sand, clay and organic material. When we dug into the hayfield that has since become our garden, what we found was pale sandy loam, so dust-dry in August that it flowed through our fingers like sand in an hourglass. Twelve years of organic enrichment now show in darker colour, better moisture retention and increasingly robust plant growth.

Over time, organic enrichment of the earth is accomplished by adding spongy, partly decayed material such as animal manure, straw, leaves or other plant remains that will replenish and boost its humus content. There was a time when, in the interests of soil improvement, my partner and I climbed the fence of an abandoned zoo and hauled burlap sacks of water buffalo and yak manure home on the streetcar to a cindery city garden; but today, our sources of organic matter are more conventional. Farmyard manure forms the foundation of our perennial beds. We look for manure that has stood in a neighbouring barnyard long enough to turn earth-dark and crumbly. Less fertile than fresher stuff, well-aged manure nevertheless mixes more easily with the soil and can be used generously without fear of overstimulating growth or burning plant roots, as the fresh manure might do. Fallen leaves, too, provide us with humus. According to tests at the University of Connecticut, newly fallen leaves exude chemicals that actually inhibit plant growth, but leaves left in a heap for a season or two break down into a finely textured fertilizer called leaf mould, which can be spread as mulch or turned into the earth for primroses, lilies, Siberian irises and others that appreciate spongy ground.

Another source of organic matter is compost, the heart of any good garden and a reminder that nature efficiently reuses everything to foster

new growth. Recipes abound for making perfect compost in a few weeks, usually by shredding ingredients, layering them with a certain ratio of fresh manure, turning the steaming heap and keeping moisture levels just so. The end result is a near-perfect plant food, crumbly, dark and moist, "like the richest chocolate cake," in the words of Vita Sackville-West.

Some gardeners, however, must rely on store-bought organic matter. Peat moss contains almost no plant food but helps to bind sandy soils and loosen clay. Although it holds 20 times its weight in water, the moss should be dampened before it is used and then mixed thoroughly with the soil; dry lumps act as wicks to steal water from the surrounding ground. Damp peat moss mixed with an equal volume of bagged, composted manure is also convenient organic matter for gardeners without access to farmyard manure. Add a spadeful each of bone meal (or rock phosphate) and wood ashes to a wheelbarrow of blended peat moss and

manure, and you have a nourishing, humusy mix that will improve the texture and fertility of any soil.

To prepare new flowerbeds at Larkwhistle, we spread a generous layer – 6 inches is not too much – of organic matter over a bed, whiten the surface with bone meal and spade the works deeply into the topsoil. Rototilling would also do the job. For deeply rooted, long-lived perennials, we prepare special planting holes, 18 inches across and 16 inches deep, by piling topsoil to one side, digging out and hauling away subsoil and backfilling with humus and topsoil well stirred together. Plants that appreciate such a spot include aconites, baptisias, the tall campanulas, day lilies, delphiniums, gas plants, heleniums, Siberian irises, snakeroot, lilies, loosestrife, peonies, tall summer phlox and Japanese anemones. Where three or more of these perennials are grouped together, consider excavating an oval 5 feet by 2 feet rather than a series of holes. Enriched to a foot deep or more,

Year in, year out, the wise gardener replenishes the earth's store of organic matter, or humus. Sources include animal manure, decayed leaves, peat moss and compost, FACING PAGE, *which can be sifted for use in seedling flats or generously added to beds and borders. Organically enriched garden soil will support a crowd of hungry perennials,* ABOVE, *and help keep them in flourishing health.*

such a space will accommodate three of the husky perennials just mentioned, with the individual plants spaced 18 inches apart.

Many perennials benefit from top dressing. If we have a goodly supply of very old, crumbly manure or fine compost, we often spread a layer around the crowns of the hungriest perennials. This ideally is done in spring, but any time is better than never. Plants that are treated in this way benefit from a shot of liquid plant food every time it rains, and earthworms eventually do the work of taking the surface organic matter into the soil.

Where topsoil is thin and starved or where unyielding subsoil ("hardpan") or bedrock lie just beneath the soil surface, raised beds are useful. Beds can be defined with low stone walls, chunky rocks, railroad ties one or two high or with 2-by-8-inch cedar boards secured with 2-by-4-inch rot-resistant stakes pounded into the ground on the outside of the boards. Fill such beds with imported topsoil mixed with organic matter, or if patience allows, use the spaces as composting or leaf storage areas for a season or two, after which the finished compost or leaf mould can be turned into whatever earth is there and the works topped up with extra soil, if necessary.

Perennials From Seed

"To begin a perennial border, certain things are necessary," says Richardson Wright in his 1924 *Practical Book of Outdoor Flowers*, "and the preparations can extend over a year or more, if experience is worth more to you than immediate effect." The first step , says Wright, is to make a compost heap – that we have done – then, buy and sow perennial seeds.

A fine idea. Growing at least some perennials from seed makes good sense on several counts. One reason is economical. Many hardy plants look their best in groups of three, five or more. With nursery plants tagged from $2.50 to $4.00 apiece, the cost of buying all of the plants for even a moderately sized flowerbed quickly escalates. Seeds cut costs dramatically. In addition, some of the

nicest perennials seldom show up on nursery benches or in catalogues. I have yet to encounter started plants of anchusa, purple coneflower or perennial flax, to name a few. Seeds bring a global selection of hardy plants – Tibetan poppies, pinks from the cliffs of Dover in England, Japanese columbines, bellflowers from the Alps and scores more. The Thompson and Morgan mail-order catalogue (see Sources) is one good source within a gardener's reach.

Although some seed-grown perennials, notably various daisies, may bloom during their first summer, most perennials spend their first year

developing a crown of foliage in preparation for next season's flowering. The more robust the first year's growth, the more prolific the eventual crop of flowers will be, so a start as early as possible in spring is advisable.

Since the wide world of the open garden is fraught with dangers – drought, deluge, frosts, earwigs and smothering weeds – I prefer to see seeds, especially tiny ones, through their tricky infancy indoors. And because I am not keen on shifting seedlings from flats to small pots to larger pots, my perennials begin life in 3-inch flowerpots and stay there until they go into the ground. A lightweight wooden flat is easily built to hold 35 square plastic pots.

Containers at the ready, the next consideration is the growing medium. Doug Green, a commercial grower of perennials, recommends a blend of one-half bagged potting soil and one-half perlite, a medium I heartily endorse for several reasons. First, the ingredients are available in March, a time when garden soil may still be snow-soggy or crusty with frost. Second, the mixture is lightweight and porous to both air and water, but still moisture-retentive. Such a store-bought blend is usually also weed-free; whatever sprouts is what you seeded, so you are not left puzzling over which tiny green bits are columbines and which are chickweed or (as I have done) nurturing some rare gentians along only to discover, after a month or so, that you have been coddling a thriving crop of common plantain. Finally, potting soil and perlite should be free of fungus spores and plant diseases, so a gardener can avoid the messy business of sterilizing soil and the discouraging prospect of watching seedlings keel over from damping-off, a fungal disease that is most often a problem in unsterilized soil.

In most areas, March and April are the months for sowing perennial seeds indoors. (The best time is about two months before the average date of the last spring frost.) Fill pots with the prepared mix. Tamp the soil lightly with the bottom of another pot, and top up with more mix if necessary. Sprinkle six or eight seeds on the soil surface, and cover the seeds only as deep as their diameter. According to Doug Green, "The main cause of failure is planting too deep —most flower growers should play the Last Post as they bury their seeds." Very fine seeds need only be pressed gently into the soil surface and left uncovered.

In nature, perennial seeds fall to the ground over summer, lie dormant for eight or nine months and germinate in spring. Gardeners can treat spring-sown seeds to a simulated (albeit much shorter) winter by sliding a seeded flat into the refrigerator for three or four weeks. We routinely set containers outdoors during March and early April. There they may freeze and thaw several times and often disappear under winter's last snowfalls. But as one early writer notes, "Snow broth is a most potent force in stirring little green souls to life and energy."

Our pretend winter over, mid-April is usually the time for a sudden spring. This translates as warm water, air and earth. Because a watering can produces a downpour forceful enough to wash seeds out of the ground and immersing flats and pots in a sink or tub is a tippy business, we prefer an ordinary hand-pumped spray bottle or plant mister filled with tepid water, which sprays a light, gently soaking rain over the seeded pots. If misting is repeated every day or so, the moisture will be retained in the soil without the glass or plastic covering sometimes recommended, which can engender overly hot and humid conditions. As Green recounts, a "thin layer of polyethylene has baked my seeds (too much sun), drowned them (too much water), steamed them and killed them with fungus." Lukewarm soil temperatures, somewhere between 60 and 70 degrees F, move perennial seeds to life and energy better than too much heat.

As a rule, seeds of hardy plants are slower to sprout than those of annual flowers or vegetables. Some seeds, such as those of gas plants, Christmas roses, foxtail lilies and peonies, may take a year or more to sprout. Who can wait? I tend to buy the slowpokes already grown. But many other perennial seeds, given first the cold treatment and then moderate warmth, show little green backs through the earth within a month, some much sooner. For a first foray into the world of seed-grown perennials, I suggest the following, all of which we have raised at one time or another at Larkwhistle using the methods described: various achilleas, perennial alyssums, anchusas, aquilegias, arabis, aubrietas, English daisies, bellflowers, perennial candytuft, dwarf catnip, hardy cornflowers, coreopsis, delphiniums, dianthus (very quick to sprout), hollyhocks, linums, lupins, monardas, painted daisies, rudbeckias, saponarias, stachys, verbascums and violas.

Gardeners like Patrick Lima, FACING PAGE, *who grow many of their perennials from seed develop a special affinity for their plants. Most seedlings will be nursed through their tricky infancy indoors, away from the dangers of weather, pests and weeds.*

35

Once seed has sprouted, cool temperatures and plenty of sunlight make for slow, steady, stocky growth. At this point, an unheated sunroom or cool greenhouse is obviously ideal, but a simple cold frame (an outdoor wooden frame with a hinged glass roof) will serve. I like to keep seedlings in a south-facing window until they show a first leaf or two and then set them in the frame, where I check them frequently for dryness—one thorough drying could mean death to the lot. As they develop, seedlings are thinned to several per pot and, then, to the strongest single young plant. Gardeners unable to observe their seedlings daily (or those apt to be forgetful) would do well to plunge the small pots up to their rims in the damp earth of the cold frame. Where slugs are a threat, a surrounding of sand is better than soil.

By nature, hardy perennials can take considerable cold, but too much heat, humidity or drought can easily kill them. As the spring weather warms up, rather than suffocate seedlings in a closed, humid frame topped with glass (or other glazing), I set over the frame a shading cover made of 1-by-2-inch lumber nailed to crosspieces; a length of snow fence would do the trick. If frost threatens, I toss an old blanket over the frame as an added precaution.

The Home Nursery

After about a month in the frame, young perennials will have outgrown the confines of the container and will be ready for the open ground. If a flowerbed is cleared, enriched and more or less planned, homegrown perennials can be put directly into their flowering positions, perhaps accompanying other plants purchased from a garden centre. At Larkwhistle, they usually make one more stop on their way to a permanent home—at a nursery bed. There is no more useful adjunct to a home garden. We routinely use one of the 4-by-25-foot raised vegetable beds as nursery space because it answers precisely the needs of young perennials.

Once young plants seem sturdy enough to fend for themselves, they

are taken from the cold frame and planted a full foot to 18 inches apart (depending on their eventual size) in the nursery, where they are treated to routine weeding, feeding and care. By the time our homegrown pinks or delphiniums take their place in the wide world of the flower garden, they are husky adolescents ready to add a splash of pink or a fountain of blue to the garden picture.

Discovering the right time to move perennials from a nursery to beds or borders entails some experimentation with plants in your own garden. In my experience, in this place, many perennials can be successfully moved any time from mid-September to Thanksgiving or early enough for them to put down some anchoring roots in their new home before winter. I am reluctant to set down hard-and-fast rules, but some guidelines are important: Lift plants carefully, with as large a ball of soil as possible intact around their roots, and set them in a hole big enough to accommodate the root ball. Tamp the earth gently but firmly around the roots with a blunt stick or trowel handle, and flood water into a shallow concave reservoir left around the plants to settle the soil and wash out air pockets. Thus treated, most plants do not wilt, a sure sign that they have not been traumatized by the move.

Shifting perennials in fall works well here because snow comes early

and stays late, thus maintaining a continuous protective blanket during the harsh months. Often the earth stays summer-soft under the snow. Seldom does a freeze-and-thaw cycle heave plants out of the ground, as happens elsewhere. In areas subject to fickle winters, try to complete transplanting before the end of September. Then in December, after the ground is frozen, lay evergreen boughs several layers deep over newly moved plants. You can also postpone transplanting until early spring, just as soon as you spy a start of new growth, but be prepared to pour on the water, especially if a sudden spring heat wave hits.

Spring or fall, the ideal time for transplanting perennials (or any plants) is in the afternoon or evening of a cool, calm, drizzly day. If several overcast or rainy days follow, newly transplanted things will be off to a good start. If the sun threatens to bake them, shade wilting plants with inverted bushel baskets, cardboard boxes or newspaper sun hats for several days.

Perennial Care

"It is one thing to make a perennial border and quite another to maintain it," says Richardson Wright. Granted, but if a garden is conscientiously cleared and generously fertilized at the start, the necessary after-care is accomplished with far greater ease. This garden maintenance includes roughly five tasks. Weeding and cultivating I count as one, because they usually happen together. Another three are watering, staking and trimming, this last job subdivided into pruning, removing dead flower heads and cutting back perennials in fall (see chapter 9). The remaining chore involves taking steps to keep plants relatively unmolested by insects and diseases.

As for the last task, the story of disease in our flower garden is, thankfully, short. In more than a decade of growing a wide variety of food and flowering plants, we have used no chemical fertilizers, herbicides or pesticides at Larkwhistle. A flourishing, healthy, abundant garden speaks volumes, I think, about the efficacy of generous and consistent organic treatment. Occasionally, a few peony stems drop from a botrytis infection, or the odd iris rhizome falls victim to bacterial soft rot; the phlox may mildew or hollyhock leaves sprout ugly orange spots. These few afflictions are fungal in nature, and while most are seasonal, none are terminal.

The old adage about "an ounce of prevention" is appropriate in the garden. Sanitation is our first line of defence. Diseased plant parts are pruned away and either buried in the centre of an active (hot) compost heap, thrown away or burned. Treating the soil kindly, too, is a preventive measure; tests have shown that plants growing in humus-rich earth are less susceptible to mildew. And fungal diseases are less apt to afflict perennials that are given adequate elbowroom or are growing in breezy gardens. Wise is the gardener who does not routinely spray a shower of water on the flowerbeds of an evening; fungus thrives where leaves are damp all night. Working in a wet or dewy garden can also abet the spread of disease.

The tale of insect pests is even shorter. For the most part, bugs are blasé about perennials; vegetables are more to their taste. In 12 years, we have yet to encounter an appreciable pest problem in the flower garden, and we have used nothing more potent than insecticidal soap to rid roses or honeysuckle of aphids or to clear out nests of earwigs. ("At least they die clean," quipped one visitor.) In damp weather, slugs munch their way through a shady salad bar of primroses and hostas. A foray into the garden after dark with a flashlight, however, brings the night crawlers to light for slippery hand-picking, an approach we also use by day to catch leaf-rolling worms and other obvious insects.

"Nature's censors," insects have been called. It is a maxim of organic culture that well-fed, strong-growing, lively plants are less attractive to bugs than any that are weak, ailing or otherwise struggling. (Could this explain why recent transplants are often chewed?) Again, selecting perennials that are suitable to your site and setting them in nourishing earth are important preventive measures. Also, a garden that grows a diversity of plants is less apt to be bothered by bugs. Grow only irises, and every iris borer around will find the place that provides their favourite food and lots of it.

Not all insects are anathema to a good garden. Ladybugs and praying mantids gobble aphids. Parasitic wasps prey on bugs that prey on plants. A gardener who hauls out the big guns to spray harsh, nonselective chemicals kills friend and foe alike and risks injuring bug-eating birds. The garden's delicate balance is knocked off kilter, and the next

At Larkwhistle, a simple cold frame, FACING PAGE, *is as useful for hardening perennials as it is for lettuce and broccoli. After the young plants leave the frame, few of them will be badly damaged by pests, but slugs and earwigs do occasionally dine on succulent hosta leaves,* LEFT.

season may bring more bothersome pests rather than fewer. Better to aim for balance and encourage birds with suitable shrubs and enticing birdhouses. Toads and snakes, too, are useful garden residents. Larkwhistle is home to snakes of several stripes. A slender sea green one lives in a dry-built stone wall; a graceful garter snake slides out from under a concealing umbrella of hosta leaves and—after a meal of slugs, one hopes—stretches over the rim of the lily pool for a drink. Tolerance, of course, has limits. Twice, after recovering from the shock, we have had to shoo away massasauga rattlesnakes, fierce-looking but timid creatures that are more than welcome to eat all the bugs and mice they like—outside the garden.

Weeds are also unwelcome in a flower garden. Variously defined as "flowers out of place" by Wordsworth and "poor creatures whose virtues have not yet been discovered" by Emerson, they mar its beauty, steal food and water from ornamentals and often host harmful insects. Like the

garden's rightful dwellers, weeds are perennial, biennial or annual. Perennial weeds, as noted earlier, had better be rooted out entirely before you set in a single garden plant, or they will trouble you ever after. Annuals and biennials should be grabbed before they run to seed because, in the words of an old saw, "one year's seeding, seven years' weeding."

There is really no shortcut here. Weeding is a hands-and-knees or a stooping job, but if it is not left until the emergency stage, it can be as relaxing and gratifying as any garden task. One garden writer tells of studying her French verbs as she worked her way along a flowerbed, the textbook open on the grass beside the weed basket. I like to listen to music or play the radio. In any case, unless weeding is done thoroughly—that means extracting interlopers root and all—it will have to be done again. "Cutting the tops off weeds," writes Louise B. Wilder, "has the same effect as cutting children's hair; it thickens the

growth." Turn weeds into the earth, and they will probably rise again.

Every gardener, no doubt, has favourite weeding tools. A curving grapefruit knife is useful for turning out plantain or other bothersome greenery from mats of creeping thyme and the like. Fingers work just fine on most weeds rooted in Larkwhistle's sandy soil, but a sturdy forked metal weeder comes in handy in clay gardens or wherever stubborn burdock—whose taproot "goes deeper than conscience," as I once read—or curled dock or bladder campion refuse to budge.

Where borders flank a lawn, encroaching grass is often a problem. If the border is edged with rocks, unchecked roots soon insinuate themselves under the rocks and become next to impossible to weed out. I once saw a gardener pouring gasoline along a stone-edged flowerbed in a desperate (and futile) attempt to kill the grass. What he ended up with was a hideous, oily edge and more grass moving away from the gas and into the flowers.

Much better, I think, to keep grass at least 8 inches from front-of-the-border plants or edging rocks at the start, and then, twice a year, to cut a scant 1-inch swath along the grassy verge with a sharp, flat-bladed spade—I am no fan of the flimsy rocking-horse tools sold as edgers—to remove the narrow band of sod along with attached grass runners that are invading the garden beds.

More Maintenance

When watering becomes necessary, it is best done deeply. Surface wetting does more harm than good by encouraging plant roots to remain shallow and thus susceptible to drought. Since we carry water by hand to our garden, we have found ways both to minimize the garden's need for water and to maximize the benefits when we do water. In areas where water consumption is restricted over summer, such methods are also appropriate.

•Add large amounts of spongy organic matter to the soil before planting perennials, and enrich deeply to encourage the growth of deep-rooted, long-lived plants.

•Early in the season, mulch thirsty perennials with compost, decayed leaves, straw or what have you. Tall, late-blooming thirsty plants, such as phlox, aconite, helenium, lythrum and heliopsis, benefit most from mulch, as do any plants that prefer damp ground, such as Siberian irises.

•Cultivate soon after a rain or an artificial watering to retain moisture.

•In a dry garden or drought-prone area, let the bulk of your perennials be drought-resistant. These include yarrows, mulleins, pinks, arabis, iberis, creeping phlox, most alliums, *Salvia superba*, bearded irises, lamb's ears and others mentioned as such in the forthcoming chapters.

•Sculpt the earth around plants so that water stays where it should. If I am hauling buckets of water to phlox, I do not want half of it running into the path or trickling around neighbouring plants.

•Add fish emulsion (or equivalent) to the water occasionally, or brew some manure tea, especially if plants are pining.

•Give watering priority to wilting plants or any that are on the verge of flowering in mid-drought.

•Learn a rain dance.

Like weeding, staking is better done before the need for it becomes critical. A budded peony is much simpler to support than one that has already sprawled. Besides top-heavy peonies, perennials that routinely need staking at Larkwhistle include tall bearded irises, delphiniums, balloon flowers, baby's-breath, the taller hardy asters, anchusas, perennial sunflowers and tall trumpet lilies growing in breezy places. Use slim green canes and twist-ties for irises and lilies, stout 1-by-2-inch lumber wound with strong string for delphiniums, and for others, follow the staking methods described in the discussion of individual perennials in the following chapters.

Once a week, during the summer, we do a "dead-heading" tour of the flowerbeds. All that is needed is a pair of pruning shears to snip away spent blooms or seedpods and a bucket or bushel basket for compostable refuse. Dead-heading not only enhances the garden picture by focusing attention on plants in bloom, it also prevents some prolific seeders from joining the ranks of a gardener's self-inflicted weeds. Dead-heading may also encourage further flowering.

Garden work is seasonal, with spring the busiest time followed by a fairly relaxed spell, once staking is done and before the fall flurry of activity. Whatever the season, garden chores are no hardship for me. The April days spent trimming and sprucing the flowerbeds, the June mornings given to shearing back early-flowering edging plants or staking peonies laden with promising buds, the late-summer evenings occupied in hauling buckets of reviving water (perhaps laced with fish emulsion) to thirsty phlox or heleniums are pleasant, relaxed times that provide opportunities to observe the garden's progress and to enjoy the flowers close up in an active, cooperative way. On the subject of garden work, Richard Eichenauer, a master gardener in British Columbia, says, "It's no bother at all. It's what I live for."

I echo the sentiment.

Where grass borders a flowerbed, its encroaching roots can be a problem. But if a thin rim of sod is sliced away from the bed edges once or twice a season, FACING PAGE, *grass roots rarely make headway. Such garden labour may seem tedious, but the necessary chores can give the gardener an opportunity to observe the garden's progress, and the flowers themselves, in an active, cooperative way.*

After the Snow
Early colour from small spring bulbs

Spring comes with dramatic suddenness to Larkwhistle. Often the earliest crocuses, such as 'Zwanenburg Bronze,' glow promisingly through the last fragile crusts of snow.

For me, the smell of spring air – "essence of fertility," one old-time garden writer calls it – has always been the season's most delicious sign. Breathing is deeper in spring. Our faces turned toward the sun, winter coats and boots having slipped away like a reptile's useless skin, we are forever filling our lungs and exhaling a satisfied, "Ah, spring." Even as a child growing up on a city street, all concrete and ceaseless traffic, I sensed this invisible signal with pleasure. Now that I tend a country garden, I welcome spring more than ever, for while my nose sniffs out the best scent of the year, my eyes quest for colour.

Spring comes with dramatic suddenness to Larkwhistle. One week the garden is snowbound and bleak; the next, if south winds and sunshine persist, there are flowers. Sparks of colour appear along the receding edge of the snow or glow promisingly just under the last fragile crusts of ice. Snowdrops (*Galanthus* spp) and winter aconites (*Eranthis* spp) are traditionally – but not invariably, in our garden – the earliest spring flowers. Under the snow, they have been silently active; spring thaw often finds these patient bulbs budded and ready, waiting for the first warm nudge.

Snowdrops
(*Galanthus* spp)

Snowdrops are not the fragile creatures they seem to be; indeed, part of their appeal lies in the contrast between their delicate appearance and their sturdy reality. Nature has fashioned these early flowers to push through crusty snow and hard ground and to cope with cold. Paired leaves, their tips sharpened to a callused beak, emerge holding the buds protectively between them. If winter returns, the buds may remain visible but tightly closed for weeks. Then, when the weather softens again, progress continues: leaves arch away, stems inch upward, and pearly buds bend toward the ground and open. A snowdrop flower – three small outer petals flaring over a tiny inner cup – is coldly white, save for three horseshoe marks of spring green on the cup; these bits of colour, says one writer, show the snowdrop's "fealty to the new order, else should we not mistake her for the child of grey old winter?"

Considering what the season throws at them in the way of snowstorms, sleet, driving rain, splashing mud and hard frosts, snowdrops last a long time in fine form. Gardeners can aid these willing early comers. Loamy ground, neither too dense with clay nor too light with sand, is what they need; a dressing of equal parts crumbly manure and peat is a help in most soils. Some shade, especially during the afternoon in warm gardens, is a must.

Early planting, too, is essential, as soon as bulbs are available and certainly no later than mid-September. "Not to do this," warns an expert, "is to court loss and a poor showing for many years." Snowdrops resent well-intentioned meddling – being dug up and moved around and, especially, being kept out of the ground any length of time. But left alone, they will increase by offsets and (if you're lucky) seeds for decades. That said, a gardener who

wants to spread an established planting or to share the wealth with friends is advised to move snowdrops either while they are flowering or very soon after. Trowel out little sods of clustered bulbs, keeping bulbs and roots intact with soil, and plant the clusters, firmly and pronto, in the new location.

Photographs of grand gardens show snowdrops naturalized by the thousands in woodlands or following the banks of a shaded stream. Most of us, however, are content to give them space on the shady side of shrubs or under deciduous trees. They are also at home in a wild corner or a shadowy border with small ferns, trilliums, hepaticas, bloodroot and the like. At Larkwhistle, snowdrops come up strongly through a cover of sweet woodruff (*Asperula odorata*) and elsewhere line the paths of an arbour that leads into the flower garden.

Winter Aconite
(*Eranthis* spp)

Picture a buttercup sitting on a frilly green ruff of leaves (botanically, an involucral bract, a whorl of leaves surrounding the flower) atop a 2- or 3-inch stem, and you have a fair view of the winter aconite. Snow melts to reveal round buds and arching stems already unfolding. In no time, there are flowers. Never mind that they will be hit with another round of winter. The flowers simply close and bide their time.

Winter aconites grow from small, brown, oddly shaped tuberous roots – "most unpromising looking," says

Larkwhistle's first spring warmth awakens a brave and patient lot of small flowers, FACING PAGE, TOP, *including the seemingly fragile snowdrops,* FACING PAGE, BOTTOM, *which hang out cold white bells, each marked with hopeful horseshoes of green. Winter aconites,* ABOVE, *also wait, budded and ready, for spring's first warm nudge.*

one writer. And indeed, eranthis tubers quickly lose all promise of flowers if they are out of the ground for very long. Commercial bulb growers know this and take some care to store and ship the tubers properly; bulb suppliers usually have eranthis on hand in August. It is up to gardeners, then, to order them early and tuck the tubers in the ground the day they arrive. Plant them 3 inches deep and the same distance apart. Since winter aconites grow best in precisely the same soil and sites that suit snowdrops and since the two bloom in sync, an early garden picture consists of a nice mingling of white and gold. Set the two thickly under a pussy willow, add a few dozen bulbs of the earliest bluebell, *Scilla bifolia*, and you have a spring scene guaranteed to lift winter-sated spirits.

Crocuses
(*Crocus* spp)

In a sunnier part of the garden, the first patches of colour are likely to be buds of wee *Crocus ancyrensis* poking through their tight bundles of spiky leaves. In *My Garden in Spring* (1914), E.A. Bowles, an English gardener and crocus fan, notes that corms of *C. ancyrensis* have "such a rough netted jacket that they are avoided by mice (have been so far, I write, for perhaps tomorrow I shall find holes, empty corm tunics and

room for repentance). I suppose it would be rather like having the tennis net entangled in our front teeth to chew such tunics."

In our garden, this 2-inch Turkish wildflower usually outpaces even impatient snowdrops or winter aconites. A single mild afternoon coaxes buds into six-petalled orange stars. Several dozen corms, 50 or so, are best, since they are inexpensive, take up next to no room and spread quickly to make a splash of warm colour in a cool spring garden.

This first crocus is followed in short order by a clutch of its wild kin. Some 80 or 90 species of the genus *Crocus* grow naturally throughout southern Europe, North Africa and the Middle East, usually in the highlands; Turkey is especially rich in wild crocuses. In some catalogues, they are dubbed "snowcrocus" because of their precipitous flowering, but by any name, they are among spring's best gifts to gardeners. A favourite of mine is *Crocus sieberi*, with its small cupped blossoms of cool lilac blue warmed by an orange centre and scarlet stigmata. Despite *sieberi's* origins in Greece, where it is said to be found at clevations of 1,000 to 7,000 feet above sea level, "disporting itself at the edge of receding snows," this crocus endures northern frosts and untimely snowfalls without flinching. "The best and most reliable of the race," Louise Beebe Wilder calls *sieberi* in

Adventures with Hardy Bulbs (1936), "and a good species to begin with, for it requires little attention and never disappoints." Our small colony, nestled at the base of a limestone rock, reappears each spring with a few more flowers from steadily multiplying corms.

From the variable species, *Crocus chrysanthus*, a host of hardy, early snow crocuses have descended, among them 'Snow Bunting,' 'Blue Bird,' 'Cream Beauty' and 'Zwanenburg Bronze.' These are the most generous of spring plants, increasing rapidly to form flowery mounds of clear colour—blue, white, yellow, cream—along border edges, down rock garden slopes or in any sunny corner where they need not be disturbed for years. All rush into bloom at the first hint of warmth. For best effect, these small corms should be planted in informal groups of, say, 25 to 50 at the front of a flowerbed. If later-flowering dwarf perennials are set between the groups, colour will carry on into summer.

Also eager to see the sun after months underground is *Crocus tomasinianus*, a slender species native to lands around the Adriatic Sea. Unpromising buds open clear blue, sparked with red stamens. At Larkwhistle, this species has grown to the clotted stage and comes up thick and strong through the reddish fleshy leaves of *Sedum album*. Like the Tommies (as we have taken to calling these old friends), many of the wild crocuses in our garden are planted under cover of some low perennial such as sedum or creeping thyme; also suitable for growing over the heads of species crocus are flat mats of *Veronica repens*, which will be sprinkled in June with tiny blue flowers, or silver spreads of pussytoes (*Antennaria tomentosa*). These covering plants not only provide the crocus with a becoming setting but also protect flowers from mud spattered during spring rains. And they may deter forgetful gardeners (a common enough breed) from accidentally slicing into corms during routine digging and delving.

Good company for soft blue *tomasinianus* is the aptly named *Crocus susianus* 'Cloth of Gold.' This Russian species has lived in gardens for

years. Records show that French botanist Carolus Clusius, the plant hunter credited with introducing potatoes into Europe, received *C. susianus* bulbs in the late 1500s, and both John Gerard and John Parkinson, writers of herbals in the 16th and 17th centuries, respectively, knew and grew it. Its small but abundant blossoms open flat and starry in spring, and a generous planting soon sheets the dark earth with brilliant orange. "As hardy as iron," Wilder calls this wild crocus; like the rest, it comes through even a last spiteful snowstorm with flying colours.

Many gardeners miss the early wild crocuses and count on the fat Dutch hybrids for first colour. While I would not forgo the species already described, I cannot imagine the spring garden without lots of these late crocuses—drifts of purple and gold, white and lavender, weaving through sprouting perennials along border edges, clustered around crimson peony shoots and emerging day lilies or skirting the sunny side of shrubs. The crocus is an informal flower; it never looks its best dotted along a single straight line (few flowers do). Rather, I like to plant crocuses in winding bands, three to five corms deep, trailing off to a few scattered flowers at the edge of a group. A mixed lot—all crocus colours are harmonious—creates a cheerful spring tapestry. Or several dozen corms of, say, 'Largest Yellow' might overlap an equal drift of white 'Peter Pan' or slate-blue 'Vanguard.' I like to see a smattering of the white-and lilac-striped 'Pickwick' lighting a shadowy mass of the large, purple-blue 'Purpureus Grandiflorus.'

Remember to associate the corms with perennials that can stay in place for many years; the crocuses themselves will not need digging and dividing until they show by fewer and smaller flowers that they are overcrowded. Many that were planted a decade ago at Larkwhistle are still in place and flourishing.

I have found that crocuses of all kinds, wild or tame, take care of themselves, provided their few requirements are met. First, they

Among the loveliest crocuses are the cool blue Crocus sieberi, FACING PAGE, *whose small corms require little space or attention yet increase steadily when planted along the edge of a border or in a sunny rock garden. Also part of a sparkling and easy-care spring picture are white 'Joan of Arc' and 'Largest Yellow' crocuses,* ABOVE, *accompanied by a stream of blue glory-of-the-snow. The bulbs push through a mat of grey-leaved dianthus that, in turn, grow and flower, obscuring the fading bulb foliage.*

45

crave sun for most of the day. Second, if protected from cold north winds, they flower earlier and longer. Finally, experts agree that the soil for crocuses should be nourishing and fairly light. Heavy clay, shade, soggy spots and soil clogged with fresh manure all lead to failure.

Crocuses are planted about 4 inches deep, from August through October. This slightly deeper planting may help to discourage chipmunks and squirrels from snacking on the corms. In subsequent seasons, a top dressing of crumbly compost or very old (or bagged) manure keeps them fit, but even if you miss this step, the crocus corms should take care of themselves. However strong the tidying urge, it is important after crocuses have blossomed to let the grasslike foliage ripen thoroughly to nourish next spring's crop of flowers; when it is withered and yellow, the foliage pulls away with a gentle tug, leaving corms in place. I get great satisfaction from going around the borders on late June mornings, yanking out handfuls of dead crocus leaves, admiring on the way the poppies and irises that have succeeded the simple spring flowers.

Early Irises
(*Iris* spp)

"Why make so much of fragmentary blue," poet Robert Frost wondered, "In here and there a bird, or butterfly / or flower . . . ." But we do. Gardeners have always been enthusiastic about any flower decked in azure. Fortunately, compared with other seasons, spring is generous with blossoms of this colour—bluebells, grape hyacinths, glory-of-the-snow and violets. A less familiar source of spring blue is an early little iris, *Iris reticulata*; the last name refers to the netted or "reticulated" coat that covers the oval bulbs.

This is a lovely creation, exotic in appearance but strong-growing and hardy in the cold. Spring thaw sees the horn-tipped, narrow leaves already through the ground. In no time, cocoon-shaped buds appear, and one morning, you wake to a south wind and find all the buds blown into exquisite, slender irises. Blossoms may be deep navy blue or

as soft as spring skies, violet-blue or purple, but on the three lower petals of each is a blaze of yellow-orange surrounded by a patch of white that is dotted with the flower's blue—"just right," says E.A. Bowles, "to attract any flying insect and please an artistic eye with its colour contrast." Bowles had been looking at one of his own seedlings ("my turquoise treasure which I call 'Cantab' ") when he wrote that and went on to say, "I think it is one of the loveliest of spring flowers." Agreed. 'Cantab' has proved a little shy in our garden so far, but other members of the reticulata group have taken off.

Especially vigorous is one tagged *Iris histrioides major*, true navy blue and always the first to bloom. Our original dozen bulbs have been in place for almost a decade; they live under mats of *Dianthus arenarius*, the sand pink, along a border edge and have multiplied at an astonishing rate. Each spring, I resolve to lift and divide the bulbs because they flower so thickly that the lovely intricacy of each blossom is lost in a blur of blue. But resolve wavers at the prospect of disturbing bulbs so obviously thriving. Maybe next year.

Reticulata irises are native to Turkey and Iran. Although they look exotic and challenging, they are, in fact, easy to grow. They need lots of sun, all day if possible. Soil of preference is a light sandy loam, well drained and sweet (no wonder they have taken to our garden). Heavier ground should be treated with a dressing of coarse sand, small stone chips, decayed maple leaves or old manure—but not peat moss; earth tending to acidity needs crushed limestone. The right setting for these gems not only shows them off but also ensures that they will grow well. I like to see the early irises nestled on the south side of good-sized limestone rocks that have been sunk partway into the ground; such rocks provide both background and safety from cold spring winds. Although a well-built rock garden is an ideal home for many spring bulbs, even three boulders arranged artistically in a corner of the yard can give shelter to several dozen *Iris reticulata* and a handful of wild crocuses. We cannot leave these irises without mentioning the fine, sweet, violetlike fragrance that some of them exhale and the small, perfect spring bouquets you can make with a cluster of irises, a sheaf of snowdrops, a twig of pussy willow or red dogwood and a few crocuses.

Glory-of-the-Snow
(*Chionodoxa* spp)

In a small town nearby, there is an expanse of front lawn that becomes a solid blue carpet for a few weeks each spring; it's as if a chunk of sky had fallen. The blue is supplied by *Chionodoxa luciliae* and *C. gigantea*. The genus *Chionodoxa* was named in the 19th century by Swiss botanist Pierre Edmund Boissier, who came upon a similar scene in the wild, "the spectacle of thousands of sky blue flowers against a background of dissolving snows" high on the slopes of a Turkish mountain. The Greek name translates literally as glory-of-the-snow. From small, pear-shaped bulbs, 4-to-6-inch stems emerge carrying clusters of two to eight flowers of clear blue, paling to a white centre. I am exceedingly fond of these simple starry things and like to see them streaming along a sunny border among drifts of yellow and

white crocuses, congregating under boughs of golden forsythia or exotic magnolias or lighting up a rock garden. Chionodoxas are determined self-sowers, but they are also so unobtrusive—at first they look just like seedling onions—that I let them stay where they settle. Their spring show is brilliant but brief, and the narrow leaves die back quickly, leaving no sign that the small bulbs are hidden underground.

Chionodoxas will take to almost any soil that is not brick-hard or waterlogged. They prefer sunshine for a good part of the day and earth that is porous with organic matter or gritty with sand or small stones. The bulbs are planted in the fall, about 3 inches deep and a few inches apart. After that, the work is done. As Louise B. Wilder notes in *Adventures with Hardy Bulbs*, "Recent plantations make little display; it is only after several seasons that those sheets of inimitable blue are produced that so richly reward the planter." Leave them alone, she advises, "to increase their lovely kind in peace." Good advice.

Scilla
(*Scilla* spp)

Like chionodoxas, scillas are small, early, self-reliant and serenely blue perennials that grow from bulbs. They flourish, however, in the shade. There is no trick to establishing a

Spring is generous with blue flowers. Exotic-looking but vigorous and cold-hardy are cultivars of Iris reticulata, FACING PAGE, *which are perfect for small bouquets and are scented like violets. None of spring's blue flowers are as brilliant as grape-scented Siberian scillas,* ABOVE, *which, left to multiply at will, soon create pools of azure anywhere in sun or shade, even under deciduous trees.*

47

small colony or even an extravagant mass of the familiar bluebells. (By bluebells, I mean the common *Scilla sibirica*, an iron-hardy native of northern Russia, as its name indicates.) Plant them in the fall, 3 or 4 inches deep and a few inches apart, in organically enriched ground (as for snowdrops), and then leave them alone ever after to increase at will. Small teardrop-shaped bulbs send up two or three narrow leaves, followed shortly afterwards by 4-inch flowerscapes hung with several dark blue bells, scented – if you stoop low enough or pick a posy, you'll detect it – of grapes. Siberian scillas, or squills, will grow just about anywhere but are at their best in shaded sites where they can spread undisturbed into carpets of blue.

Alternatives are *S. sibirica alba*, which is a white bell, and the flowers of the cultivar 'Spring Beauty,' which are darker blue than usual and have taller stems.

Earlier even than *Scilla sibirica* is *S. bifolia* (two-leaved), like the Siberian in habit and height but more tolerant of sun and less tolerant of damp or heavy soil. A sandy loam is best for this species, and given its early flowering, a site sheltered from harsh winds is preferred.

Scilla nutans is the common English bluebell or wood hyacinth. Recently renamed *Endymion nonscriptus*, it is also called ring-o'-

bells, an apt name for "the curving shepherd's-crook stalk with its dangling bells." In its native soil, this species is so common that "scarcely a copse can be found throughout our land that is not blue with its flowers," according to Anne Pratt in her 1840s book, *Wild Flowers*. Predictably, in our cold northern garden, the English bluebell lags far behind the Siberian in the matter of increase. Still, we enjoy a small colony of *S. nutans* growing in the shade of a cedar-log arbour, with a few native hepaticas and bloodroot for company; this modest woodlander is no match for the rough-and-tumble crowds of the perennial border. Bulbs go 4 or 5 inches deep and about 3 inches apart. English bluebells have a fresh scent, a gift you may miss unless you pick a few stalks for the house.

Big bear of the scillas is *Scilla campanulata*, the Spanish bluebell, last of all to bloom and an important element in our May garden pictures in the perennial beds. Bulbs of this species are large (several inches across), white and fleshy; the long, smooth leaves lie close to the ground. Sturdy flower stalks grow all of 18 inches tall, their upper halves decorated with many pure blue flaring bells. This is a showy plant for flowerbeds in light shade or sun, provided that the soil remains evenly moist. Spanish squills combine beautifully with cream or yellow

intermediate irises or tall late tulips of any colour; the white-flowered variety gleams among ferns, primroses or trilliums. Plant bulbs of *S. campanulata* 4 to 6 inches deep – the larger the bulb, the greater the depth – in well-drained loam fattened with humus.

Grape Hyacinth
(*Muscari* spp)

Earlier blue is supplied by several species of grape hyacinth, or muscari. The common name alludes to the arrangement of the small, rounded flowers in tapered clusters, like bunches of grapes, atop 4-to-6-inch stems. Even the rankest novice will succeed with grape hyacinths. The accommodating bulbs thrive in almost any soil short of swampland, take to any reasonably sunny site and return with vigour after even the harshest winter. In several seasons, they increase to form satisfying pools of blue among the white and yellow daffodils, blue ribbons binding shrub borders where polyanthus primroses grow or small fountains of azure between the crimson peony shoots just unfurling. In our garden, a favourite spring picture combines grape hyacinths with the burnished orange cups of the early tulip 'General de Wet' and clumps of the narcissus 'Yellow Cheerfulness.' This easy scene is a treat for the nose as well. The grape hyacinths and narcissi flood the air with sweetness, while the tulips smell of oranges.

Several species of *Muscari* are listed in bulb catalogues. *M. azureum* is small, early, very blue and the only species restrained enough to be admitted to a rock garden (if you hope to grow much else there). There is a white variety, too, that looks, as someone has said, "like a little wedge of seed pearls." The common grape hyacinth is *M. armeniacum*, a species so tough that it has lived untended for decades in the coarse tangle of grass and weeds which surrounds several uninhabited farmhouses nearby; it has a double form that seems congested to me and several cultivars of deeper or lighter blue.

A word about situating grape hyacinths in a border: because their foliage is uninteresting and their

lingering seedpods downright ugly, muscari bulbs are best planted where they will be hidden by perennials that leaf out after the blue show is over. Peonies are perfect for the task, as are day lilies, phlox, yarrows, hardy geraniums or Siberian irises. Remember, too, that (unlike other bulbs) all species of grape hyacinth send up leaves in the fall. This is a handy trait; the foliage indicates the bulbs' location so that one is not tempted to tuck a few crocus corms in that "empty" space.

The first flowers are a brave lot, valiantly testing the field long before fickle spring has settled in for sure. I can only admire their courage and tenacity. As I go about the cool garden in April and early May, tidying up winter's debris of snapped branches and flattened flower stalks, pruning roses or planting peas and spinach, I am heartened to see the slow, steady progress of snowdrops and crocuses, bluebells and sweet-scented muscari. Perhaps some of these small, early blossoms would go unnoticed in the flowery chaos of June and July, but after looking out on the white and grey winter garden for so long, I turn eagerly to each colourful expression of the new season.

Essentially informal, spring's small flowers never look their best dotted in a single line; rather, a mixture of colours such as those of several different crocuses, FACING PAGE, *can mingle in overlapping drifts. Since all crocus colours are harmonious, it is easy to create a cheerful tapestry. Sweet-smelling grape hyacinths,* ABOVE, *can be tucked around the crowns of vigorous summer perennials for early colour.*

49

The Primrose Path
A celebration of springtime perennials

Prolific and long-flowering, primroses are the quintessential spring flowers. Their common name means "the first rose," and indeed, the double varieties do resemble small roses. A shady site and moist organic soil are all that are necessary for a gardener to grow these "first roses" to perfection.

Spring is a gentle season. Against the dark earth and a backdrop of fresh green, the early garden is a harmony of yellow, white and orange flowers complemented by lavender and blue petals that match the sky in brilliance. All the colours of this cool spring spectrum are represented by just one plant group, the primroses, among the most generous of the early comers but so quiet and dependable that they are perfectly in tune with the unfolding season.

No spring perennials bloom as long—a full five weeks on average—and no perennials at all, with the exception of bearded irises, display as wide and lovely a colour range as primroses. A late-April walk along our little, ambling primrose path—a curving, yard-wide border skirting the shady side of budding lilacs—takes us past flowers that are pink, mauve and wine-purple, butter-yellow and cream, Indian-red, toffee-brown, golden tan and all shades of blue from light to navy. Most have been raised from specks of seeds (Michigan's Far North Gardens catalogue is a primrose treasure trove), and favourites have been split and resplit to extend the display.

Primroses are more than willing to add their fresh, simple flowers to the spring scene, provided their two needs, shade and moisture, are met. In their native lands from Europe and northern Asia to the Orient, primrose species congregate in moist meadows and shadowy woodlands, follow the courses of streams or hide in shaded swamps. To give their best in gardens, they ask for roughly the same environment. This may translate into a north- or east-facing border against a house or fence, the cool side of shrubs or a bed of humusy loam under the flickering shade of birch trees. Any gardener blessed with a damp, wooded corner by a stream or pond is set to grow primroses supremely well.

The lowly primrose has a big appetite for organic matter. After stripping away the turf from our prospective primrose path, we set about turning in an 8-inch layer of crumbly, dark cow manure mixed with dampened peat moss. That done and the border raked fine and smooth, we tuck in seedling prim-

roses about 10 inches apart—three to five yellows overlapping an equal drift of white or reddish brown. A manure mulch laid down the next spring and the next helps to maintain fertility and conserve moisture. With such encouragement, stripling primroses soon wax into robust clumps, sending up perfect fountains of multihued flowers.

But sooner or later, even the most pampered primroses begin to show a weakened ring of leaves around an increasingly bald and woody centre. It will be time then, sometime in June after the current crop of bloom is over, to renew a patch. After prying the shallow-rooted primroses out of the ground with a sturdy trowel or hand fork, ease a clump apart by hand—the dividing lines are easy to see—into one- or two-crowned divisions. Retaining only the liveliest outer growth, reset the plantlets in freshly enriched earth. If organic matter is in short supply, consider spot-enriching—several trowelsful of humus under each primrose—rather than applying a thin dressing over all. Water with dilute fish emulsion or manure tea, a brew made of manure dissolved in plenty of water, and see that the plants do not lack for moisture over the summer.

At present, our garden is home to ten species of primula, ranging from the tiny 2-inch *Primula rosea*, a hot pink eye-catcher and first to stage its

small brilliant show, to a lone, lovely *P. apicola alba*, a shy 2-foot Tibetan that brings the primrose season to a close with clustered, flaring, creamy white bells in late June. If these primroses intrigue only insatiable plant collectors, other species are more suited to creating sheets of colour in any garden not completely sun-scorched and dry.

Toward the front of a fairly sunny border at Larkwhistle, a half-dozen cowslips (*Primula veris*) make a spritely spring picture with tumbling white arabis and flame-coloured wild tulips (*Tulipa praestans*). Least fussy of primulas, cowslips do well enough with a modicum of shade and moisture but respond to better conditions with exuberant and extended spring bloom. Above typically tongue-shaped, crinkled leaves ("ovate" and "rugose" to the botanically minded), 8-to-12-inch stems carry side-swinging clusters or umbels of small, pendulous five-petalled flowers, freshly fragrant and coloured soft yellow with five tiny red dots ("rubies, faerie favours," according to Shakespeare). There are also rusty orange and scarlet cowslips.

Where the environment suits them, cowslips naturalize freely. Under the trees that line a local farm driveway, scores of them, self-sown like any native wildflower, light up the shade. Also, in a nearby village, cowslips, English daisies and, yes, dandelions annually transform one lawn from the usual plain green expanse into a flowery quilt patched with widening colonies of rose, red, yellow and white. The considerate gardener waits until the flower show subsides before bringing out the lawn mower.

More demanding of moisture, oxlips (*Primula elatior*) carry clustered soft yellow flowers that are larger and flatter than cowslips. But of all the wild primulas, the sentimental favourite of old-world gardeners is the common or English primrose (*P. vulgaris*), whose typical tuft of wrinkled oval leaves all but disappears under a swarm of flowers of simple primrose yellow, the colour of fresh butter, one to a stem.

Crosses between primula species have given rise to a sturdy race of garden primroses, the polyanthus of

countless colours and many variations in form. One seed-raised novelty, a hands-down favourite with garden visitors, is the gold-laced polyanthus. A sharp, light yellow edging laid over a blackish background gives this flower's 5 petals the appearance of 10. Then there are the double primroses, like small true roses of pink, peach or lavender. Our one specimen of a nameless wine-purple cultivar, bought five years ago for a hefty six dollars, has proven so vigorous that it has since been conjured into 11 fat clumps and could very well yield 50 or more divisions this summer.

As cowslips, oxlips, English primroses and polyanthus complete their blooming season, the star primrose of Japan (*Primula sieboldii*) begins to open elegant flowers — white, shell-pink, mauve or deep rose — as lacy as snowflakes. Rather than forming crowded clumps, this easiest, hardiest and most beautiful of primroses has the unusual attribute (for a primula) of a creeping rootstock that travels just under-ground and re-emerges as a new tuft of softly crumpled foliage a little way from the mother plant. Our patch of five seed-grown plants has been in place for four years with no sign of decline. When we think of it, we simply spread a manure mulch around the plants to maintain soil fertility. This primula retreats underground entirely during the hot summer months, only to show its lovely leaves and blossoms again next May. Our star primroses thrive in sun — since sun is all we have to give them — but according to all accounts, they would appreciate a half-day's shade in warmer gardens.

Two more oriental beauties complete our list. *Primula denticulata* is among the loveliest of spring perennials. Atop 10-inch stems, many small white, lavender or purple-red flowers, each petal notched or toothed as the Latin species name suggests, are arranged in perfect balls of bloom. It flowers very early, so we keep flowerpots on hand to pop over our *denticulatas* to ward off frosts that would spoil the bloom.

Rarely seen in gardens these days, the spritely, old-fashioned gold-laced primrose, FACING PAGE, *is as easy to grow as any other if given moist earth and some shade. Sharp yellow outlines on a black background give its 5 petals the appearance of 10. Better known are yellow cowslips,* ABOVE, *which create a fresh picture with tumbling white arabis, tulips, fragrant orange wallflowers and lingering grape hyacinths. Cowslips are among the few primroses that will tolerate the sun and dryness of an open border.*

Primula japonica, a tall late-flowering species belonging to the "candelabra" group, hoists strong, 2½-foot stems bearing intense magenta-crimson flowers in ascending tiers—a whorl of flowers, several inches of bare stem, another flowery whorl—above lush rosettes of lettuce-green leaves. A true bog primula, *japonica* is at home on the banks of a stream but can be made comfortable in well-manured loam that is kept nicely moist the season through. Our dozen clumps, again raised from seed, share space with hostas, Jacob's ladder and spiderwort in an 18-inch-deep raised bed filled with topsoil, manure and peat moss. All of them seem to enjoy a drink of cooled dishwater.

A challenge to grow in our sunny, sandy garden, primroses of all sorts merit special attention at Larkwhistle. Colourful and floriferous, they are not overly difficult to raise from seed but quicker and more certain from starter plants. In response to generous organic treatment and careful siting, all of them are capable of the most gratifying returns.

Species Daffodils
(*Narcissus* spp)

If I could grow only two spring perennials, primroses would be one of them and daffodils the other. When the flowerbeds are alight with daffodils swaying above simple blue-green leaves, I am almost ready to agree with an early writer that "the high point of the year has been reached, that all that follows is anticlimax." These are the quintessential spring flowers, fresh and in harmony with the gentle colours of leafing trees.

The genus *Narcissus* is a relatively small one containing perhaps 40 species all told; some botanists recognize as few as 12, since it is not clear where wild narcissi leave off and cultivated sorts begin. These wildflowers, the so-called "species daffodils," are the parents of all of our cultivated daffodils, of which there are thousands. The habitats of the wildlings range as far north as Scandinavia, as far south as the Canary Islands and eastward through Morocco and Algeria to the Orient. Many more daffodils grow in the mountains of Spain, Portugal and France. I find these wild sorts an intriguing lot because, growing in the same garden as the bold trumpets and the exotic crowned sorts, they illustrate just how much the small and simple flowers have been changed by hardworking hybridists and keen amateur gardeners. And the species are precious in their own right.

"When I first saw *Narcissus minimus*," says Louise B. Wilder in her *Adventures with Hardy Bulbs*, "I had the Alice-in-Wonderlandish feeling that I was gazing through the wrong end of an opera glass." Standing all of 3 inches tall, with flowers no larger than a dime, *N. minimus*, the smallest and earliest to bloom of all daffodils, is a perfect replica in miniature of the tall yellow trumpet types.

In the late 1800s, plant explorer Peter Barr discovered this wildling in the mountains of Spain, "growing freely on south-facing slopes among the gorse bushes." For years now, it has grown freely in our chilly garden, where it stages a brave small show in mid-April. The soil recommended for the little bulbs is gritty and neutral (a pH of around 6 or 7), not clogged with manure or overly sweetened with lime. Our colony grows in unimproved sandy loam with a surface mulch of stone chips; for company, there are the silver rosettes of encrusted saxifrages and other scaled-down alpine plants. Each year, a few more small trumpets sound a silent fanfare for returning robins and bluebirds.

Close to *Narcissus minimus* grows another Spaniard, *N. triandrus albus*, poetically called angel's tears. The name is apt. Its tiny ivory cups turn gracefully downward, the perianth petals flaring back like small wings. Several flowers hang from most of the 8-inch stems.

Although we give this bulb the recommended shady spot and good soil, it seldom stays more than two seasons in our garden. I suspect our winters are too much for it. But since it grows well in containers and responds to gentle forcing, the delicate flowers can be enjoyed close up indoors.

Triandrus is the parent of many hybrids, and those that we grow have proved hardy and increase freely. *Narcissus* 'Thalia' I particularly like for its white nodding flowers, like a flock of doves, several to each foot-high stem. We situated 'Thalia' behind a clump of *Erica carnea* (easiest of the heathers and one of the few species that will tolerate our nonacidic soil). When the daffodils are out and for some time after, its evergreen branches are lined with small mauve bells.

One of the strangest wild daffodils is *Narcissus cyclamineus* – the last name indicates that the flowers resemble cyclamen blossoms. A "little horticultural joke," one writer calls this 4-to-6-inch species, with its long, narrow trumpet below petals that are turned sharply back "like the ears of an angry mule." The flowers are clear yellow. It thrives in a cool, moist (but not waterlogged) site. One Upstate New York gardener says *cyclamineus* is quite hardy, seeds freely and does not mind a dry summer "as long as the ground is damp in spring." Another expert says, "not frost-tolerant." What's a gardener to do? For us, it grows and flowers at the base of an east-facing rock but has not yet increased.

Certainly prolific and enduring are cultivars derived from *cyclamineus*. The optimistically named 'February Gold' and 'February Silver,' yellow and creamy white respectively, are very flowery in May. In size and colour, these two show their link with the later trumpet daffodils. Our colonies of 'Silver' and 'Gold' push strongly through a dense ground cover of sweet violets (*Viola odorata*) that bloom with them and add fragrance to a fresh spring picture of white, yellow and purple. Often, these early daffodils are caught by frost or a late snowfall, but I have never seen them damaged. Both increase generously.

With its reflexed yellow perianth and longish nose, 'Peeping Tom' betrays its wild origins. But perhaps my favourite *cyclamineus* hybrid is wee 'Jack Snipe,' a 9-inch toughie with white, slightly turned-back petals behind a neat yellow cup. It blooms for as long as three weeks in May and is especially nice mingling

with grape hyacinths and cowslips.

Narcissus bulbocodium, a 6-inch species that hails from mild Mediterranean lands, seems a little dubious about staying in a northern garden. Every spring, there are a few flowers from our original dozen bulbs, but certainly no increase. Quaint is the word for the small yellow blossoms with their flaring conical cups, like windblown skirts, and very thin perianth petals streaming behind; the hoop petticoat is this bulb's descriptive common name. In chilly gardens, a warm sheltered spot in moist but well-drained ground keeps this species comfortable. If soil is not up to par, a special pocket of loam, leaf mould and sand can be made for the bulbs. Like *triandrus*, these, too, are fine for forcing, six or eight bulbs to a pot.

Many daffodils, wild or tame, are fragrant. Some exhale a rough, earthy scent; others are quite sweet. But best of all, at least to my nose, is the perfume of jonquils. Fragrance, in general, is hard to describe, and this is no exception. I can only say, plant a few bulbs of *Narcissus jonquilla*, and you are in for a spring treat. I am always amazed that such a small flower can pour out a scent that is at once so delicate and strong, so freshly sweet – I want to say innocent – but never cloying. I like to pick a jonquil for each Larkwhistle visitor to carry while touring the garden; most keep it close to their

Blooming later than most primulas, the Japanese bog primrose, FACING PAGE, LEFT, *must have damp earth and partial shade to thrive. In a dry garden, it is worth creating a pocket of humus-rich soil for this tall oriental beauty. Blooming concurrently with the primroses are lesser-known species narcissus such as 'Thalia,' a hybrid of* Narcissus triandrus, FACING PAGE, CENTRE, *and the diminutive* Narcissus bulbocodium, ABOVE. *This 6-inch wildling has an unusually shaped trumpet that has inspired the common name, hoop petticoat daffodil.*

short – 8 inches, tops – with small flowers. I am intrigued by the sound of *Narcissus juncifolius*, a "baby jonquil" with yellow, intensely fragrant flowers, a grand three-quarters of an inch across on 4-inch stems. Where in the garden could such a mite go without getting lost? Most wild daffodils are out of scale with fat border perennials. They are safe, however, in a rock garden and are at home with wildflowers such as Dutchman's breeches, spring beauty, hepatica, dog's-tooth violets and bloodroot, with the caveat that the site must not be too densely shaded. Little clearings can be left in a border of primroses for a dozen bulbs of some species. Wild narcissi are plants for gardeners who appreciate beauty in small packages, for those willing to get close to the earth to observe the finely wrought form of this small bit of spring gold.

Hybrid Daffodils

Horticulturists are not always kind to flowers. The search for bigger, bolder, brighter – even weirder – has changed many a simple blossom into a puffed-up caricature of its wild self. Those who fiddle with genes and chromosomes have inflicted on gullible gardeners black tulips, blue roses and floormop dahlias, not to mention peonies, gladioli and delphiniums that can't get through life without a sturdy crutch. But as far as I can see, daffodils have survived centuries of breeding unspoiled. Even the grandest of them retains a measure of natural grace.

In 1936, Louise B. Wilder wrote, "Gerard, who gardened in the time of Elizabeth, named twenty-four kinds as commonly grown about London. There are now something like six thousand." And that was then. Who knows how many daffodils have appeared since? It would be impossible for the average garden to grow even a small fraction of them. But if I take a walk through the spring garden, certain varieties stand out from the flowery crowds for their exceptional beauty, sturdiness, unique colour or the fact that they bloom earlier or later than the rest. Using the Royal Horticultural Society's narcissus classification as a

noses the whole time.

Jonquils open after the other species have come and gone – mid-May here – and last for weeks in good condition. The waxy flowers, clustered in twos and threes at the top of 8-inch stems, are bright yellow throughout, as round as pennies, with overlapping petals behind a tiny flat cup (the source of all that sweetness). The leaves are dark green and very narrow – rushlike is the usual description; the word jonquil is derived from the Latin *iuncus*, a rush. Any decent, well-drained soil will grow jonquils, and according to one expert, they "can stand a good deal of

undiluted sunshine." A rock garden is a good home for them, as is the sunny side of shrubs or border edges. To please the eye as well as the nose, jonquils ought to be planted in close groups of a dozen or more. Here, we grow them at the front of a perennial border near clumps of creeping phlox (*Phlox subulata*), one of the best spring edgings; the prickly phlox foliage is lost under pink, lavender or white flowers, while the jonquils provide colour contrast – and, of course, fragrance. The bulbs are hardy and multiply in a way that may prompt a gardener to generosity.

As a group, wild daffodils are

map through that maze of cultivars, I have listed here some that have proven hardy, healthy and vigorous in our garden for many years.

•Division No. 1: trumpet or crown as long as or longer than the perianth segment.

'Unsurpassable' is a classic yellow trumpet daffodil, tall and strong. I especially like it when it reaches the stage of staring straight at the sky.

'Mount Hood' is a fine white trumpet, very crisp and formal and both shorter and later-flowering than the forgoing. Each spring a corner of our garden is freshly red and white when clumps of 'Mount Hood' open behind crimson early tulips 'Couleur Cardinal.' Over the border edge tumbles a mass of double arabis (*Arabis albida flore-pleno*), also white and just the right frothy foil to the upright flowers behind.

Four years ago, a single bulb of *Narcissus* 'Fortissimo' arrived as a bonus with a fall bulb order. Tucked in a corner of the vegetable garden, the lone bulb soon formed a strong clump. Each spring, there were a few more of the largest, brightest daffodils I have ever seen, with yellow perianths 6 inches across and enormous reddish orange trumpets. Somehow, they are not too much of a good thing. Last fall we lifted the clump carefully with a spading fork, separated the matted bulbs into 12 or 15 two-nose divisions and set these in a flowerbed with some

crown imperials to match the daffodils' boldness.

•Divisions No. 2 and 3: cup or crown less than the length of the perianth.

For more than a decade, 'Carlton' has flourished for us, forming stout clumps of soft yellow, large-crowned daffodils fairly early in the season. We call it "the pump yellow" when we forget its real name, because it once thrived unattended in the grass around the ancient hand pump that supplies our house and garden with water.

'Silver Standard' is a tall beauty with white petals and a cup that starts out yellow and turns creamy white. And as one catalogue promises, it blooms for an exceptionally long time. We find this cultivar much better than the look-alike 'Ice Follies,' which is prone to topple in a spring shower and fades rather quickly.

'Belisana' is another favourite, different from the rest with its ivory-white perianth and flattish, flared yellow crown dressed up with a frilly orange rim.

'Mrs. R.O. Backhouse' has lived in gardens since the 1920s, a sure sign of merit. Its flowers are smallish with a narrow, fluted trumpet coloured soft apricot-pink, sitting on a white background. This is a reliable late bloomer that we grow with sky blue Virginia bluebells in the light shade of a budding lilac.

Last of the hybrid daffodils to bloom (and one that seems to have

A springlike colour harmony of purple and gold is produced by such plants as the Narcissus cyclamineus *cultivar 'February Gold,'* FACING PAGE, *growing through a carpet of fragrant sweet violets,* Viola odorata. *Daffodils are not always entirely gold, however. While the big yellow trumpet sorts are the most familiar, other cultivars such as 'Silver Standard,'* ABOVE, *display attractive white, cream or apricot shades, which are nevertheless in keeping with the springtime colour theme.*

disappeared from catalogues) is 'Ultimus,' a lovely flower with a creamy perianth and soft orange crown on a 2-foot stem. Blooming beside a group of yellow 'Golden Melody' triumph tulips with wands of blue grape hyacinths at its feet, 'Ultimus' is part of my favourite spring picture. The emerging foliage of wormwood (*Artemisia absinthium*) and a nearby peony provide a dash of silver and bronze to the scene and later hide the yellowing bulb leaves.

And we must have a representative of the small-cupped sorts. 'Edward Buxton' is one such old friend – "Ed B." now – which crops up each spring around two sprouting peonies; his perianth is buff-yellow behind a buttonlike orange cup that tends to fade at the edges in the sun. After nine years in the same spot, Ed needs lifting, splitting and replanting in enriched ground.
• Division No. 4: double daffodils.

Of the few double daffodils that we grow, only 'White Lion' has stems sturdy enough to keep the top-heavy flowers from falling over. It is a camellialike flower coloured white, cream and pale apricot. The double yellow 'Dick Wilden,' very showy but a bit too fat, always falls over in the first shower and usually ends up filling jars and vases indoors.
• Divisions No. 5, 6 and 7: hybrids of *Narcissus triandrus*, *N. cyclamineus* and *N. jonquilla*, respectively.

Some of these I have already mentioned. As a rule, they are smaller-flowered and relatively short, dainty treasures for rock gardens, city yards or intimate corners of larger gardens with plants in scale. 'Suzy,' however, is fine for perennial

beds or borders; a jonquil by birth, she shows little family resemblance with her flashy red and yellow flowers and lanky stems. Only the cluster of flowers on each stem and a sweet scent betray her origins.
• Division No. 8: poetaz.

The poetaz narcissi are crosses between the tender 'Paper White,' so popular for growing in pebbles and water indoors during the winter, and the hardy poet's narcissus, *Narcissus poeticus*. This last species, recognized by its pure white petals and red-rimmed, buttonlike crown, often survives around old farmsteads long after the inhabitants have left. In the tangle of grass, burdock and briar roses that would become our garden, we found clumps of "poets" languishing under lilacs and half choked by day lilies but still flowering valiantly. Those that we divided and moved into a new flowerbed have responded with lots of flowers late in the daffodil season and a quick increase of bulbs. They bloom in the filtered shade of a dwarf 'North Star' cherry tree whose lace of white flowers appears at the same time.

'Cheerfulness' and 'Yellow Cheerfulness' are floriferous poetaz cultivars that I would miss if they were not in place every spring. Both are multiflowered, double (but small) and very fragrant; both are indispensable in May garden pictures. 'Cheerfulness,' white with a few buff and reddish petals tossed in for warmth, gleams behind early orange 'General de Wet' tulips, with a smattering of blue grape hyacinths winding through all. Elsewhere, hot pink creeping phlox contrast with this narcissus, while tufts of blue forget-me-nots lighten the scene.

Narcissus Culture

If you have ever dug up a clump of daffodils during September in the process of reorganizing a hardy border, you'll have noticed that the bulbs are already well supplied with new white roots. It is their nature to root early in the fall, a sign that one should have daffodil bulbs in the ground as soon as possible. October planting is still on the safe side, but any later is risking failure. Be guided in planting depth by both the size of

the bulbs and the nature of the soil. Generally, 4 to 6 inches of earth is enough over the round "shoulders" of most daffodil bulbs, although the smallest species go only 2 or 3 inches deep, while the very long-necked sorts and the largest bulbs of the biggest trumpet daffodils go down 6 or 9 inches. For all types, relatively deeper planting is suggested in lighter soils and shallower planting in heavy ground. And remember to allow each bulb space to multiply; 6 to 8 inches between them is not too much. The effect will be a little spotty the first spring, but after a few seasons, each bulb will yield a veritable bouquet of flowers. "Close massing" – again, the observation of Louise B. Wilder – "results in an unhappy effect not unlike a feast of scrambled eggs set for a giant."

The best soil for daffodils is loamy, nourishing and well-drained. "They delight in cool conditions," says one expert, and "on hot, starved soils, cannot thrive." Both heavy clay and light sand are improved by generous dressings of organic matter – but

fresh manure is not on their diet.

Daffodils are encouragingly easy to grow. True low-maintenance plants, they are cold-tolerant, insect-proof, healthy and enduring. Nor are they overly fussy about soil and site. For instance, they can bloom through emerald green *Vinca minor* – the familiar myrtle or periwinkle – under a clump of white birches. Other ground covers and other trees, especially fruit trees, provide a fine setting for them too, if the shade is not too dense. In light woodlands, they seem at home where other plants would look out of place. They can decorate the banks of a pond or stream, provided they are out of the way of standing water.

At Larkwhistle, the perennial beds appear full to overflowing with daffodils in April and early May. A month later, however, the scene has changed: a new wave of early summer flowers has succeeded the daffodils, and the promising greenery of even later-blooming perennials is very much in evidence. The beds once again appear full but this time

with different plants. At first glance, you might not guess that the garden has already yielded an abundant crop of daffodils. Traces of them have all but disappeared – a neat bit of garden magic.

The trick is to plant the bulbs in the company of later-sprouting herbaceous perennials that will ultimately grow up and out to obscure the fading bulb foliage with an umbrella of their own leaves. Suitable plants to use in conjunction with daffodils include: peonies, phlox, painted daisies, day lilies, gas plants, purple loosestrife, baptisias, tall yarrows, aconites in variety, Siberian irises (but not the bearded sorts), hostas, snakeroot, the larger artemisias and *Sedum spectabile*. These are all mid- to back-of-the-border perennials. To accomplish this kind of interplanting, we set the perennials, three or five of a kind grouped together, slightly farther apart than usual – generally a full 2 feet. We then plant daffodil bulbs about 8 inches apart in a weaving fashion among the crowns of the

Baptisia

One of the last daffodils to bloom, 'Ultimus,' FACING PAGE, *is a tall, stately cultivar that increases to a generous bouquet after a few seasons. It is part of the spring picture at Larkwhistle,* ABOVE, *where white, yellow and blue appear against a background of budding green. Later, this garden will be filled with irises, peonies, lilies, loosestrife and many other perennials that are just emerging between the blossoming bulbs.*

59

perennials, being careful to keep bulbs at least a hand-span from the herbaceous plants. Voilà, no ugly yellowing bulb foliage ("their last state is not as lovely as their first," as Wilder puts it) and a second crop of flowers in the same spot.

Virginia Bluebells
(*Mertensia virginica*)

Daffodils are also enhanced by the company of other spring flowers. Nothing could be finer planted alongside them than Virginia bluebells, a gift to gardeners from eastern American woods. Early in spring, intriguing purple shoots sprout from chubby, blackish tubers planted the previous fall. By daffodil time, shoots have become 18-inch stems clothed with tongue-shaped, blue-green foliage. At the end of each stem, a tightly packed spiral of mauve buds gradually unfurls into a succession of bells tinted the most glorious turquoise, a blue not matched by any other flower I know. In our garden, Virginia bluebells grow practically on top of crowded bulbs of the "pink" daffodil 'Mrs. R.O. Backhouse'; they push through to make a favourite picture in a corner bed backed by a cedar rail fence and the hazy green of a leafing shrub. I recommend mertensia, a clear favourite with visitors, for any lightly shaded site in cool, moist earth. With us, it seeds freely. Each spring there are lots of single oval leaves – bluish green, purple-tinted – that are a welcome promise of more blue next year. By early summer, the foliage dies away. Plant mertensia tubers several inches deep; the end of the tuber with the little pointed "eyes" (next year's shoots) goes up. If you have no choice but to move this plant in years to come, September is the month.

Lungworts
(*Pulmonaria* spp)

Mertensia's spiralled arrangement of pinkish buds and blue flowers reveals the plant's ties with borage, comfrey and anchusa, all members of the family Boraginaceae. Several kindred plants bring more blue to the spring garden – just the colour we need to set off the prevailing scheme of yellow and white. The lungworts, for example, are enduring, easy plants for almost any soil in light shade.

Pulmonaria officinalis is the ubiquitous spotted dog of older gardens, sometimes known as Jerusalem cowslip. It grows dusty-looking greenery mottled with dots and blotches of creamy white. Typical of many family members, its buds are mauve, but the bell-shaped flowers turn gradually blue. This plant is sturdy enough to be grown as a ground cover in difficult corners and can be divided to any extent in fall to increase its scope. Clumps of daffodils will flower through it.

The jewel of this genus, however, hides under the ponderous name of *Pulmonaria angustifolia azurea*, or, not very poetically, blue lungwort. Sprays of brilliant blue, funnel-shaped flowers, as deeply tinted as the famous Alpine gentian, sway over bristly, dark green leaves that are oblong and pointed. Bring this plant together with soft yellow English primroses (*Primula vulgaris*) and white narcissus 'Thalia' for a spring picture that sparkles in filtered shade.

Forget-Me-Nots
(*Myosotis alpestris*)

I know one gardener who is so fond of the modest blue forget-me-nots that she can't bear to root out a

Among late spring's blue flowers is brilliant turquoise Mertensia virginica, FACING PAGE, *perhaps the loveliest accompaniment for daffodils such as the (supposedly) pink 'Mrs. R.O. Backhouse.' Virginia bluebells grow from elongated tubers best planted in the fall; left to seed, they create ever-widening stretches of blue. More modest (but also apt to create increasingly wide patches if allowed to go to seed) are forget-me-nots,* LEFT, *which nicely accompany primroses. Forget-me-nots can become one of the gardener's self-inflicted weeds.*

single one. This presents a problem, since the pretty *Myosotis alpestris* – the first name means mouse's ear in Greek, which is just what the leaf resembles – is easily the garden's most unrestrained seeder, a real self-inflicted weed. At last visit, her spring garden was alight with blue, but what happens after the forget-me-nots are gone? We are strict with this spring flower; most of the seedlings are rooted out in the course of regular weeding, with only a few left to fatten up for next year's bloom in places where we think a little blue would help the picture.

Dwarf Anchusa
(*Anchusa myosotidiflora*)

Forget-me-nots are best treated as biennials. But the big blue borage family includes a fine perennial substitute in *Anchusa myosotidiflora*, a plant whose cumbersome last name says simply that its flowers look like forget-me-nots, or are myosotislike. This foot-high herb was new to us last spring (after a decade of searching in catalogues and nurseries) and promises to be a sturdy, trouble-free and long-flowering addition to the spring scene. Its leaves, slightly coarse and hairy like those of many of its kin, are heart-shaped and dark green. The small, intensely blue flowers come for six weeks or more through May and early June. When flowers are past, the leaves keep growing large and lush; if they threaten to overshadow smaller plants, some can be snipped off with no harm done to the anchusa.

Anemones
(*Anemone* spp)

Named for the Greek *anemos*, or wind (hence "windflowers"), anemones of one kind or another inhabit meadows and woodlands throughout the earth's temperate lands. Two species, so distinct that you would not guess they were related, colour at daffodil time. Both are so lovely, it is hard to choose between them. First to flower is *Anemone blanda* and specifically, the cultivar 'White Splendour'; the other is *A. pulsatilla*, the pasque flower.

We had heard that spring anem-

ones were tricky in the north and had repeatedly planted *Anemone blanda* without so much as a rewarding leaf. But hope springs eternal. Three falls ago, we tucked a dozen brownish *blanda* tubers, like gnarled bits of wood, in a sunny square foot of ordinary sandy earth in front of some heather bushes. Luck attended us. We later read that this 6-to-8-inch-tall Grecian windflower enjoys "a good loamy soil and the twiggy protection of little bushes against the blustering winds" and that it "craves all-day sun." By chance, too, we had planted the tubers where they are covered (quite literally) by tons of snow over the winter, thus ensuring that they do not freeze and thaw repeatedly. An equivalent protective mulch is necessary in gardens where winters are cold but the snow cover is iffy. Now every spring, we welcome back the mass of shiny white, thin-petalled flowers, like the most delicate daisies, each warmed by a centre of yellow stamens. The blossoms open widely in the sun, all but hiding the pretty, cut-leaved bronze-green foliage, and close protectively each night. Flowers last for a gratifyingly long time, in spite of fickle spring weather. I don't know if there is another spring flower that gives me as much pleasure as this animated anemone.

More certain is the pasque flower, a graceful, foot-high alpine that has settled comfortably in our garden. Finely incised leaves are silky with tiny hairs, and even the flower buds are furred. Blossoms, usually light violet but in some varieties wine-red or purple, are deep, six-petalled cups filled with contrasting yellow stamens. Each bloom sits neatly in a feathery green ruff. Anyone who has seen the related Prairie crocus (*Anemone patens*), the provincial flower of Manitoba, knows something of the pasque flower's charm. This plant is decorative for many weeks. The plumed seed heads that follow the flowers are sought by visitors for dried winter bouquets. The pasque flower takes to dryish, rather stiff ground in full sun. Tricky to grow from seed that is not ab-

A furious self-seeder, forget-me-nots can become the ground cover for an entire garden, FACING PAGE, *although after they finish blooming, the plants become unsightly and must be sheared back. More dignified is* Anemone pulsatilla, LEFT, *whose finely cut leaves and flower buds are silky with tiny hairs. This dependable windflower follows its bloom with decorative feathered seed heads that dry well for winter bouquets.*

solutely fresh — and even then not a sure thing — this plant regularly crops up in nurseries. Once planted, it should be left for years to increase in stature and beauty; the ranging roots cannot be divided with any success. Our five or six plants grow in a 3-foot border on the sunny side of a honeysuckle shrub. Somehow, I would not trust them to a crowded perennial border.

Fritillarias
(*Fritillaria* spp)

Behind the tall hybrid daffodils, no plant is as striking as tall *Fritillaria imperialis*, the regally named crown imperial. John Parkinson, botanist to Charles I, thought fit to give this "jocund herb" the place of honour in his 17th-century book of plants: "The Crowne Imperiall for his stately beautifulness, deserveth the first place in this our Garden of Delight." Native to the ancient land of Persia and points east, exotic crown imperials seem to belong to myth and romance — even after you get a whiff of them.

At all stages, whether in or out of the ground, this plant gives off a very unflowerlike scent. The smell, strongest just as shoots emerge in spring, has given rise to the name "stink lily" in some quarters. It is

astonishing, then, to read in one old herbal that the blossoms were once used "to adorn the bosoms of the beautiful." In its proper place — that is, the garden — I have no objection to the perfume this bulb wears and agree with Parkinson that the scent is "not unwholesome."

Early in spring, fat pointed noses, bronzed and polished, push aside the earth in a determined reach for light. Before a month has passed, leafy stems are standing 3 feet tall and are preparing to ring their clusters of large blockish bells, brick-red, yellow or orange, the works capped by a topknot of greenery. If you tip a flower gently upward, you'll see five conspicuous drops of pearly nectar at its heart. If you're lucky, you will also see hungry Baltimore orioles find your fritillarias, cling to the strong stems and all but disappear into the flowers in search of nourishment.

As might be expected from such a stately plant, the grapefruit-sized bulbs of crown imperials are larger than any others northern gardeners are apt to handle. The plant has a correspondingly large appetite. Soil of preference is a sweet loam, fattened with spongy organic matter down a foot or so. Into this nourishing stuff, they are planted 4 to 6 inches deep and a good handspan apart. Bulbs should be planted

at least 3 feet from shrubs and trees, which would rob them of necessary food. At least six hours of sunshine is essential.

Groups of three or more crown imperials are obviously more striking than a single specimen, but gardeners with more patience than cash — bulbs sell for about $5 apiece — could plant one bulb and wait for the increase. As one expert notes, "Newly planted bulbs flower magnificently for several years . . . then they begin raising a leggy family." In midsummer, after the foliage has yellowed, it is time to ease a clump out of the ground, separate bulbs one from the other and replant them in freshly enriched earth. A single bulb may yield five or six in several years.

Catalogues list a number of crown imperial varieties. Here, 'Maxima' red has proliferated to such an extent that the original group of three is now five groups of a half-dozen bulbs each — with a few left over to sell. At the same time, a lone 'Maxima' yellow has only just maintained itself and seldom flowers in a less-than-ideal spot. I have seen thriving clumps of this variety in Hamilton's Royal Botanical Garden, so perhaps our experience with it is not typical.

A second species, *Fritillaria meleagris*, is so slender of leaf and stem that I seldom notice it until it is actually in bloom. The flowers are squarish bells—the name fritillaria comes from the Latin *fritillus*, or dice box—curiously coloured with a grid of purple lines on a white background. The odd markings have inspired the names guinea hen flower, snake's head and checkered-lily.

In its native Norway and in the meadows of Europe and England where it has taken up residence, *meleagris* grows thickly in damp, sandy loam. Where it is content, it increases quickly both from bulb offsets and seed. Our bulbs, growing at the bottom of the flower garden with primroses and dwarf daffodils under the light shade of a cedar arbour, have even sent a few scouts into the adjacent hayfield. How they will fare in the dense grass is anyone's guess, but this plant is often recommended for naturalizing in grassy orchards or damp meadows. Perhaps a stretch of tame lawn would serve.

Rock Cress
(*Arabis* spp, *Aubrieta* spp)

The diverse family of Cruciferae gives the vegetable gardener broccoli, cauliflower, cabbage and a host of other practical plants. For the gardener keen on decorating the early garden, there are the related rock cress (*Arabis albida*) and purple rock cress (*Aubrieta deltoidea*), which, being fibrous-rooted, provide welcome contrast to the otherwise bulb-dominated spring palette. Arabis and aubrieta both hug the ground closely and gradually creep outward to form mats of greenery and flowers along border edges, down the small hills of a rock garden or in festoons at the top of a retaining wall.

Aubrieta thrives in fertile, well-drained earth and is far better off if it has reasonably consistent moisture. It takes to full sun or light shade. Although this Mediterranean native, evergreen at home, is hardy in northern gardens, it is apt to brown badly in a damp winter. Tidy it up with a shearing, and see if the dead-looking stems aren't soon bristling with new leaves. Aubrieta sprouts quickly from seed—what else would you expect of a radish relative?—and

grows into a neat green tuft the first summer. If set out firmly in its permanent home in early September, it is ready to meet spring with a bright bouquet.

Arabis is like aubrieta in all ways save that its scalloped leaves are slightly larger and greyer and its typically four-petalled flowers are usually white. Easiest of border plants to grow in any well-drained loam, it needs only a close haircut after flowering to keep it thrifty and dense. With daffodils and cowslips, it creates a fresh spring trio. The simple early flower has given rise to a double sport: a frothy, cheerful plant decorated with many spikes of small, full-petalled blossoms that visitors have likened to tiny roses or stocks. I think they look a lot like popcorn. Our showy edger came from a rough-and-ready gardener who yanked a handful of stems from her patch and said, "Stick 'em in the ground. They'll grow." And so they did and have provided plenty of slips for other gardeners. Double arabis— it goes by the surname *albida flore-pleno*—can be propagated vegetatively only; the single sort, however, is easy to grow from seed. Both are excellent ground covers for dryish, sunny sites, providing suitable backgrounds for the taller flowers of a gentle and colourful spring.

Striking and exotic, the crown imperial fritillaria, ABOVE, *looks every bit the Persian native that it is. This impetuous bulb accomplishes 3 feet of growth by daffodil time, thus adding height to an early border. At the front of a border, purple rock cress,* FACING PAGE, *blooms at the same time as orange cowslips, grape hyacinths and daffodils. Purple rock cress, or aubrieta, sprouts quickly from seed and grows into a neat green tuft the first summer.*

May Days

Tulips and their contemporaries

Tulips are not known for their sweet scents, but both the orange 'General de Wet' and yellow 'Bellona' are fragrant early hybrids that bloom with the late Narcissus poeticus 'Cheerfulness' to create a crescendo of spring colour at Larkwhistle. There are hundreds of cultivars of tulips early or late, single or double, fringed or striped, short or tall, traditionally cup-shaped or flared like lilies.

May is tulip time at Larkwhistle. By the middle of the month, the early Dutch hybrid tulips are blooming with the last of the narcissi to create a crescendo of spring colour among a bewildering array of other hardy plants, tall and dwarf, sun-loving and shade-tolerant. But weeks before the hybrids appear, small wild tulips have been popping up through mats of creeping thyme and at the base of the large rocks that define the flowerbeds.

Wild tulips. The very words seem incongruous because we are accustomed to thinking of tulips as the late hybrids that fly their red and yellow flags in park beds and gardens. But the tulip was not born bold, overblown and loud; it has been bred that way, groomed and gussied by generations of hybridists. Every fancy garden flower—rose, iris, dahlia or gladiolus—has wild roots, and the tulip is no exception. If one traces tulips back to their places of origin, one lands not in Holland but in the meadows of Turkey and Yugoslavia; on rocky Asian moun-

tainsides; in the olive groves of France, Italy and Spain; in hot North Africa; and in the ancient land of Persia. Here, wild tulips—there are about 150 species of the genus *Tulipa*—still have a home. Far away at Larkwhistle, any that we have grown have proved to be lovely little bulbous plants that recommend themselves to gardeners keen on early colour.

Ranging in height from all of 3 inches to a scant foot, wild tulips are much smaller than the Holland hybrids, but all flower weeks earlier; so while they may not create the colour masses of the hybrids, they *do* flower when you most appreciate them. Size, too, is in their favour. Species tulips, as they are called, are in scale with the smallest gardens—urban growers take note—or intimate corners of larger plots where the hybrids would appear awkward. In addition, many are reliably perennial, while the big late tulips tend to deteriorate after a season or two.

I never met a wild tulip I didn't like. Spring garden visitors seem to

share my enthusiasm for these little savages, even if the visitors don't recognize them as tulips at all. I list them, below, in order of appearance.

Species Tulips
(*Tulipa* spp)

Always the first to flower—and it may be my favourite—is *Tulipa kaufmanniana*, 8 inches tall and, quite simply, a beautiful bulb. From the centre of broad, blue-green leaves, each smartly edged with a pencil line of red, emerge tapered buds that open into gold-centred, cream-coloured flowers marked with a stroke of soft red on the outside of the petals. Flowers grow larger and more luminous daily as they mature and finally open almost flat, suggesting the common name water-lily tulip. A Turkish native, *kaufmanniana* has proved hardy in our northern garden, returning every spring for the last seven. Interplanted with the small bulbs of glory-of-the-snow (*Chionodoxa* spp), the creamy tulip cups above sky blue stars make an easy spring picture anywhere in sun.

On the heels of *Tulipa kaufmanniana* come *T. turkestanica* and *T. praestans*, both multiflowered. The first carries 6 to 12 nodding, bronze-green buds on each foot-tall stem. The six-petalled starry flowers, ivory white with yellow centres, are enlivened by dark brown stamens. One writer calls *turkestanica* "a nice little species for a choice nook in the rock garden." With us, however, it flourishes at the edge of an ordinary flower border, even pushing its way through a cover of woolly lamb's ears (*Stachys byzantina*).

The buds of *Tulipa praestans* are little flames in the chilly spring garden. Its flowers are scarlet, "not deep, but high and thin, a lovely flashing colour," an observer once wrote. Either of these two species shows well just behind white rock cress (*Arabis albida*). Nearby might grow orange and yellow cowslips (*Primula veris*), one of the few primroses that, given decent soil, will thrive in the sunny spots that wild tulips need.

Variations on a tulip theme continue with the appearance of *Tulipa tarda* (sometimes listed as *T. dasy-*

stemon), a sprightly small thing, generous with its annually increasing clusters of 2-inch white and yellow flowers that open flat and starry from deceptively dowdy buds. This tiny Turk reaches all of 3 inches, but in a few seasons, a dozen bulbs form a continuous band of white and gold down a rock garden slope or along a border edge. *Tulipa urumiensis* is like *tarda* in all ways save that it is entirely yellow with sombre bronze buds. I would never trade it for *tarda*.

Hardly sombre, though, is little *Tulipa linifolia*, a gemlike species with ruby cups that flare widely in the spring sun. We smothered this

6-inch mite under a dense cover of sedum, and it gradually disappeared – a lesson learned. In general, however, delicate shallow-rooted plants growing over the bulbs are a comfort and protection for wild tulips; any of those suggested to overlay the species crocuses (see chapter 3) would do.

The 8-inch *Tulipa chrysantha* repeats (but softly) the red and yellow colouring of many big late tulips. If some of the later hybrids are too blatant, "a wildflower," as Eleanor Perenyi says in *Green Thoughts*, "is never vulgar." In the wild, *chrysantha* climbs the Himalayan slopes into

The home garden is not a park. There is no point in lining up tulips like stiff floral soldiers. Rather, they should be allowed to break rank and congregate in informal groups of 10 or 20, in company with early irises, pink creeping phlox, lavender dwarf catnip and tumbling white arabis. At Larkwhistle, FACING PAGE, *the silver foliage of* Artemisia *'Lambrook Silver,' dark clumps of peonies and the leaves of upcoming perennials create a fresh setting for tulips and their contemporaries. Among the tulips are the lesser-known species such as* Tulipa tarda, ABOVE, *which might not be recognized as a tulip at all by those who know only the opulent Dutch hybrids.*

Tibet, but it is more than willing to settle in lowland gardens. The bulb of *T. chrysantha* has a woolly lining in its papery jacket that protects it from rotting in overly damp earth, a sign that the bulb should be planted in warm, dry, well-drained soil. In common with other wild tulips, this species runs on a finely tuned internal thermometer. You can almost see it expand when things warm up a bit, close a little when a cloud passes over and shut up shop completely at sunset. No sense staying open, in any case, if all the pollinators have gone home.

Seemingly fashioned of pale spring sunlight, *Tulipa batalinii* looks ethereal but is as rugged as you would expect of a 5-inch mountaineer. Its light yellow petals display the graceful outline of a Turkish mosque, and I would not be surprised to learn that Eastern architects took their inspiration for their pointed domes from such tulips. In one bulb catalogue, the true species has been superseded by varieties called 'Bronze Charm' and 'Red Jewel,' both

no doubt jazzier than the original — but are gardeners to be denied *batalinii*'s quiet grace?

French botanist Carolus Clusius, a 16th-century plant explorer in Asia, has given his name to *Tulipa clusiana*, the lady tulip, one of the few wild tulips that also have a common name. Its slender, crimson and white buds open into elegant white flowers with a wine-dark centre. Although one catalogue states that the lady tulip "will give years of pleasure," this species has not lived as long as others in our garden. Taking one expert's advice that "new conditions should immediately be tried when a situation does not bring success," we have *clusiana* down for another try in a warmer spot.

The rounded flowers of *Tulipa sylvestris*, copper in the bud but deep yellow when open, smell like sweet violets. Although their second name suggests a woodland home, *sylvestris* grows plentifully in Mediterranean fields and olive groves. It, too, wants a hot spot where drainage is good. What it does not want, as we found

out, is a top-heavy peony lolling over it all summer. Our little colony all but disappeared until we moved the survivors into the open.

The small bulbs tagged *Tulipa aucheriana* have lived in our garden for five years under a flat carpet of creeping thyme, and each spring they push through in numbers that have increased enough to let us know that they plan to stay. I hope they do, because I look forward to the small galaxy of light-centred pink stars on 3-inch stems above narrow grey leaves. This one is a favourite with garden visitors.

Two additional pink species, *Tulipa pulchella* and *T. saxatilis*, sprout from between flat stones that pave our front porch. Somehow, the tulips, as well as the dwarf columbines, thymes and bellflowers that share its porch space, are nourished by sun, sand and stone.

Finally, we come to two species that prepare us for the imminent parade of hybrid tulips. Both species have been tampered with by gene jugglers and show it. *Fosterana* 'Red

Emperor' is as flushed and angry as Lewis Carroll's Queen of Hearts. As one old-time writer says, "The gardener who likes any colour so long as it is red will adore this tulip." Catalogues wax ecstatic in describing this "brilliant, dazzling scarlet giant, larger than any other tulip." *Greigii* hybrids will also "ignite your garden with flame-red bloom." Once, we planted them, but when they flowered, everything else in the garden seemed to pale – or cringe. Who wants some red-faced tyrant dominating the gentle spring show? I'll wait for the Oriental poppies to provide the razzle-dazzle.

Species Tulip Care

Early fall planting is not necessary for wild tulips and may even be detrimental. November is the month to tuck them in place. They do best with deeper planting than most small bulbs; a full 4 inches of soil should top the little bulbs of *tarda*, *pulchella*, *linifolia* and the like, while 8 inches down is not too deep for *kaufmanniana* and *praestans*. In the matter of soil, wild tulips are not fastidious. Although one expert recommends "a rather heavy soil, rich in humus," they make do nicely in our light, sandy loam. Swift drainage, in any case, is essential; in damp earth, surround the bulbs with a cushion and cover of sand.

All wild tulips crave a place in the sun, and none like strong-growing neighbours to blanket them in shadow. A sunny rock garden is the perfect home for them, but we grow the largest species at the edges of perennial beds and smaller sorts at the base of edging rocks or in intimate corners of the garden with alpine gentians, edelweiss, the lowest thymes and other scaled-down plants.

I have found wild tulips gratifyingly easy to grow, as care-free and self-sufficient as any plants in the garden. Although they hail from far-off lands, most have adapted nicely to a northern site. Our seasonal weather patterns suit them well: hot, dryish summers that provide the "good baking" that bulbs need for health and a thorough ripening, winters that offer a continuous deep-freeze or safety under snow to ensure their survival.

Hybrid Tulips

I am of two minds about hybrid tulips. After the quiet hues of daffodils and other early flowers, I welcome, with reservations, the bold and varied colours that tulips add to the spring picture. Although I concede that tulips play an important role in the May scene, my enthusiasm for them is not unbounded. I still associate them with formal beds and stiff, uninspired plantings. Every spring, in every park and in front of

Among the small early tulips are the pink stars of Tulipa aucheriana, FACING PAGE, LEFT, *and the crimson and white lady tulip,* T. clusiana, FACING PAGE, CENTRE. *Both are unusual changes from the white, scarlet and yellow that predominate among wild tulips. One of the yellow sorts is* Tulipa kaufmanniana, LEFT, *whose flaring cups grow larger and more luminous daily, until they open almost flat in a way suggesting the common name water-lily tulip. All of the wild tulips will grow through a protective covering of creeping thyme.*

71

every public building, thousands of tulips line up like so many soldiers – strictly regimented, uniform in height, bold colours clashing – precursors of the equally stiff wax begonias or scarlet salvias that will replace them. The tulip parades are a vestige of the old "bedding out" style – a triumph of control over grace and naturalness – that was so decried in the last century by Gertrude Jekyll and William Robinson, English master garden-makers and champions of hardy perennials, permanent plantings and gardens that took their cues from nature.

But perhaps my biggest grudge against tulips has to do with their lack of health. For all their bold looks, tulips fall easy prey to several fungal diseases that curtail their stay in the garden. Although a number of cultivars have remained hale and sound at Larkwhistle for as long as five years – and one catalogue offers a new breed as "perennial" – for the most part and in most gardens, tulips simply refuse to settle in for a long run. This means that gardeners who want to include them with other perennials in a Maytime composition must be continually rethinking and renovating the picture.

For all of that, we still succumb to the blandishments of catalogues and plant a few dozen new bulbs each fall. No other flower of the season can match the tulip's colour range. Few are as tall; at a season when dwarf perennials predominate, tulips lift the colour above ground level and take the eye from dwarf border plants up to that old apple tree blossoming pink against the blue spring sky.

One bulb catalogue lists 16 full pages of tulips – early or late, single or double, fringed or striped, short or tall, traditionally cup-shaped or flared like lilies. Clearly, drastic editing is in order. The doubles do not draw me; I'll wait for peonies or roses. Any tulip with two colours is too much for me. Parrot tulips are strange, twisted creatures, a bit too exotic, although the 'Blue Parrot' has a nice slaty lavender tint rare in tulips. Green tulips leave me cold, and the multiflowered sorts lack impact. The bizarre Rembrandts are two-toned, feathered and streaked – enough said.

At Larkwhistle, we grow a few groups of single early tulips to extend the season and spark up the daffodils. 'General de Wet,' soft orange overlaid with copper-red veins, is particularly luminous and smells sweetly of citrus. 'Bellona' is a good early yellow above blue grape hyacinths, while 'Couleur Cardinal,' wine-red, stands out against white daffodils behind a border of double arabis. Triumph tulips flower between the earlies and lates; 'Apricot Beauty' is just that (but little more than an annual here), and 'Golden Melody,' the most perennial tulip we grow, glows against the bronze early leaves of peonies above a floor of forget-me-nots.

The early and midseason sorts are a prelude to the full May symphony of tall Darwin, cottage and lily-flowered tulips. Pink cultivars such as 'Esther,' 'Rosy Wings' and 'Smiling Queen' and the lavender-blue sorts are lovely in the company of bleeding hearts, blue intermediate irises and many of the spring border plants, save for acid-yellow alyssums. With the alyssum, we grow 'Dillenburg,' a very late tulip shaded like a ripe peach; the delicate lemon and cream of 'Sweet Harmony' would do here

too. Ivory-coloured and egg-shaped 'Maureen' fits in anywhere but is especially effective tucked into a quiet corner of green and silver foliage and white flowers.

Lily-flowered tulips, with their out-turned, pointed petals, are among my favourites. The clear yellow 'West Point' is perfect behind bushes of *Euphorbia polychroma*. By late May, this last perennial has grown into a neat, symmetrical mound of blue-green leaves, 18 inches high and wide, topped by flat heads of cool greenish yellow flowers. Even after the flowers are gone, the euphorbia — "a sterling plant, long-lived and trouble-free," according to English perennial expert Alan Bloom — persists as a fine foliage mass until fall. The yellow flowering currant, *Ribes aureum*, an extremely hardy and adaptable shrub, forms an admirable backdrop here.

Hybrid Tulip Care

Fall is the time to tuck tulips in place, and late rather than early is the recommendation. The bulbs can be set aside in a cool, dry place until as late as December (provided the earth is not frozen), while you get daffodils, crocuses, lilies and the rest into the ground. For tulips, the ground ought to be loamy, sweet and well-drained. A dusting of crushed limestone should be dug into acidic soil to raise the pH to neutral or just above. Tulips do well in rather heavy soil that has been loosened somewhat with well-decayed organic matter; fresh manure is definitely not to their liking.

Tulips need a place in the sun. In shade, they stretch and bend in a valiant effort to see the light. Here, we plant them in sunny perennial borders in oval groups of 10 or 20 bulbs, each about 6 inches from the next. If the bulbs are tucked close by clumps of *Sedum spectabile*, day lilies or silver-leaved yarrows, these perennials will soon grow up and out to conceal fading tulip leaves and renew colour in that same spot.

The recommended planting depth moves up and down according to whom one hears or reads. Tulips have a remarkable ability to push their way through as much as 12

inches of soil. Some experts suggest that this very deep planting helps keep tulips in the garden years longer, providing there is plenty of rich soil beneath the bulbs. We have tried deep planting and find that, yes, bulbs stay healthy for a season or two more, but when the inevitable decline comes and they must be lifted, they are that much harder to get at. Now, we plant tulips about 6 inches deep, count on them for two or three seasons, then dig them up and toss them out when the flowers grow few or small and the foliage shows signs of spotty fungus. If we want to put fresh tulips back in that same spot, we dig out a bushel or two of soil and replace it with fresh rich earth from the vegetable garden. Once the flowers are spent, tulip leaves must be left to yellow and ripen thoroughly, in the process feeding the bulbs that will produce next spring's flowers.

Spring Edgings

Tulips show their real worth in garden pictures when they are planted, not in the splendid isolation of a separate bed, but in association with other spring perennials, flowering shrubs or blossoming trees. In our garden, they are allowed to break rank and congregate in informal groups here and there in the mixed borders. For example, in May, several dwarf perennials are in full

A familiar rite of fall, tulip planting, ABOVE, *takes place in earth enriched with rock phosphate, bone meal and very old manure. Trowel out individual holes 6 to 12 inches deep, and press the bulbs firmly in place before covering. The returns, after a cold grey winter, may be the familiar red and yellow hybrids or something less common, such as the lovely lily-flowered tulips,* FACING PAGE, *effective here above a sea of blue forget-me-nots planted over the bulbs in fall.*

73

bloom along the border edges. Behind each mat of creeping phlox or each cushion of dwarf catnip, 10 to 15 tulips are planted in a close colony. Tulips are chosen to harmonize with border plants so that, for instance, a bright yellow cultivar does not fight with hot pink phlox (we might go for lavender instead) and the ruby cups of another will highlight the china white of candytuft.

Creeping Phlox
(*Phlox subulata*)

Perhaps the most effective of spring edgings is creeping phlox, also commonly called ground phlox, moss phlox or moss pink. Its greenery is narrow and pointed, a mass of little needlelike leaves that appear prickly but are soft to the touch. The wild species, an American native that flowers dim magenta in rocky places, along roadsides and in untended fields from New York State to Florida, is parent to a handful of cultivars, all better for the garden than the original.

Garden-bred phlox vary in habit of growth. Some are loose, lax and springy, others close and compact like dense green mosses, but none grow taller than 6 inches. Flowers range through all shades of pink, to white, to a lovely silvery lavender best described as "moonlit blue." Few perennials are as floriferous; for three or four weeks in late spring,

phlox stems are hidden under countless crowding flowers – flat, round as a penny and formed of five notched petals – equally effective edging a flowerbed, covering a stretch of sunny ground or cascading over a wall top or down a rock garden slope. Doug Green, a commercial grower of herbs and flowers, comments that *Phlox subulata* is his best-selling perennial. I can understand why.

At intervals along the front of our hardy borders, great cushions of creeping phlox lie contentedly sunning themselves. We have continued to propagate our first few plants so that now each variety has a yard of border space to itself and tumbles in a flowery fall over the rock-raised edge. This plant lends itself perfectly to early picture making.

Once planted, creeping phlox requires minimal attention, only a single close shearing of foliage once the spring flower show is over – no watering, no spraying, no coddling.

Seed will not grow the named varieties, but a single nursery plant, after it has been growing in the garden for a season or two, can be turned into any number of new ones. Here's how: Like many ground-hugging plants, phlox fans out from its centre on laterally moving shoots that eventually put down roots of their own. This natural layering process can be encouraged and hastened if the little side branches are held snugly to the earth with a

small stone or hairpin and some soil is firmed over the contact point. Layer 10 or 20 shoots while you're at it. In two months or so, roots will have formed. Snip the layers from the mother plant with scissors, and using a small trowel, ease them out of the ground and plant them firmly and immediately in a new locale. For a more immediate effect from this deliberate grower, I like to plant a half-dozen shoots, set about 4 inches apart, in a close group that I consider as one new plant. Three groups spaced a foot apart make a generous drift. Creeping phlox take to any soil short of soggy; rich earth is not a prerequisite, but lots of sun is a must. If after some years plants tend to grow leggy and leafless along the lower part of their stems, sift some sandy loam or fine compost right over them, and work this material into the network of criss-crossing branches with the fingers. This is a sure way to rejuvenate a patch of creeping phlox.

Gardeners who enjoy a floral treasure hunt might be on the lookout for: magenta *Phlox amoena*, *P. stolonifera* 'Blue Ridge,' with its lavender flowers, and *P. divaricata*, the wild blue phlox.

Dwarf Catnip
(*Nepeta* × *faassenii*)

Much less showy than phlox, but useful for variety and misty blue accents among brighter flowers, is a decorative dwarf form of catnip called *Nepeta × faassenii* (listed in old gardening books and some current catalogues as *N. mussinii*). Early each spring, this easy-care, drought-resistant perennial sprouts a fresh crop of fragrant, pebbled grey-green leaves. By tulip time, there are lots of slender foot-high stems set with many small lavender-blue flowers, like mint blossoms magnified. I like single specimens of this neat, mounding plant at regular intervals along a border edge, with a dozen pink, pale yellow or crimson tulips behind each.

Dwarf catnip can be raised from seed to flower in 12 months. Sow seed in spring, and expect your first crop of blue a year later. Nursery plants are a shortcut for impatient or busy gardeners or for those who shy away from seeds. The soil and sites suggested for creeping phlox are just right for this modest perennial too. Maintenance is the same—a close haircut after flowering. New leaves soon sprout and stay fresh until fall.

Candytuft
(*Iberis sempervirens*)

If it flowered in colours other than white, perennial candytuft would rival creeping phlox as the best spring edging. The first Latin name tells us that it comes from the Iberian peninsula, or Spain; the second means "evergreen." Our original clumps, still flourishing after almost a decade, seem to be aiming for just that. Here is a little bush (8 to 12 inches tall and, eventually, 18 inches or more across) that is presentable year-round. Spring thaw sees the small, narrow leaves still dark green and fresh. By late May (here in central Ontario), the foliage is obscured by a mass of chalk-white flowers. After an early summer shearing, the plants lapse into neat green again. If foliage should become

Spring edgings are lovely on their own in a rock garden, but they also complement other flowers. Pink and white creeping phlox and china-white candytuft, FACING PAGE, LEFT, *require a sunny, well-drained site and shearing back by about half once the flowers have faded. Both maintain a show of greenery from spring until late fall. The flowers of creeping phlox,* FACING PAGE, CENTRE, *all but obliterate the mounds of needlelike foliage in May, while dwarf catnip,* LEFT, *adds gentle colour and a contrast in form to a harmonious Larkwhistle picture that includes creamy intermediate irises, Spanish bluebells, sparks of wallflowers and Darwin tulips.*

brown or shrivel in a damp, snowless winter, a spring trim will encourage fresh growth.

We began growing candytuft after some small plants had popped up in a neighbour's gravel driveway from seed scattered by flowers spilling over the top of an adjacent retaining wall. It can be raised easily from seed. Give seedlings at least a foot between them, and in a season or two, they will grow together. Although not picky about the soil it grows in, candytuft does need a warm, sunny spot where water drains away quickly.

Basket-of-Gold
(*Aurinia saxatilis*)

Candytuft is perhaps better known in its annual guise, as is our next spring border plant, perennial alyssum. Many gardens grow sweet alyssum, a fragrant annual that flowers either white or purple the summer through. Few include the hardy perennial alyssum, *Aurinia saxatilis* (formerly *Alyssum saxatile*), commonly known as basket-of-gold.

We have had trouble with this

one. The grey colour of its leaves indicates a need for warm, dry conditions of both soil and atmosphere. Summers here fit the bill, but four months of being crushed between soggy snow and wet earth is too much for this plant. By spring, the promising silver tufts have usually melted to mush. Thinking to get alyssum off the ground and give it a drier surface, we tucked a few seedlings in the vertical face of a dry-built rock wall. Against the warm stones, they grew strongly over summer into leafy rosettes. The next spring, some were there, others gone. A few tufts of yellow were all that materialized. Nevertheless, some gardeners grow basket-of-gold without trouble.

Perennial alyssum, an 8-inch relative of mustard, broccoli, arabis and kindred Cruciferae, is a froth of small, deep yellow, four-petalled flowers every May. Its colour is a trifle harsh to harmonize with the pinks and reds of tulips, creeping phlox or bleeding hearts—better to keep it in the company of white and lavender, with perhaps some orange tulips to rival its brilliance. A cultivar, 'Silver Queen,' less robust than the species, flowers soft butter-yellow, a shade that gets along with any other. This plant has lived with us for five years but never waxes strong or blossoms exuberantly.

Quick and easy to raise from seed, basket-of-gold is a perennial favourite with nursery growers. If it takes to your garden, perennial alyssum will soon set about raising a family of seedlings in far-flung corners. An early summer shearing of spent flowers and straggly stems does alyssum a world of good.

Leopard's Bane
(*Doronicum* spp)

A sparkling spring picture has golden alyssum (where it thrives) and candytuft in the foreground, a mass of soft orange tulips behind and, still farther back, leopard's bane, the first of the garden's daisies to bloom. This is an easy perennial whose deep yellow flowers and 3-foot height are appreciated at a time when low plants and soft colours predominate. From spreading, turniplike tubers,

heart-shaped (in botanical terms, "cordate") leaves sprout, followed by branching stems topped with thin-petalled, golden—well, frankly, dandelion-yellow—daisies for many weeks in late spring.

Leopard's bane—the name comes from a legend that leopard hunters once dipped their arrowheads in juice pressed from its roots—responds to decent soil but makes the best of the less-than-perfect stuff. In addition, this hardy plant can be set in either full sun or fairly dense shade any time, spring to fall, and divides more easily than most. A single plant looks a little forlorn and weedy, but a massed group, say, 3 feet long and 2 feet across, will light any dim garden corner. English gardening books speak enthusiastically about named cultivars, including a dwarf sort, another as double as a dahlia and one with flowers tending to orange; but as far as I know, none has crossed the ocean yet. However, seeds and plants of *Doronicum plantagineum* and the shorter *D. cordatum* can be found.

Early Irises
(*Iris* spp)

To this same picture could be added a few irises. June is the iris month, but weeks before the parade of gorgeous, tall bearded irises arrives, scaled-down versions, called dwarf (10 to 15 inches tall) and intermediate (15 to 28 inches tall), wave advance flags. Like the tall bearded irises in all ways save size, the dwarfs and intermediates move along on expanding rhizomes and produce the typical fleur-de-lis—three upper petals (standards) and three lower petals (falls) on which sit the furry "beards." The shorter irises are self-supporting (in contrast to the taller, which usually need a prop), drought-resistant, exceedingly hardy perennials that soon increase to form pools of clear colour in the May garden. Their reduced stature makes them suitable for smaller gardens, and their early flowering extends the iris season in gardens where there is room for all kinds.

The shorter the iris, the earlier it flowers. Dwarfs come first, often blooming with the daffodils. The intermediates are in sync with tulips,

Among the sunniest of spring flowers are leopard's bane, FACING PAGE, ABOVE, *and basket-of-gold,* FACING PAGE, BOTTOM. *Leopard's bane is the first of the daisies to flower, a no-care perennial that is more effective in a broad mass than as a single specimen. Frothy basket-of-gold is a natural in a rock garden or can edge groups of white and orange tulips.*

and the two set each other off uncommonly well in both form and colour—sky blue irises with pink tulips, dark purple irises with yellow tulips or any mix that takes your fancy. Colours range from white, cream and yellow through peach and orange to almost red, and there are many shades of blue, lavender and violet.

All of the bearded irises, early or late, require a sunny site and swift drainage. Otherwise, they are adaptable and need only a bit of tidying—removal of spotty leaves and spent flower stalks—in summer and division when the rhizomes start to crawl all over each other and flowers grow sparse. A few weeks after flowering is the right time for division, a process described fully in chapter 9.

Bleeding Heart
(*Dicentra* spp)

The genus *Dicentra*—from the Greek *dis*, twice, and *kentron*, a spur—includes three perennials for the early garden. Few plants are as glorious in May as well-grown clumps of bleeding heart (*Dicentra spectabilis*), their arching stems hung with fanciful deep pink and white hearts, like some exotic confection, above elegantly divided blue-green foliage. All my old gardening books speak of it as an old-fashioned plant "too well known to need description, as nearly every garden is adorned with its singular flowers." Maybe so, but bleeding heart was new to me a few years ago and has been a revelation in perennial beauty every spring since.

Here is a neat, minimal-care, long-lived 3-foot plant for many sites, sunny or shaded, formal or natural. I like to set single clumps, just back of front, at intervals in a mixed border, with tulips and early dwarf perennials for company. In a spacious foundation planting or corner of a city yard, the same arrangement would work. Bleeding hearts can be used as accents on either side of a path or doorway or in woodland or semiwild gardens where ferns and wildflowers live.

Bleeding hearts grow from pronged, tan-coloured rhizomes, not unlike peony rootstocks. Like peonies, too, these roots are planted in the fall, their season of dormancy. Handle the brittle roots gingerly to avoid snapping them. Alternatively, actively growing (sometimes even flowering) potted plants can be found in nurseries in spring and can be set out, soil and all. The initial work of turning a half-bushel or so of decayed manure, compost and/or peat moss into the earth for each plant will be rewarded with stronger growth and more flowers over a longer time. In seasons to come, an organic mulch will maintain moisture and fertility. Since a large part of this plant's charm comes from its graceful,

fountainlike form, I suggest a spacing of 1½ to 2 feet between clumps or an unplanted area 2½ feet wide around a single specimen, so that plants can arch out naturally. Keep tall, flopping perennials such as anchusas or delphiniums—unless they are conscientiously staked—well away from bleeding hearts. Another tip: Bleeding heart foliage, lovely as it is in spring, dies away by midsummer. If a plant of baby's-breath occupies the space behind, the misty veil of its bloom can be drawn over the bare space.

Two years ago, we set out three plants of white bleeding heart (*Dicentra spectabilis alba*) in a newly made garden bed. The earth was fertile and deep, the site lightly shaded by a trelliswork fence and protected from cold winds by lilacs behind. Never have plants taken off with such enthusiasm. In a season, the three were linking branches and hanging out an incredible succession of white hearts. I would rate the white bleeding heart as one of the loveliest and most elegant perennials we grow. If its foliage lasted until fall, it would be the perfect plant.

Another species, *Dicentra eximia*, recommends itself to gardeners looking for dwarf, low-maintenance, long-flowering perennials for shade—not an easy bill to fill, as many city gardeners know.

Not unlike *eximia* is the new hybrid *Dicentra* 'Luxuriant.' This one, too, has silvery, incised leaves and 12-inch stems of hearts, but this time the flowers are a deep purple-red and the plants entirely comfortable in sun. Useful for the front line of borders or just back of front, 'Luxuriant' does not spread like *eximia* but remains as a distinct clump.

Columbines
(*Aquilegia* spp)

The first time I saw clumps of soaring columbines blooming in a city front yard—this was years before I had a garden of my own—I was completely taken with the flowers, with how the petals, spurs and sepals fit together like an artfully wrought puzzle. Since then, it's been my pleasure to grow many clumps of columbines, many kinds and colours,

Columbines such as 'Olympia Red and Gold,' FACING PAGE, are best raised from seed, a method that lowers the cost of furnishing a perennial garden. Bleeding hearts, however, are purchased as rhizomes, similar to peony rootstocks. Unusual and lovely, the white bleeding heart, LEFT, is a perfect background for tulips of any colour. Add a floor of forget-me-nots to complete a spring picture.

but I am still smitten. I sometimes think I'd like to devote a whole garden bed to them, growing the finest cultivars from seed, mixing up a special humus-rich soil to keep them in flourishing health, giving the plants lots of room and moisture. But since both space and time are limited, I content myself with growing columbines as well as I can in a mixed hardy border.

The genus *Aquilegia* may take its name from the latin *aquila*, eagle, alluding to the similarity between the columbine's hooked-back spurs and the eagle's talons. Various species live all through north temperate regions, from the Rocky Mountains to Siberia and Japan. Most gardeners start with the elegant long-spurred hybrids, but if the reaction of visitors here is typical, few can resist the charm of the small alpine species. Just outside our garden gate grows a pert native columbine, *Aquilegia canadensis*. (Why do some wildflower guides call this the *American* columbine?) Its nodding red and yellow flowers appear in the most unlikely and seemingly inhospitable places—gravelly roadsides and mossy fis-

sures in limestone boulders—but this wild thing can be tamed if you collect ripe seed. As well, in untended old gardens nearby, rather stodgy, short-spurred columbines (*A. vulgaris*) in shades of purple and pink have seeded and reseeded themselves for decades.

Recently, we've been thrilled by the performance of 'Olympia Red and Gold' and 'Olympia Blue and White' hybrid columbines (from Stokes Seeds). The plants are vigorous (as promised) and a yard tall; the abundant flowers are large yet graceful, the colours vivid. 'Mrs. Scott Elliot' has given her name to another popular strain of columbines, and 'Mc-Kana Giants' appear in most catalogues. Both flower in a range of colours and bicolours. George W. Park Seed Company also lists 'Snow Queen,' a lovely white cultivar, and *Aquilegia chrysantha*, a fine yellow.

Many perennials we buy as started plants, but columbines we always raise from seed, for several reasons. First, they are so easy that any gardener who has seen parsley or broccoli through these steps has the patience and know-how to achieve a

fine crop of columbines. Second, seeds open the door to a wider world of columbine beauty. Finally, they are lovelier in groups of three, five or more, and a $1.50 packet of seeds will grow at least $15 worth of plants. Columbines commonly do not live more than three seasons in the garden, so we keep a batch of new plants coming along from seed to replace any that succumb to stem borers—columbine enemy number one with us—or winter.

Columbine seeds are shiny and black and not too small. April is the month to sow them; indoors is the place to start. To grow, say, six each of the red and gold and of the blue and white 'Olympias'—if you get the lot from seed to full flowering, you can pat yourself on the back, enjoy the compliments and marvel at the blossoms—you'll need two 8-inch bulb pots (shorter and broader-based than ordinary flowerpots) filled with the porous medium described in chapter 2 and two packs of seed, which you are advised to chill in the refrigerator for five days. At seeding time, do not cover the seeds, but simply press them lightly into the soil surface. Space the 15 or so seeds several inches apart; you'll want to keep every seedling that sprouts. Water the pots from beneath, and drape a piece of clear plastic (or use a pane of glass) over them. Set pots in a warm place, but not in full sun. In several weeks, little green backs will show through the earth. Remove the plastic or glass, set the pots in a very sunny window, and see that seedlings stay moist—but not sodden—as they grow.

When the seedlings have sent up five or six small ferny leaves, the time has come for the move outdoors. Lift seedlings carefully out of the pot—an ordinary dinner fork or teaspoon is a good tool for the job— and set them firmly, a full foot apart, in the friable earth of a nursery bed or, even better, in a sheltering cold frame fitted with a slatted shade. Pick an overcast day for the move, and if several days of cloud and showers follow, so much the better. In any case, some artificial shade is a help for a few days.

Once they take hold, the seedlings should shoot up over summer. Fertilizer will fatten the clumps, of course. In early September, they are lifted once more with as many roots intact as possible—this time you'll need a shovel—and set out in their permanent places. I like to dig oversized transplanting holes in the border and stir a spadeful of crumbly manure or compost deeply into each before lowering in the columbine. Backfill with earth firmed around the roots, and water generously to settle the works. Columbines thrive in earth that contains enough organic matter to stay nicely moist and well-textured. "It is not generally realized how cruelly [they] suffer in dry weather," says one expert, who also recommends liberal watering during drought. A leaf or straw mulch is useful. Plants should grow 12 to 18 inches apart. Sun or partial shade is all the same to them, provided the earth is fertile and moist.

Jacob's Ladder
(*Polemonium* spp)

In an arbour-shaded raised bed flanking our door-side herb garden, columbines grow next to Jacob's

ladder, whose common name refers to the precisely ascending arrangement of the leaflets. Jacob's ladder is among the first perennials to sprout in spring. Its greenery, fresh, dense and tidy, lasts in good condition the summer through and is in large measure a reason for the plant's appeal. The 3-foot stems, upright and self-supporting, are each topped by clustered flower buds that open successively over six to eight weeks into pretty, 1-inch, sky blue cups sparked with yellow stamens. A single plant makes little impact, but four or five in a group—planted a foot apart—create a haze of blue in any lightly shaded place.

Native to European mountains, and also found in the Himalayas, Jacob's ladder grows best in the fertile, humusy soil that suits columbines and bleeding hearts; it is also well-placed with hostas and ferns. So far, our clumps have been in place for five years and show no sign of decline, nor can I recall giving them any attention at all save for the usual cutting back in fall. All in all, a first-class hardy plant, not brilliant or spectacular, but elegant in its way

Because they are native to woodlands and mountains, plants such as columbines, FACING PAGE, and Jacob's ladder, ABOVE, prefer moist, humusy soil. Dig oversized planting holes in the border, and stir a spadeful of crumbly manure or compost deeply into each before lowering in the plant. Provided the earth is fertile and damp, sun or partial shade are all the same to columbines, while Jacob's ladder prefers some shade.

and quietly decorative all season. A dwarf polemonium (*Polemonium reptans*, 10 inches), also blue, was new to us last year but seems sturdy and self-reliant. Plant it with *Dicentra eximia* for a long-flowering duo, pink and blue, in partial shade.

Yellow Fumitory
(*Corydalis lutea*)

No better companion for Jacob's ladder could be found than a fore-planting of *Corydalis lutea*. Kin to the Dutchman's breeches of northern woods, corydalis has similarly dainty foliage, grey-green, much divided and fernlike. But there its daintiness ends. The plant is vigorous and quick and more generous with its dangling clusters of yellow flowers than any other perennial I know—literally non-stop blossoms from May until September. All those flowers, of course, mean seeds. Little silver seedlings, incipient corydalis, pop up by the hundreds around a parent plant. Not difficult to weed out, a few can be left to extend the drifts of silver and gold into a ground cover where space allows. Corydalis likes to get a foothold in a dry-built stone wall, and if given free rein, this rampant seeder will completely veil the wall in feathery foliage and flowers in a few seasons. A good perennial, this, sun- or shade-tolerant and showy.

Violets
(*Viola* spp)

Almost every garden grows a crop of violas of one kind or another, usually bold-faced, multicoloured pansies, hybrids of *Viola tricolor*, bought in bloom every May. But there is a host of other violas, both garden-bred and wild, to colour spring days. Not unlike pansies, but prettier to my eye (not so big and blotchy), are cultivars of *V. cornuta*. These we count on for a long-lasting ribbon of colour—white, yellow, apricot, rusty red and, best of all, clear blue—along the edge of a lightly shaded primrose border. With generous soil preparation at the start, a few deep drinks during drought and removal of withered flowers, these violas carry on flowering all summer. As often as not, the plants

survive winter and resume blooming in spring if last year's straggly stems are snipped back to the tufts of fresh green.

Viola cornuta and *V. tricolor* cultivars are very easy to raise from seeds, a project worth undertaking if you want plants in quantity. The timing, however, is a little different from most. Mid-August is the time we sow short rows of seeds—among violas, perhaps yellow 'Lutea Splendens,' red 'Arkwright Ruby,' apricot 'Chantreyland' and always 'Blue Heaven' along with 'Imperial Blue' pansies—in the previously watered soil of an empty cold frame. In 10 days or so, seedlings are showing through. As they grow, we thin and/or transplant them to stand 4 inches apart. When the weather turns chilly in late September, we cover the frame with its storm window sash to keep things summery under the glass for a while longer, but come November, the sash is removed entirely to accustom seedlings to the impending winter.

Snow-blanketed or straw-mulched, viola or pansy plants come through the winter green and ready to flower.

Just as soon as the snow is gone, we replace the glass on the frame to give the plants a jump on spring. By early May, most are showing a first flower. Setting out the violas has become part of our spring ritual. One of us trowels out a series of holes among the blossoming primroses and stirs a double handful of humus—a mix of crumbly manure, damp peat moss and a little bone meal—deeply into the hole; the other lifts the violas from the frame, one by one, plants them in the prepared places and waters them with fish emulsion. A little fluffing and levelling of the earth, and the job is done. Pert, friendly violas are with us for months to come.

If *Viola cornuta* and *V. tricolor* cultivars are best grown as biennials, other members of the genus are hardy perennials that take to the most northerly gardens. *V. odorata*, the sweet-scented violet of English gardens and spring nosegays, flowers profusely in shady places and then flings hardy seeds far and wide. It can be a (lovely) pest, as can Johnny-jump-ups (*V. tricolor*), a sassy small viola that will stretch (or jump) right through a peony, if it happens to lodge underneath one, in an effort to see the sun. A good carpet for daffodils, tulips or lilies, purple and gold Johnnies flower blithely from spring thaw to snowfall. Start this one from seed once, and it will stay in and around the garden ever after. But be warned, it can cause some confusion in a perennial border if you are keen on every plant in its allotted place.

Years ago, we brought seeds of the true *Viola cornuta alba* (as opposed to its cultivars discussed above) home from a tour of English gardens. Ever since, it has lived and flowered in a pocket of deep, fertile moist earth. For weeks in late spring and into summer, the plants are covered with white, smallish flat-faced pansies. 'Papilio,' among my favourite violas, is a longer-flowering lavender and white sport that I like to use in groups of 8 or 10 in a perennial bed as a ground cover for yellow lilies. From other gardens have come other perennial violas, nameless as yet or, rather, known simply as "the white one from the Hansons'" or "the blue and white violet from Ger and Don."

May is as generous to gardeners as our friends have been to us. Which of these hardy May-blooming perennials—from tulips to violets—would I pick for a friend who owned a smaller garden? Not an easy decision, but I am drawn first to *Tulipa tarda* and *T. kaufmanniana* and then to a few representatives of the later hybrid tulips, probably pink, white and lavender. With these, I would go for pink and "moonlit blue" creeping phlox and the old-fashioned bleeding hearts, both pink and white. Partial to blue, I would need a clump of azure intermediate irises in the picture and, of course, columbines. If there were also a rosy crab apple to overlook the scene, my friend would have a May garden as lovely as any.

The yellow fumitory, Corydalis lutea, FACING PAGE, *starts to bloom in May and continues well into summer. Left to seed, it will spring up thickly enough to form a ground cover in partial shade. Another shade-loving ground cover is the violet, one of the longest-blooming perennials.* 'Papilio,' LEFT, *and other cultivars of* Viola cornuta *are dependable edging plants wherever the ground never becomes completely dry.*

Sweet Harmony

A June garden of complementary tones

A planting scheme as simple as a single peony backed by a flowering rose creates a picture that typifies June's easy bounty. Colour-conscious gardeners should take a hint from nature: settle on a rosy theme for the solstice garden, then add touches of white, yellow and blue to enhance the warm tones of early summer.

"It is easy to have a beautiful garden in June," one expert gardener has written. The days grow steadily longer and warmer, frosts are over, and gentle rains fall often; everything, in fact, conspires to accelerate growth and spur flowering. Whatever pests and problems may be in store for us in July and August, the solstice garden is generally fresh and flowery, a fulfillment of earlier promise and a gift to hardworking gardeners.

The June garden was the first to repay us at Larkwhistle. My partner and I had worked for four seasons digging borders, forking out quack grass roots, turning under manure and decayed leaves and hauling limestone rocks to raise and define the planting spaces. We had been reading about perennials in treasured turn-of-the-century gardening books and scouring catalogues and nurseries for seeds and plants. With paper planning, a fair bit of on-site impromptu planting and some subsequent rearranging, the garden took shape.

Irises set out in two 5-by-30-foot beds gave a smattering of bloom the first year, an encouraging hint of what we could expect. As the seasons turned, the perennials fattened up to fill their allotted spaces—and sometimes more. The garden was maturing. And then, quite suddenly one June morning (or so it seems in memory), we awoke to find flower borders brimming with blossoms: dianthus studded with round fringed flowers, pink or white, and irises a harmony of deep purple, lavender and pink in one bed, cream and yellow in the other. At the back of one border, there was a blur of blue anchusas. Through the middle, there were fountains of pink and crimson painted daisies, with sparks of red coral bells along an edge. A sea of rose pink poppies rippled behind silvery stachys. Everything seemed to be happening at once, a picture of colour and freshness beyond anything we could have imagined when we were planting small seedlings or skinny roots. I remember trying to get some work done—after all, there was a house to build, a vegetable plot to tend—and being drawn back to the flower garden every few minutes. There I wandered, almost bewitched, around the paths or retreated to the arbour seat to absorb the colours and scents of a June garden, all with the accompaniment of bobolinks calling and meadowlarks whistling in the field beyond.

I wanted to shout, "Perfect! Stay just as you are." But, alas, as one gardener has observed, "The wretched plants will not stand still." The flowers that bloom on either side of the summer solstice came and went, leaving gaps where there had been loveliness and sending us back to the books and out to other gardens in search of follow-up perennials. But we had seen the magic that June can work with a gardener's helping hand.

Oriental Poppies
(*Papaver orientale*)

Whatever the calendar says, I always think that summer starts when the first Oriental poppy bursts its furry bud. There is nothing quite so spectacular as the big flaunting flowers of *Papaver orientale* tottering on yard-high stems; the four-petalled crepe-textured cups, a hand-span across, are filled with quivering purple-black stamens that give way to little pepper shaker pods dispensing poppy seeds to the winds.

Few gardeners are without a plant or two—and sometimes many more if they are left to seed—of the ordinary scarlet-orange poppy. Near our place, this species has taken possession of a gravelly bank in front of an old farmstead, where for two weeks every June, the roadside is stained red with hundreds of fluttering flowers. In the garden, these brilliant things must be placed more carefully if they are not to dominate the scene. At Larkwhistle, scarlet Oriental poppies accompany cream-coloured bearded irises and blue anchusas or mingle with the ferny greenery and white lace caps of sweet cicely (*Myrrhis odorata*).

But in other parts of the garden, pink cultivars of *Papaver orientale* steal the show. These were new to me some years ago and continue to surprise visitors who only know the

red. 'Betty Ann' is as pink as an old-fashioned rose; 'Cheerio's' light pink petals are marked at their base with a blotch the colour of Bing cherries. Either combines beautifully with blue, lavender or inky violet bearded irises and pink or crimson coral bells. Set a plant of lacy valerian behind and an edging of silver-leaved lamb's ears in front, and you have a picture to satisfy any gardener's soul.

It is tempting to fill a flowerbed with gorgeous—for once, that over-worked adjective applies—pink poppies. But keep in mind that they are an ephemeral lot, here for a few weeks, then gone. Even their foliage is fleeting. By midsummer, it has disappeared underground, leaving no trace of former glory—leaving, in fact, a gap in the border, unless we have thought to plant other perennials fore and aft of the poppies to mask their defection. Baby's-breath, showy stonecrop, heleniums, late-blooming day lilies and several of the taller yarrows are useful for that job.

Oriental poppies have a nap during July and August, then wake up and sprout new leaves during cool, damp fall days. The time to move them is in late summer, just as they show above ground. Like peonies and gas plants, they are among the perennials

As the solstice approaches, the perennial garden bursts into lavish rose-toned bloom. Along the edges of Larkwhistle's flower borders, FACING PAGE, *white cerastiums, blue veronicas and airy pink coral bells enhance full-blown peonies. Continuing the rosy theme are Oriental poppies, which bloom in more colours than just the familiar brilliant scarlet. This showy but fleeting perennial may be decked in rose pink,* ABOVE, *and salmon as well. Clumps of baby's-breath set among the poppies fill the gap left by disappearing poppy foliage with a cloud of misty white.*

that can stay put, undisturbed, for decades. But to increase a favourite cultivar, gently dig up a clump when you see a start of new growth. Likely, the earth will fall away from the thonglike roots. Then, using your fingers and a small, sharp knife and being careful not to snap the brittle roots, split the clustered shoots into one- or two-crowned divisions. Plant these right away, firmly and at least a foot apart, with the juncture of leaves and roots 2 inches below ground level. Water to firm the soil, then hope that the roots take hold. In my experience, Oriental poppies are practically indestructible once established, but more reluctant than other perennials to settle in at first.

Bearded Irises
(Iris spp)

From early spring until well into July, irises of one kind or another are in bloom. And June is the month for tall bearded irises and Siberian irises to shine. Each type has specific requirements, and each fills a different niche in the landscape.

Bearded irises, highly bred and exceedingly fancy, have been derived over decades from crosses between three faithful "flags" of old gardens: *Iris germanica, I. pallida* and *I. florentina*, source of the herbal fixative orrisroot, which is much used in potpourris and perfumery. These erstwhile favourites, softly tinted

lavender, purple and grey-white, have been ousted from catalogues by modern fleurs-de-lis in all the colours of the rainbow — and then some.

For once, I favour hybrids. I like their frills and ruffles, even if a few are so crimped along their petal edges that they have a hard time opening without a hand. I like the larger flowers and stately stems, the branching and multiple budding. And I am completely taken with the array of colours available. But enough is enough: I read that the bearded iris now appears in more than 20,000 different variations, with 700 new cultivars introduced annually at the inflated prices — as much as $25 for one root — of recent fashion. I've also heard of a gardener who, every three years, rips out his iris beds and replaces his poor passé sorts with the latest developments. It is foolishness, I say, and not even gardening as I know it.

And yet, the June garden picture would lose much of its sparkle without bearded irises. All of our sunny flower borders have a core group or two of irises, their colours chosen to complement the perennials blooming with them. A favourite picture combines a soft pink, semi-double peony with creamy yellow 'Southern Comfort' and sky blue 'Eleanor's Pride' irises. Double white dianthus spill over the raised border, and coral bells add sparks of red. Towering over the works — or, if

we've neglected our staking, flopping through everything — are bristly stems of dark blue anchusa. Elsewhere, iris 'Esther Fay' unfurls pure pink flowers near 6-foot spires of white eremurus, an exotic desert plant from Turkey commonly called the foxtail lily. Anchusa is here, too, behind a few plants of ivory lupins, with azure delphiniums just showing a hint of colour in the background.

Deep violet iris 'Matinata,' a 10-year resident here, blooms with single pink peonies ('Seashell') behind an edging of rosy Cheddar pinks. And 'Shipshape,' as blue as the sea, waves above a froth of white sand pinks and rippling flax blossoms that match its blue; a clump of Oriental poppies adds a touch of pink. Iris-time pictures are limited only by a gardener's imagination, colour preferences and space. It isn't sensible to pay huge sums for novelties when older, cheaper cultivars are all you could ask for in iris beauty.

Iris Care

"What are you planting those for?" a visiting friend asked one July morning as he watched us tucking iris rhizomes into a new border. "You'll never get rid of them." Irises have an unfair reputation for spreading their fat rootstocks beyond control. In truth, they are no quicker to increase than many other perennials and much easier to check than some;

invasive they are not. Besides, if you are growing some of the showier sorts, you'll have a list of fellow gardeners waiting for any excess.

Bearded irises sprout fans of flat, blue-green sword-shaped leaves from elongated rhizomes, which are thickened underground stems, rather than from roots. The actual roots, thin, white and very tough, spread down and out from both sides of the rhizome—which gives us a clue about planting irises. For each rhizome, trowel out two holes (rather than one), side by side and about 4 inches deep with a narrow ridge of earth between them. Set a rhizome on the ridge with roots parted naturally into the holes, then backfill with soil firmed over the roots and just covering the rhizome. A few rain showers will wash some soil away to expose the tan backs for the sun-baking they need for health.

Midsummer is the time to set out new irises. Mail-order roots generally arrive in August, but if one is dividing from the garden, July (or several weeks after the current crop of flowers) is a better time. Nurseries usually send single rhizomes with a short fan of leaves. For best effect, I prefer to set three to seven rhizomes of one colour, 10 inches apart, in an oval group with fans turned outward to avoid later crowding. In narrow borders (3 to 5 feet wide), such groups could alternate with single plants of late-blooming perennials such as day lilies, lythrums or yellow yarrows, which provide not only contrast in plant form to the stiff iris swords, but also give colour in July and August. In a wider border, low pinks, sedums, thymes or coral bells could run along the edge. For a sunny site, just a few plantings are easier to maintain.

In untended gardens, old clumps of bearded irises often grow merrily on from year to year, but like most plants, they are better for a little care. Sun is essential, at least six hours a day. See, too, that the soil is well drained and sweetened with lime if necessary. Soil texture is less important—light or heavy loam is much the same to irises—but soggy spots are fatal.

Care includes the removal of badly spotted or withered brown leaves

from the outside of the fans once or twice during the summer and the clearing of debris from the rhizomes so that they can breathe and sun-bathe. Otherwise, you're apt to get soft rot. If a rhizome goes mushy— "the consistency of a rather nasty cream puff," says one author—cut it back to hard, sound tissue, and discard (not compost) the affected part. Occasionally, iris borers show up; moist "sawdust" and droppings on the fans are clues. Again, minor surgery should bring the culprits to light and to a quick end underfoot. I have never sprayed irises for any-thing, nor do I intend to start. In the fall, scissor the leaves back to 3-inch fans to avoid a major spring cleanup of soggy leaves. Thus nurtured, a collection of tall bearded irises will bring a rainbow of colour in June.

Siberian Irises
(*Iris sibirica*)

Quite different from bearded irises in terms of foliage, flowers and needs, Siberian irises are extremely hardy, fibrous-rooted perennials that soon form stout clumps of elegant leaves—thin, reedy, dark green and gracefully arched—topped by fleurs-de-lis coloured conservatively in shades of blue, lavender, mauve and white. These take to partial shade as well as to sun, but in the dry soil that suits bearded irises, the Siberians pine and dwindle. They luxuriate in

Irises of various types are highlights of the June garden. Flowering best in full sun and well-drained soil, hybrid bearded irises, FACING PAGE, LEFT, *which bloom in all colours of the rainbow, are among the few plants best divided for propagation in midsummer, a few weeks after they have finished blooming. A long-term Larkwhistle resident is the dependable iris 'Matinata,'* FACING PAGE, CENTRE. *Less opulent than their bearded relatives, Siberian irises,* ABOVE, *produce clumps of elegant, long-lasting foliage with lightly made flowers in shades of blue, lavender, mauve and white.*

moist, fertile ground and even in fairly wet sites. Ordinary garden soil usually requires the addition of peat moss, decayed manure, compost or rotted leaves – but not lime. A leaf mulch (provided you are not plagued by slugs) helps retain both fertility and moisture.

A noninvasive habit of clumping and persistently good foliage make Siberian irises appropriate for important focal or accent points in the garden, alternating with hostas at regular intervals along a shaded path or on either side of an entrance to the house. Their healthy constitution and 3-to-4-foot height recommend them for the middle sections of low-maintenance perennial borders where they can be interplanted with daffodils for spring colour.

Pinks and Sweet William
(*Dianthus* spp)

As the flower gardener's year moves along, certain colours tend to predominate for a while and then give way to others. Much of June's rosy glow is provided by pinks, species of dianthus valued both for their neat mounds of silver or green foliage and their extravagant crop of spice-scented flowers. Our garden suits pinks to a tee: the soil is warm, sweet, sandy and quick to drain, and the site is fully open to the sun. Dianthus gives up in cold, heavy or waterlogged ground and steadfastly refuses to grow in shade.

Although we have grown about a dozen species of dianthus over the years, four stand out from the rest for beauty, hardiness, ease of culture and suitability for general border use. *Dianthus caesius*, the spicy 6-inch Cheddar pink said to decorate the white cliffs of Dover in silver and rose, is equally comfortable hanging from a chink in a sunny rock wall or sprawling over the edge of a flowerbed. *D. arenarius*, a white pink, sends up hundreds of flat, fringed flowers, like scented snow-flakes, above its short turf of green. Mats of this excellent edging plant have lived for eight years along an iris border, with only the attention of a short haircut after flowering and a top dressing of crumbly loam worked in among the leaves every few years if the plants show patchy spots.

Then there is *Dianthus allwoodii*, a garden-bred strain that fringes one of our borders with silver and seems to explode into fireworks of fragrant flowers – in shades of pink and crimson, single-toned or dark on light, penny-round or fringed, single or double – to celebrate the summer solstice. Because our 40 or 50 plants, all raised from one packet of seeds, vary not only in flower colour but also in vigour and hardiness, we like to take cuttings from the best of them every summer to have replacements for any that do not survive the winter.

Very nearly indestructible, the maiden pink (*Dianthus deltoides*) seeds with weedlike abandon and can be used as a ground cover or edging. Its leaves are dark green and dense below smallish flowers of a most piercing, almost neon crimson. This is the only dianthus I know of that lacks scent.

Few plants make such dramatic drifts of clear colour as sweet William, *Dianthus barbatus*, an old-fashioned biennial available also in cultivars such as 'Newport Pink,' 'Scarlet' and the wine-dark 'Crimson Velvet.' (The dwarf "wee willies" and annual midgets are not as effective.)

Biennials like sweet William produce vegetative growth the first year, flowers and seeds the second; they are not perennials, the plants to which this book (like Larkwhistle) is dedicated. Over the years, we have tried to plant the flowerbeds so that they will take care of themselves as much as possible. Accordingly, we cultivate predominantly plants that return faithfully year after year — low-maintenance, hardy, noninvasive perennials. But in the process, we have neglected a few of our old favourites — none so missed as sweet William — that used to decorate the June garden in the early days.

Quite easy to grow from seed, sweet William is worth including in perennial gardens. It is sown indoors in April or outdoors by mid-May. Plants are grown over summer, 12 inches apart, in a nursery bed where they develop into strong, leafy rosettes ready to go into their flowering quarters in September. Next June, and probably well into July, they will shoot up 18-inch stems topped by flattish flower heads — like exotic broccoli — of rose, red or blackish crimson. Three or more clumps set just back of the front of a border make a solid band of colour.

Pyrethrums
(*Chrysanthemum coccineum*)

All through June, clusters of pink and crimson pyrethrums, or painted daisies, sway in the borders with spice-scented dianthus in front and a flock of blue Siberian irises fluttering behind. Pyrethrum flowers may be as simple as roadside daisies — one row of petals around a yellow disk — or fully packed with petals, and they may be white, lilac or reddish. In whichever combination, the flowers top 2-foot self-supporting stems with dark green carrotlike leaves.

Among the most steadfast, useful and care-free of perennials, pyrethrums sprout quickly from seed

(within three weeks), develop in one season into flowering-sized clumps and return more strongly in seasons to come. If necessary, they can be propagated by root division in early spring, just as new leaves appear. Fertile loam well supplied with nourishing organic matter grows the best painted daisies; they resent dry ground and respond to thorough watering or mulch with a fuller crop of showy, long-lasting flowers. Nothing could be finer for early summer bouquets. Plant a few clumps in the vegetable garden for cut flowers.

Coral Bells
(*Heuchera* spp)

Coral bells add a touch of lightness to the front of flowerbeds and more rose colour to June and beyond. A strong contender for Best Edging of the Summer, this plant would earn garden space even if it never flowered, on account of its decorative dark green foliage marbled and zoned with white or bronze. But flower it does. For almost two months, the lovely leaves provide a setting for a generous crop of sparkling small bells, shaded pink and red, hung along slender swaying 18-inch stems. A single plant is nice enough, but a drift of five or more, each a foot apart from the next, makes a more effective sweep of misty colour in sun or partial shade.

Bouquets of bloom come from pinks such as Dianthus allwoodii, FACING PAGE, *and pyrethrums,* LEFT. *Fragrant dianthus flowers can be expected the second season from seed, and favourite varieties can be propagated from summer cuttings. Also excellent as cut flowers, pyrethrums, or painted daisies (accompanied here by the single peony 'Mahogany'), bloom year after year when planted in fertile, humus-rich soil.*

Nor is it difficult to work up a stock. The 20 or so clumps that now front a corner of old roses, foxgloves and alliums at Larkwhistle are off-shoots of five plants purchased in full bloom, wrapped in newspaper, from a flower vendor at Hamilton's farmers' market. Where the sales-woman got such a variety I'm not sure, but the plants, each different in bloom size and shading, must have been grown from a packet of mixed seeds. Seed-grown coral bells are possible for meticulous, patient gardeners, but since seed takes its sweet time sprouting and the young plants are frail and slow at first, division is the obvious method.

Once our first five had been in the garden for a few years and had fattened into multicrowned clumps, we lifted the lot and gingerly eased the individual tufts apart, careful to ensure that each had a few roots attached. We then set the divisions in earth that had recently been dressed with a generous layer of manure, peat and bone meal turned in to a depth of 8 or 10 inches. Coral bells, in fact, bloom better if divided every three years or whenever diminished flowering tells you they are over-crowded. Only the liveliest outer crowns are retained in the process, and the spent woody centre is com-post material. Cared for in this man-ner, they will be the jewels of the June garden and will go on flowering longer than most other perennials, all the while drawing in passing hummingbirds to sip nectar from their bells.

Geum
(*Geum quellyon*)

Northern gardeners have a distinct advantage when it comes to growing perennials, many of which thrive better in cooler locales than in areas where summers are excessively hot. Such is the case with geums, pretty perennials belonging to the vast family Rosaceae, which includes such diverse plants as apple trees, strawberries, spirea and, of course, roses. Two cultivars of one species, *Geum quellyon*, a Chilean native, are classic border inhabitants and the best of geums for general garden use. 'Lady Stratheden' tops 2½-foot

stems with bright yellow, round double blossoms. Another cultivar, 'Mrs. Bradshaw,' has remained, ac-cording to one expert, "one of the most popular of all herbaceous peren-nials" since it was discovered by chance in 1906 in a London garden.

Last summer was the first time I ever saw 'Mrs. Bradshaw' in the flesh (so to speak)—a single plant full of flowers obviously thriving in the dark, moist loam of a friend's rather shady garden. It was love at first sight. The basal clump of lobed leaves grew beneath branching stems decorated with brilliant scar-let semidouble flowers, like little open roses, set off with a central mass of straw-coloured stamens.

Geums present no real difficulty. Like many perennials, they require humusy garden loam that drains well but holds a steady reserve of moisture. Light shade is fine in hot gardens, full sun in cooler sites. Seeds will grow both the 'Lady' and the 'Mrs.' true to form and colour. An indoor spring start is recommended —soil temperature hovering around 70 degrees F for three weeks or so— for flowers the next summer. "Plants are best the third season," according to the Stokes seed catalogue.

Foxgloves
(*Digitalis* spp)

In all my gardening days, I doubt that any crop of flowers has given me

as much pride and joy as last year's 8-foot-tall 'Excelsior' foxgloves hung thickly with darkly freckled cream, yellow, pink or magenta tubular or finger-shaped (hence, digitalis) flow-ers. They were spectacular towering behind old rosebushes billowing with bloom, with the June sky for a backdrop.

If only they would come back every year. But, being biennial, foxgloves, like sweet William, grow a rosette of greenery one year, flower the next and then, after scattering their tiny seeds, disappear. Wise are the gardeners who avail themselves of some of the many seedlings left behind. These can be tucked into a corner of the vegetable garden to fatten up in fertile soil and then, come early September, lifted care-fully and transferred to a flowerbed for next year's colour. Seed is a better way to bring foxgloves into the garden initially, and the method described for anchusas, below, will do as well for digitalis.

Seldom seen in gardens where prim, predictable annuals are the mainstay, foxgloves are naturals for half-wild or woodland sites where they can be left to roam at will. Once while on a bicycle tour of English gardens, my partner and I passed through a shadowy forest where ivy grew thickly up the tree trunks and purple foxgloves congregated by the hundreds. Given their woodland origins, foxgloves grow to greater heights in a home garden if the earth is humus-rich and moist; compost, leaf mould, peat moss and old ma-nure all help. Although foxgloves thrive in shade, they also do well in sun in our coolish garden.

Anchusa
(*Anchusa italica*)

All of June's rosiness needs complementary blue, and few plants wear the colour as well as anchusa. In fact, "no plant," according to one old-time writer, "not excepting the delphiniums, decks itself in a more truly azure colour." A seldom-grown 4-foot perennial, *Anchusa italica*, or *A. azurea*—its common names in-clude Italian bugloss and alkanet— shows its family ties to both borage and comfrey in rather coarse, rough

hairy leaves and stems and spiralled clusters of mauve buds that unfurl into five-petalled blue blossoms.

And what a blue – clear, deep and visible from a distance. I always think of anchusa as the plant that stopped a bus. One June morning some years ago, 20 or 30 people came tumbling out of a tour bus passing our place and swarmed into the garden, all wanting to know the name of "that incredibly blue plant." Searching the back roads for birds and wildflowers, the group of naturalists had spotted anchusa in full glory from 100 feet away.

Nurseries seem to ignore this showy plant, but anchusa is not difficult to grow from seeds. Start plants in 4-inch pots, a few seeds per pot, thinned eventually to one plant, and set seedlings in the garden before their searching taproots become cramped in the containers. Listed as a biennial in some catalogues, anchusa is more accurately a short-lived perennial, in the manner of columbines, flax or Iceland poppies; in our garden, it usually re-

appears for three or four years. But if older clumps deteriorate in the end, there are always seedlings left behind – sometimes far too many – that can be lifted when still fairly small and transplanted toward the back of flowerbeds, perhaps behind pink peonies or rosy pyrethrums or near a drift of yellow irises.

Anchusa has but one fault. In full flower, the top-heavy stems tend to topple, smothering nearby plants and generally creating confusion in a border. The remedy is to hammer two or three slender stakes – 1-by-2-inch lumber works well – around each clump and to wind the stakes round with strong cord to help corset this brilliant but untidy plant.

Flax Flowers
(*Linum perenne*)

More blue for June comes from the pretty flax flowers of *Linum perenne*, an 18-inch plant as delicate and airy as anchusa is large and sprawling. Garden flax is a perennial counterpart of the blue-eyed annual flax, *L.*

Classic border perennials demand only moist, fertile soil to produce a lavish crop of summer flowers. Slender foxglove spires can decorate the back of a border behind peonies, old-fashioned roses, Siberian irises and the like, or, FACING PAGE, they can be left to seed in half-wild garden corners. Geum, ABOVE, is a less familiar but equally easy plant. 'Lady Stratheden' tops 2½-foot stems with double flowers.

usitatissimum, whose Latin name, meaning "the most useful," is truly appropriate for a plant that yields not only fibres to weave into linen, but flaxseed and linseed oil as well. If you have ever seen a farm field as blue and rippling as a summer lake, chances are you were looking at a crop of annual flax.

In a flowerbed, perennial flax serves to lighten more massive and complicated flowers such as peonies and irises, much as baby's-breath

does in a bouquet of roses. Linum's graceful spray of thread-fine stems carries clusters of drooping buds that open successively every morning into simple, round clear blue blossoms. Finely tuned to the natural cycle of light and dark, flax flowers start to unfurl about an hour before dawn and are wide-eyed and perky by sunrise. By noon, however, the ground is littered with their petals. Flowers last a few short hours each day (unless the sky is overcast), but

the next morning and the next for many weeks to come sees a fresh crop of blue.

Perennial flax sprouts quickly from seed scattered in the garden. Young plants are thinned to 8 inches between them. Seeds sown outdoors in late spring will yield flowers 12 months later, but impatient gardeners might seed indoors in March —3-inch peat pots are suitable containers—for first-season bloom.

Linum will make itself at home in

any sunny corner, lodging among the iris rhizomes, at the edges of paths or wherever the feathery seedlings get a roothold in well-drained earth. Unless they are too thick or sprout in mats of creeping thyme, I let them be. The plants are so delicate and unobtrusive that they are no threat at all to most other perennials.

Cornflowers
(Centaurea montana)

Many gardeners know cornflowers as easy 3-foot annuals that grow quickly from May-sown seed and decorate the garden for a single summer with fluffy round flowers so distinctly blue that they have given their name to a shade of that colour – cornflower blue. Less fleeting and not quite as vivid is a perennial counterpart, *Centaurea montana*, known commonly as the mountain-bluet or, simply, perennial cornflower. The leaves are elongated, oval, pointed and grey with fine hairs – pubescent, botanists say. Early in June, here in central Ontario, and for almost a month, 2½-foot stems rise up, carrying the many dark blue thin-petalled blossoms that always remind me of little jets of flame.

Perennial cornflowers look best set in groups of three or more – a single plant makes little show – just back of front in company with poppies, irises of any colour, dianthus and the like. Since they spread from both roots and seeds, they might be left out of smaller gardens in favour of something showier and more stay-at-home; but our travelling bachelor's buttons are a good choice for next-to-no-maintenance flowerbeds that could include Siberian irises, day lilies and rose loosestrife for later colour. Although they are not spectacular, perennial cornflowers are practically indestructible; A. Clutton-Brock says in *Studies in Gardening* (1916) that if the hardy cornflower "were not so easy, it would be prized, and it deserves to be more prized for its easiness."

Ornamental Onions
(Allium spp)

My favourite flowering onion, *Allium aflatunense*, is a contempo-

rary of perennial cornflowers, and the two planted together make a close harmony of purple and blue. This perennial bulb, recently dubbed "purple sensation" by bulb hawkers who were perhaps concerned that buyers would be deterred by the Latin, is decorative through all its phases from budding to seed-making. Early in June, stiff leafless stems lengthen to 3 feet, each supporting a tight round package of flowers-to-be wrapped in a papery husk that splits to free the unfolding buds. Soon stems are swaying with the weight of perfect 5-inch globes composed of many small lavender starts all shooting out from a central point on thread-fine stems. Once flowers fade, pods rattling with black seeds take their place, unless the seed heads are cut for dried bouquets.

Our original half-dozen bulbs of *Allium aflatunense* have increased at least threefold in as many years. I find this one a good substitute for the larger, later and considerably costlier giant flowering onion *A. giganteum*, which has so far refused to stay with us for more than a season. All alliums appreciate fertile loam and a place in the sun. Needless to say, most bugs give them a wide miss.

If I could grow only two of the decorative alliums, my other choice would be *Allium albopilosum* – the Latin means "white, shaggy onion" – a rather strange plant that sends up foot-high stems topped by gleaming

Blue flowers are often rare and almost always valuable additions to garden pictures. Dainty dime-sized flax flowers, FACING PAGE, *are produced on 18-inch plants so fine-stemmed and airy that they are never in the way, even if they seed down among other perennials, and since plants commonly last no more than three seasons, self-sown seedlings help to carry on the colour. The subtle shades of* Allium aflatunense, ABOVE, *best of the flowering onions, and of blue perennial cornflowers could be sparked by an edging of pink or red coral bells.*

8-inch globes of sharply pointed, starry flowers apparently cut from some ghostly lilac-tinted metal. All of the flowers radiate from a central point like some vegetable sparkler.

Lupins
(*Lupinus polyphyllus*)

Photographs of grand English borders at their peak of early-summer bloom often include masses of multicoloured lupins. Pictures of parts of the North American wilderness show vast stretches afloat with the blue and white spikes of this legume. But before you attempt to duplicate the display at home, take heed of one expert who says, "Not all districts are suited to the cultivation of lupins, and even the magnificent modern hybrids can be capricious if conditions are not exactly to their liking."

I expect he means the 4-foot Russell hybrids. Magnificent they are, with their fanning hands of dark green leaves below tapering candles of pea-shaped flowers variously tinted white, cream, shades of pink and red, blue or purple. Capricious, too, they have proven in our garden, growing beautifully some seasons and in some parts of the garden, dwindling unaccountably other years elsewhere. Lupins are not usually long-lived in a garden. If they linger for four years, count yourself lucky.

Once you have a sunny site, soil

pH seems to be the crucial variable. Lupins do not tolerate alkaline earth well; too much sweetness, in fact, can do them in. They are said to thrive in moist, humus-rich soil that is a little on the sour side. No wonder, then, that our best crop grew in a bed that had been liberally fertilized the previous fall with a thick layer of decayed leaves, a process that no doubt lowered the pH of our sweet, sandy soil. Peat moss does the same.

One additional difficulty arises in the cultivation of lupins: the taprooted plants do not recover well from root disturbance. It is best, then, to sow the quick-sprouting seeds directly into 4-inch pots, several seeds per pot, thinning to the single strongest seedling, and to transfer the young plants to the garden before the taproot winds itself around the bottom of the pot. The Stokes seed catalogue recommends freezing seeds for two days, then wrapping them in a damp paper towel for a day before sowing. A cool germinating temperature (54 degrees F) is also called for because "higher temperatures will actually prevent sprouting." Another tactic is to sow seeds directly into the prepared earth of a flowerbed, three or four seeds in a group, 18 inches between groups. Again, thin to one plant per station. The best lupins I have ever seen grow in a local garden where they have been allowed to seed and re-seed for years. Fortunately, the

border is large enough to accommodate their roving ways.

Blue False Indigo
(*Baptisia australis*)

If lupins have proven iffy at Larkwhistle, blue false indigo, a related legume not unlike lupins in growth and flowers, has been with us from the start. Baptisia never needs dividing. For nine years now, a single 4-foot plant has sat comfortably in a sunny border where it adds multiple 10-inch spikes of dim lavender pea-shaped flowers to June's rosiness. The nicely rounded bush of pale grey-green alfalfa-like leaves stays in good condition the season through and provides a pleasant screen for tall, possibly shabby delphiniums or hollyhocks behind it. If only baptisia flowers were true blue, red or pink, this easy plant would probably live in more gardens.

An American native, false indigo grows in woods and along streams from Pennsylvania southward. In the garden, it seems to thrive in almost any soil, in sun or light shade.

Foxtail Lily
(*Eremurus* spp)

Few of our perennials are as astonishing in full flower as the towering spires of eremurus, the upper third of their 6-foot leafless stems crowded with hundreds of small stars—white,

yellow or rose, depending on the species. These vegetable skyrockets hail from Turkey, Central Asia and the Middle East. A visitor told us that she saw eremurus growing wild on dry, stony, heavily grazed hillsides in Israel.

In the home garden, they must be sited in fullest sun well away from shadowing neighbours and planted in earth that drains water like the proverbial sieve. Sandy ground is almost a must, but a light loam is possible with crumbly cow manure or compost added to nourish these robust giants. Fall is the time to plant foxtail lily roots (listed in some bulb catalogues, but not cheap), which are fleshy, brittle and splayed like elongated starfish. Take care not to bend the easily broken roots but to set them as received in an ample hole so that the crowns, or eyes—little nubs like asparagus tips at the hub of the roots—are 3 inches below ground. If there is any doubt about drainage, an inch or so of sand above and below the roots is a help. Next spring, fat pointed noses will push through the earth—only the impetuous crown imperials make such a dramatic entrance—and with luck, their numbers will increase slowly every spring thereafter. "Once well planted," says William Robinson in *The English Flower Garden* (1883), "they should never be disturbed."

Hardy Gloxinia
(*Incarvillea delavayi*)

At the feet of our foxtail lilies grows a little colony of hardy gloxinias, a misnomer if ever there were one for a plant that is neither a gloxinia (not even a relative) nor a particularly hardy plant in cold gardens. And yet this 12-inch Chinese native is worth a go—even if it manages to survive only one or two winters—for the sake of its exotic tubular flowers coloured glowing pink with a yellow throat above decorative, dark green, deeply cut leaves. Every garden needs a bit of exotica, every gardener a challenge. The hardy gloxinia provides both. I expect that on the balmy West Coast

Tall elements in the garden picture may be provided by spectacular, towering foxtail lilies and the more familiar lupins. The former, FACING PAGE, LEFT, are sun-loving desert denizens that rise from brittle starfish-shaped roots planted in fall. Many-hued lupins light up the garden behind a clump of crimson sweet William, FACING PAGE, CENTRE. Given slightly acidic soil and careful planting, lupins are dependable and lovely, but they can pine and fade away in sites not to their liking. Even harder to please is the exotic, mis-named hardy gloxinia, ABOVE, which is neither a gloxinia nor particularly hardy. A challenge to grow, it should be left in place if it thrives.

and anywhere south of Maryland, this plant would be as easy as any.

Generally, incarvilleas are listed with dahlias, gladioli and begonias in spring catalogues, and like these definitely tender tubers and corms, our almost hardy gloxinias are planted sometime in May. Last spring, a local supermarket was selling little moss-filled plastic bags containing, according to the tag, three roots of the "Exotic Chinese Trumpet Lily." Since our original planting of incarvillea was on the wane after four seasons—the plant lasts longer if snow-covered or straw-mulched over the winter—I brought home some replacements. Planted a foot apart in fertile loam in the sun, the skinny tubers yielded a nice crop of flowers for many weeks that same summer.

Soapwort
(*Saponaria ocymoides*)

Once, in distant, simpler days, a washing powder was made of soapwort, a European perennial whose roots yield, according to one source, "a suds-producing substance particularly effective for dissolving fat, grease and resins." The same sudsy roots have been used to produce a head on beer. Today, this 10-inch plant is a showy June edger or rock garden dweller that foams with five-petalled pink flowers above a tangle of wiry stems clothed in small oval leaves. Few plants are as decorative,

spilling over a sunny retaining wall or lodged in the wall face.

Easy to raise from either seed or starter plants, mounds of soapwort widen eventually to fill a square foot or more of space. A shearing, as for pinks, keeps soapwort thrifty and dense. If after a damp winter, plants look like soggy mats of straw rather than their usual perky green, don't be too quick to rip them out. They may put on new growth as spring warms.

Gas Plant
(*Dictamnus fraxinella*)

Here is a perennial that, like a peony, can live in a garden for decades without lifting, dividing or other kindly meddling on a gardener's part, provided it is set in deep, fertile earth at the start and given its own yard-wide circle of space in a sunny or partially shaded flowerbed. Foliage, dark green and leathery, stays fresh from spring till fall and makes an attractive setting for the foot-long, tapered spires of florets, either white or rosy purple, that decorate the plant in June. Its height when in flower is 3 feet, making the gas plant a mid-border selection. Both foliage and flowers are aromatic, smelling bittersweetly of citrus and spice.

By some accounts, the flowers give off such a quantity of fragrant, volatile oils on a sultry summer night that if a lighted match is held to one,

a little puff of flame will shoot out from the flower's mouth—hence the common name. But since one gardener reports only singed fingers, "and that from holding the match too long," I have not been tempted to experiment. Fireworks or not, this care-free perennial, at once elegant and sturdy, deserves to find a home in more flowerbeds, where it blends nicely with irises, peonies, foxgloves and pinks.

Perennial Salvia
(*Salvia superba*)

Flower borders need the shadowy effect of deep dusky colours among the light yellows and rosy pinks. Few perennials glow as darkly brilliant as a mass planting of *Salvia superba*, a 2½-foot-tall, self-supporting, drought-resistant, bug-proof and long-flowering relative of cooking sage. It returns year after year, with no designs on more garden space. Each June, its aromatic grey-green foliage is topped by a thick crop of purple-violet flower spikes that remain colourful while irises and poppies come and go. Much of this salvia's show comes from its bracts, modified leaves under each flower that continue to be decorative even after the flowers have faded. The cultivar 'East Friesland' is the one to look for in nurseries. Once in the garden, it is easy to increase into three- or four-shoot divisions in spring or fall. A good thing, too, because purple sage is that much more effective in a group of three or more.

Silver-Dollar Plant
(*Lunaria biennis*)

Most folks know lunaria's brittle branching stems hung with round, parchmentlike seedpods as dust-gathering dried material for winter bouquets. I wonder how many gardeners would buy these "silver dollars" if they knew how easy they are to grow. In fact, this seed-scattering biennial, also called money plant and pennies-from-heaven, can soon become one of a gardener's self-inflicted weeds. In a neighbouring garden, lunaria has claimed a whole rocky hillside, where each June it

In order to reveal the "silver dollars" of dried-flower arrangements, the green seed-covering of Lunaria biennis, FACING PAGE, *must be peeled away. Another garden oddity is the 3-foot gas plant,* LEFT. *Its white or rosy purple flower spikes look ordinary enough, but the flowers are said to give off such a quantity of fragrant volatile oils that if on a summer night a match is held to one, it will produce a little puff of flame.*

shines purple and white among grey boulders and scrubby sumachs. If your space is limited, it might be better to buy a few dried silver-dollar stems rather than introduce this pretty pest into the garden. But if you can handle the increase, money plant grows quickly from spring-sown seeds, flowers a full year after and then disappears from that spot only to spring up elsewhere. Any soil short of soggy in any site will do.

Snow-in-Summer
(*Cerastium tomentosum*)

Another inveterate spreader, but this time underground, grey-leaved cerastium insinuates its twitchlike runners into the affairs of neighbouring plants or weaves its way down a rock garden slope. While it is useful for low-maintenance plant-ings—a good ground cover in sun, for instance—it must always be kept well away from smaller things. We grow cerastium along the edge of a flower border and pounce with the trowel if it gets out of bounds. Its

grey-white foliage is effective from spring to fall, and the crop of fluffy white blooms, truly like a little drift of snow in summer, adds to June's bounty. Seeds or starter plants grow in any dryish soil in sun.

Veronica
(*Veronica* spp)

Veronica can be confusing simply because the genus contains so many garden-worthy species that vary a good deal in height, habit of growth and flowering time. Currently, our garden grows at least six species and as many named varieties, ranging from half an inch to 4 feet tall and colouring in sequence from late May until August. Three belong to June.

Veronica repens hugs the ground closely as it creeps outward to form flat mats of minute, shiny leaves sprinkled in season with small pale blue flowers. This one is safe only among scaled-down alpine plants or wedged between paving stones where foot traffic is light. Some shade is best.

More at home along a border edge or in a rock garden is the elegant *Veronica incana*, whose tufts of elliptical silver leaves, presentable year-round, provide a setting for the slim 8-inch spikes of many small amethyst florets.

Perhaps better still, due to the clarity of its blue, is *Veronica teucrium* (*V. latifolia*) in cultivars such as 'Shirley Blue' and 'Crater Lake.' If they stood upright, they would reach 18 inches, but the lax, wiry stems tend to tumble; twiggy branches pushed into the earth around the clumps keep them from sprawling on the ground. Noninvasive and hardy, this species has proven easy to cultivate in the fertile sandy loam of a sunny flower border. Nothing could be finer adjacent to pinks or coral bells than little rounded clouds of blue veronica. Aside from a bit of propping, maintenance means only trimming away the spent flower spikes in July, after which the plants revert to neat green mounds. In one season, and for many thereafter, three plants set a foot apart—crocus corms tucked between them flower while veronica is in its first stages of spring growth—create a solid path of blue for a few weeks in early summer. The brief flowering may be a drawback for some gardeners, but any lover of blue flowers cannot help appreciating their jewel-like colour.

Yellow Loosestrife
(*Lysimachia punctata*)

Yellow flowers are not plentiful in June—and just as well; this gardener is content to revel in rosiness and enjoy the subtle harmony of blue, lavender and white flowers with silver foliage. But the 3-foot yellow loosestrife, as frankly golden as any of August's sunflowers or heleniums, can be sited near scarlet Oriental poppies, navy anchusa and white or blue irises (Siberian or bearded) for a striking June combo. Gardeners who love boldly contrasting colours might set a group of purple *Salvia superba* in front. Thriving in any decent soil in sun or light shade (but with a preference for moist ground and partial shade), this tall sibling of the prostrate and wide-ranging creeping Jenny (*Lysimachia nummularia*) is a tough, care-free perennial that needs no staking or watering. Whorled leaves, dusty green and undistinguished, fan out below 18-inch tapers—more each year from a rapidly expanding rootstock—of deep yellow florets. Although yellow loosestrife can be divided with ease, you are more apt to have to check its spread than to propagate it.

Peonies
(*Paeonia* spp)

When the peonies flower, Larkwhistle reaches one of its high points, a celebration of the coming of summer with a spectacular burst of crimson, pink and white. I always wonder how such opulent blooms can grow from such sturdy, no-nonsense plants; hardy far into the north, they are almost invariably vigorous and healthy and are capable of keeping their corners of the garden full and fresh six months a year and of standing their ground for decades when left to their own wild ways.

I doubt that there is such a crea-

ture as an unattractive peony. Even nameless nursery varieties or chunks of roots split from a neighbour's trusty old plant are sure to beautify a garden for many years. A specialty catalogue filled with enticing cultivars plunges a peony fan into a pleasant quandary and prompts one to start digging holes. The surest way to extend peony times is to plant early, midseason and late-blooming cultivars. At Larkwhistle, peonies span five weeks or more, from the end of May until about mid-July.

First to flower, along with the late tulips and lilacs, is a strange and wonderful peony that came to us one fall as a gift from visitors who said it had grown in their grandparents' garden: "We've never seen it anywhere else and thought you would like a root. This way we know somebody will keep it going." Accepted with thanks, the root was tucked into an open place in John's "rosy border"—chances were it would be pink or crimson. Next spring, several stems emerged dressed in the most unpeony-like leaves, thread-fine and

Apparently delicate, snow-in-summer, FACING PAGE, *is a determined creeper that can soon infest a rock garden or perennial bed but also has a place as an indestructible ground cover in dry, sunny gardens. Also fragile in appearance are pink coral bells,* ABOVE, *which, when accompanied by a stream of blue veronicas, set off the bearded irises and peonies that provide much of June's splendid colour.*

fringed like fennel. By May, the stems were topped with intriguing crimson-satin buds and, not long after, with full-petalled, fragrant, cherry-red blooms. There is hardly a spring visitor who does not ask what it is—"Looks like a peony, but with that foliage, I wasn't sure . . ."—and most ask for a piece of it. But knowing that peonies like to be left in peace once they have settled in and recognizing that there would never be enough bits to go around anyway, we have been reluctant to dig up and divide the "fringed" peony, close kin (we have since discovered) of a wild European species, *Paeonia tenuifolia*.

At the turn of the century, hybridists turned their attention in earnest to peonies and left gardeners with a splendid legacy of still-celebrated cultivars such as 'Sara Bernhardt,' 'Philippe Rivoire,' 'Mrs. F.D. Roosevelt,' 'Kelway's Glorious' and a host of others. 'M. Jules Elie' is the first of the old favourites to flower for us; its double-scoop strawberry-pink flowers are so outrageously overblown that they are in danger of toppling in the lightest breeze unless the plant is "bundled up like a mummy," as someone once said. Once, after a June rain, poor old Jules was so battered down that it took a first-aid treatment with various crutches, splints, slings and cloth ties to get him on his feet again.

Rain or shine, double peonies are sure to be the first flowers to fall over. After watching our peonies trail sodden blossoms on the lawn for several seasons, we decided that the few minutes it takes to support them is time well spent in view of the splendid effect. To that end, we now hammer three lengths of 1-by-2-inch lumber around each peony, close enough that the wood is partially hidden by leaves but not so close as to damage the peony crowns. We then wind three levels of sturdy string from stake to stake, making sure that the top string comes to within 8 inches or so of the flower buds—I say "buds" because staking is done before the flowers open. See that the cord is not so tight that it keeps the bush from assuming a relaxed natural shape. Garden centres sell special tapered wire peony cages too, and homemade versions, reusable and

easy to install, will do as well.

Not all peonies need staking, however. Gardeners who know only the heavy doubles will find nice surprises in the single peonies (poppylike with a row of petals cupped around conspicuous central stamens) and the semi-doubles (with several overlapping rows of petals). Delicate and shell-like yet needing no support, these peonies include: 'Krinkled White,' whose profuse single blooms with textured petals around a golden centre make classic cut flowers; 'Dainty,' whose smallish, bowl-shaped flowers have two rows of

rosy petals that fade to the merest blush; and 'Sea Shell,' with big, blowsy mauve-pink flowers.

Whether single or double, no perennial known to me is as steadfast as the peony. Given their longevity, peonies deserve thoughtful siting and careful planting in earth that will nourish them for many years; they prefer to sink their roots into what has been described as "fat, greasy loam," a rather heavy soil well supplied with organic matter. At Larkwhistle, we have planted something like 70 peonies in improved sandy soil with excellent success. We order the roots in summer for dormant delivery in fall; mid-September to mid-October is peony planting time. For each root, we dig an oversized hole, 2 feet or more across and 18 inches deep, piling the topsoil to one side, but hauling subsoil away. The excavation is backfilled with a mixture of about two-thirds topsoil—sometimes we borrow a wheelbarrow load of our best loam from the vegetable plot—and one-third very old, black cow manure, avoiding anything approaching fresh. Three or four shovelsful of peat moss, a shovel of wood ashes and a few trowels of bone meal are all thoroughly stirred into the blend. With planting holes topped up, we tamp the humusy mix with a blunt stick to settle things and then do a little dance to consolidate the earth further and press out root-drying air pockets.

Planting depth is critical. Set too deeply, peonies may never bloom. If you have a clump that has been in place and flowerless for two years or more, consider lifting it in fall, cutting the roots gingerly into three-to-five-eye sections—larger clumps may not recover for several years—and replanting the divisions at the right depth. The hard-and-fast rule is to place a measured 1½ to 2 inches of earth over the topmost buds—little reddish nodules that will be next year's shoots. In preparation for peonies, we trowel out enough of the prepared soil to accommodate the root at the required depth and, with the root in place, gradually fill in and firm the soil around it—fingers are the tools for this—until it is secure. A half-bucket of water settles the works.

Once established, peonies seem to thrive on benign neglect. But one expert recommends a handful or two of bone meal "about the time the leaves begin to unfold." Water seems to be even more necessary for peonies than surface fertility. Although the plant itself will endure drought, its buds need moisture to mature and open. If an early dry spell hits, a few deep drinks could mean the difference between a full crop of flowers and a meagre show. Late-summer moisture, too, ensures that activity continues underground in the cause of next season's bloom. Also in aid of next season, late mulching may be a good idea. Peonies remain hardy to at least minus 20 degrees F. Winter temperatures at Larkwhistle are often colder, but because we can count on snow cover, we have never protected them. In snowless regions, however, a mulch of straw or evergreen boughs laid on in December after the ground is frozen keeps newly planted roots from heaving during a freeze-and-thaw cycle.

Generally, peonies enjoy the best of health, but if stems grow a bit of fuzz at their bases and then keel over, suspect a fungal blight called botrytis. Prune away infected stems and burn or otherwise dispose of them. And a word about ants: Despite stories to the contrary, these busy bugs do not do a thing to help peony buds open. All the ants are doing when you see them, inevitably, on the buds is helping themselves to a meal of the sugary bud coating.

As landscaping tools, peonies are more versatile than most perennials. In addition to spectacular blooms, the symmetrical yard-high growth of elegant, long-lasting leaves makes the plants naturals for focal points or massed display. At Larkwhistle, peonies are a stable, persistent presence in beds and borders among more flighty or floppy perennials. Where they are grown in groups, they should be planted 3 feet apart, and the same distance should be left between peonies and other robust perennials in a mixed border.

I readily admit a passion for the peony. If I could grow only one perennial, this would be it. I agree with G.A.R. Phillips, author of *Aristocrats of the Flower Border*, when he notes that because of the flower's lovely blossoms, combined with "elegance of foliage that is never other than pleasing throughout the season, its delicious fragrance, its ease of culture, freedom from disease, hardiness and permanent effect, we have indeed something very nearly approaching the perfect perennial." At Larkwhistle, the nearly perfect perennial's many attributes combine with the other harmonious colours and textures of June to create garden beds that approach the sublime.

Opulent, heavy-headed double peonies must be supported while still in the bud, or they will topple in the first rain shower. Three 1-by-2-inch stakes wound around with twine will do the job nicely and will be practically invisible within the lush peony foliage.

Midsummer Magic
Lilies and more for the hottest weather

Exotic in appearance yet hardy even in cold prairie gardens, lilies add a note of elegance and dependable midsummer colour to a garden. Some, such as 'Bronze Queen,' turn downward and curl their petals back, while others face outward or up, but all grow from bulbs best planted in fall.

Years ago at Larkwhistle, May and June's exuberant flowering gave way to a subdued and rather shabby midsummer garden. To say that the flower borders lapsed into green after the last peony had faded would be a polite way to describe the patchy plots of none-too-interesting foliage separated by gaps of bare earth where spring bulbs and Oriental poppies had flowered and then gone underground. With three months of decent growing weather still to come, July seemed too soon for an anticlimax.

Annual flowers, we discovered, are one option for extending the colour, since most of these garden transients come into flower fairly late and then carry on until frost or beyond. But annuals were at odds with our aim to grow a garden of hardy, relatively permanent perennials that would follow each other in successive waves of colour from spring till fall, plants chosen and arranged with a view to masking the inevitable gaps with either persistently fine foliage or later flowers.

Clearly, we had some homework to do if we wanted to avoid the mid-summer doldrums. We checked back into our favourite garden books and poked around in other gardens to see what was happening in July and August. Over several seasons, we expanded our repertoire of hardy plants to include a greater complement of late-bloomers. Once new plants – scrounged, seed-grown or mail-ordered – were at hand, we began the process of shifting things about so that perennials that were at their best at different times alternated with one another throughout a border. Sometimes we would completely replace, say, a clump of irises or a group of sweet Williams with later-blooming lythrums or day lilies. More often, we would reduce the scope of early plants to make room for hardy geraniums, scarlet bergamot or balloon flowers. Wherever there were a few square feet of empty border space, in went a clutch of lily bulbs, often with the likes of flax or violas planted over their heads for a cooling ground cover and

extended bloom. Dwarf early perennials that continued to flower into July and beyond – violas and coral bells come to mind – were given places of prominence along the fronts of borders.

Becoming acquainted with the many fine perennials that bloom in midsummer was the surest way of all, we found, to keep a garden fresh and flowery after June's opulence.

Lilies
(*Lilium* spp)

As the seasons turn, each phase in a bed of hardy flowers has its primary perennials around which garden pictures are composed. In April, daffodils star; in May, tulips; in June, irises, with poppies and peonies sharing top billing in some gardens. At Larkwhistle, July sees lilies in all their exotic forms and stunning colours, blooming in the company of sky blue delphiniums, misty baby's-breath, fragrant scarlet bergamot and dependable day lilies. The garden that grows a crop of lilies cannot help making the transition from June's abundance to midsummer in the most beautiful way.

In the last few years, lilies have become something of a passion with us. Besides including them in all of the flowerbeds, each fall we fill a 4-by-25-foot vegetable garden bed with several hundred bulbs, many of them offshoots from crowded older clumps, which we then sell to garden visitors the following October. I would not hesitate to rank lilies among the top five hardy perennials.

More than most perennials, lilies vary among themselves in flower form. The short but treasure-packed catalogue put out by Honeywood Lilies, a specialty nursery in Riverside, Saskatchewan (if bulbs are hardy there, they're likely to be hardy almost anywhere), distinguishes four types:
•Down-facing lilies. Honey-coloured 'Bronze Queen,' 'White Gold' and the deep maroon 'Butterfly' are sterling examples of the type, as are the ubiquitous tiger lilies. Their often smaller blossoms are arranged in a multi-flowered, conical head or panicle of as many as 20 flowers. Petals turn back gracefully, suggesting the common name Turk's-cap lilies.
•Out-facing lilies. Among the showiest, they "look straight at you," tilting their flowers perpendicular to the ground and turning back petals only a little. Of these, we grow 'Embarrassment,' which, when well grown, can produce as many as 50 bright pink blossoms on or near the tops of 4-foot stems; and scarlet 'Brenda Watts,' which, according to the Honeywood catalogue, remains "healthy and vigorous" in their lily fields even after 40 years.
•Up-facing lilies. This type looks at the sky with chalice-shaped flowers, six or eight in a cluster. 'Wanda,' among my favourites, is a startling, glossy maroon red, and the "orange lilies" of older gardens have this form.
•Trumpet lilies. In form like the tender white Easter lily, these flowers have proven more difficult. Except for the truly glorious 'Regale' lily, which endures and increases with us, the hybrid trumpets such as 'Black Dragon' and 'Golden Splendour' seem reluctant to stay. But one catalogue insists they are "sturdy,

vigorous and prolific," so perhaps we should prepare a patch of fertile soil for our remaining bulbs away from the competitive roots of clematis vines and Russian olive shrubs.

The fact that lilies bloom in various sizes and conformations and in a colour range rivalled only by irises makes them equally amenable to harmonious associations with other plants. As with tulips and irises, the possibilities for lily-based pictures are limited only by imagination, preference and the scope of a gardener's plot of land.

A lily grows from a bulb composed of many overlapping fleshy scales, the whole looking rather like a buff-coloured globe artichoke. Nestled at the heart of each bulb are next season's stem, leaves and flowers in embryo form. Attached to the bulb's base are stringy pale roots. Like most other hardy bulbs, lilies are generally planted in fall, but I have also had good luck with peat-packed lily bulbs bought from local nurseries in spring. If I see shoots pushing at the confining plastic bag and fresh roots among the moss, I reckon that the bulbs are lively and raring to grow. Spring or fall, it is important that bulbs be plump, firm and supplied with some roots.

Sound bulbs in hand (or in the bag), we turn our attention to the earth that will best nourish them. With bulbs ranging from $2 apiece to $35 for 12, most of us will want

Blooming in a range of colours rivalled only by bearded irises, self-sufficient hybrid lilies, FACING PAGE, thrive when their roots are in cooling shade and their flowers are in the sun. At Larkwhistle, LEFT, wine-red 'Wanda' and soft yellow 'Dawn Star' lilies create a midsummer picture with climbing rose 'New Dawn' and sky blue delphiniums. When lily clumps grow crowded after five or six years, they can be lifted and split in fall to extend the colour.

to see that they live in suitable soil. Decent loam well supplied with organic matter is the medium for lilies, while heavy, excessively damp, dry or very sandy soils are to be avoided – or improved. Heavy clay needs an admixture of gritty sand or even crushed stone to lighten it and improve drainage. Since most lilies respond to a soil pH of neutral to slightly acidic, lime is usually not called for.

To plant lilies, trowel out an oversized hole to accommodate the roots without cramping, and see that soil – again, fattened with organic matter if it is your basic garden-variety earth – is gently firmed all around the bulbs to avoid root-drying air pockets. In one of her many books, Gertrude Jekyll describes digging out a long wild lily bed (or, to be precise, having it dug) to a depth of 3 feet and filling it with all manner of sappy green stuff, spent mushroom compost and the like, before planting the bulbs. Good old "Bumps," as her friends called her, never was one to do things on a small scale.

Most lilies sprout roots not only from the bottom of the bulbs but also from the underground portion of their stems. These "stem-rooters" are planted with 3 or 4 inches of earth over the tops of the bulbs to give stem roots somewhere to go. As with other bulbs, be guided in depth of planting by their size, with larger ones going relatively deeper. Some lily bulbs grow to softball size, notably those of tiger lilies, plants scorned by some but still among my favourites for August pictures with blue and white aconites. An exception to the rule of deep planting for large bulbs is the classically lovely white Madonna lily (*Lilium candidum*), which must be planted in August or early September with a scant inch of earth over the bulbs. This species produces a fall growth of leaves. If Madonna lilies thrive for you, let them be and resist the urge to dig them up and divide them.

Conventional garden wisdom has it that lilies like their roots in the shade and their heads in the sun – that is to say, they prefer cool moist soil to hot sun-baked sites. Clearly, a mulch is in order, either living or inert. Dwarf, shallow-rooted plants such as violas,

flax or Carpathian harebells set among the lilies help to shade the ground, or (more easily accomplished) a mulch of cocoa bean shells, chopped straw or compost can be laid down. Lilies will adapt to flickering sun or shade for half a day but flourish in sun in our relatively cool garden. Any planted in even a modicum of shade tend to lean out toward the light and are in danger of toppling when the stems are laden with flowers.

Sooner or later, a single lily bulb will grow to be a cluster. One bulb becomes two in a season, two become four and so on. When you see a plethora of leafy stems but a dearth of flowers above ground, you will know that the bulbs have increased to the overcrowded stage below. The time has come, once foliage has ripened to brown and yellow in fall, to lift a clump. Pry up the works delicately with a spading fork, being careful not to aim too close or you'll shish kebab some bulbs on the fork tines. What you will find is an aggregate of tightly packed bulbs, as well as a handful of pea-sized bulblets. If your garden is full, you'll have an embarrassment of riches to deal with, because each bulblet, like any onion set, is potentially a big flowering bulb in one season. Unless you plan to sell lily bulbs – at several dollars apiece, among the more profitable home-garden cash crops – you'd better compost or give away the bulblets and

concentrate on the big ones. After snipping off the current stems close to the bulbs, ease bulbs apart carefully by hand. If the roots are long and unwieldy, shorten them a little. Replant bulbs right away – if they must stay out of the ground for a while, damp peat moss is the storage medium, a cool shed or garage the place – in earth that has been heartened once more with humus. If, during the summer, you had noticed signs of botrytis infection, such as spotty leaves that die back exceptionally early, consider a shake-'n'-plant solution of garden sulphur in a plastic bag, in which bulbs are gently tossed before being planted.

Delphiniums
(*Delphinium* spp)

Once during a tour of English gardens, my partner and I happened to arrive at Wisley garden, showplace of the Royal Horticultural Society, just when the delphinium trials were in full glory. Row upon row, fountains of flowers bloomed in every shade of blue, mauve and lavender, darkest violet, white and cream, but none was as beautiful as the clear, true blues. Surely any gardener who has seen well-grown clumps of delphiniums standing tall and stately, their reaching spires mirroring the blue of the summer sky, must yearn to grow them. The fact that they are not to be won with the mere scattering of a few seeds in any out-of-the-way corner makes them all the more enticing.

We have had good success with this showy perennial by paying attention to its few reasonable requirements. Our route to decent delphiniums usually starts with seeds of the 'Summer Skies,' 'Black Knight' and 'Blue Jay' cultivars of the Pacific Giant hybrids, although I hear that the 'Blackmore & Langdon' strains are also excellent. All of our old gardening books suggest ordering fresh seeds in midsummer for August planting. But who can remember to order a few packets of seeds in July? Besides, although plant expert John Bradshaw suggests that August sowing is a tradition from cool old England, delphinium seeds sprout poorly if at all in the heat of a North Ameri-

Depicted in many religious paintings of the Renaissance, sweet-scented Madonna lilies, FACING PAGE, *must be planted in August or September with only a scant inch of earth covering the scaly bulbs. They bloom concurrently with delphiniums,* LEFT, *whose tall spires are worth the extra effort of preparing an especially fertile spot and of supporting the plants with stakes and string. Since the lower leaves are apt to become tattered and mildewed, bushy foreground plants such as earlier-blooming* Baptisia australis *or red-flowered rose campion (*Lychnis coronaria*) serve as leafy screens.*

I am not partial to dumpy recent delphiniums that grow full-sized flowers on yard-high plants—surely a delphinium's glory is its skyrocket spires—but truly dwarf selections such as the bushy foot-high 'Blue Mirror' and 'Blue Butterfly,' both easy to grow from seed, are delightful rockery or edging plants with the same intense navy blue as the alpine gentian.

One writer's comment about spring bulbs—"Their last state is not as lovely as their first"—applies equally to delphiniums. By the time the flowers have faded to ashen tints, the foliage is usually wind-ripped and mildewed. This is the time to cut clumps back close to ground level. With decent soil and extended growing weather, there may be a second show of flowers in October.

Delphiniums, especially the modern hybrids, cannot be counted on to stay for many years. After three or four seasons, one needs to give some thought to replacing clumps that may be deteriorating. Since they do not divide particularly well, it is back to the seed catalogues or off to a nursery for starter plants.

can summer. Growers must have learned something about seed storage over the years, though, because spring-sown seeds sprout well enough, provided we give them a full day in the freezer beforehand to break dormancy and thereafter keep the soil temperature between 55 and 60 degrees F. After that, we follow the usual method of growing perennials from seed (as detailed in chapter 2), then setting the leafy clumps in flower borders, where they go a full 2 feet apart in September for colour the next year and the next.

Delphiniums take to full sun, especially in cool northern gardens, but I have seen them bloom beautifully in a foundation bed along an east-facing house wall where they caught the morning sun only. In hot gardens, some afternoon shade is a comfort, provided it is not cast by large trees close enough to steal moisture and soil nutrients. More important than site, however, is soil. Bulky, sappy perennials, delphiniums must sink their roots into deep, moist, fertile loam to rise to their full potential. It is hardly possible to make the soil too rich for them. I use the method of preparing a spot for lily bulbs: digging out a deep hole, removing subsoil and backfilling with topsoil and humus to give a single delphinium full-course fertility. Well-rotted cow manure is especially recommended, and a sprinkling of wood ashes is said to heighten colour intensity. Drainage must be reasonably good, and a surface mulch of manure or compost, laid down anytime, can only help.

Lanky 6-foot delphiniums must have some support, or they will be on the ground after the first windstorm. We make an inconspicuous truss by hammering three pieces of 1-by-2-inch lumber (or strong, straight branches, old rake handles or what have you), each 5 feet tall, firmly into the ground around the outside of a clump. Then as the stems lengthen, we wind stout cord from stake to stake and tie the plant in at several ascending levels, but not so tightly as to give it a Scarlet O'Hara waist. Support is the goal, not strangulation.

Bergamot
(*Monarda didyma*)

Fertile earth and moisture, too, are needed for *Monarda didyma*, a perennial of many names—bergamot, bee balm, Oswego tea. The whole plant smells deliciously of citrus and spice, and the leaves add a unique bouquet (similar to the flowery essence of Earl Grey tea) to a homemade herbal brew. A member of the mint family, bergamot is a first-rate plant for midsummer colour as well. Atop 3-to-4-foot stems, the crowns of tubular flowers, sometimes one whorl above another, are always alive with the aerial acrobatics of hummingbirds. Expect flowers the first season from seed-grown plants of the 'Panorama' strain—a March or April start indoors is recommended—in shades ranging through mauve and purple to white. 'Croftway Pink' and 'Cambridge Scarlet' are better still. Bergamot blooms gloriously for weeks in July and early August for us. Each season, I find a new corner that would be brighter for it.

Bergamot is more than willing to contribute its colour to the garden if its few specific needs are met. Give it humus-rich earth that does not dry out, or it will lose its lower leaves and never attain its full height. Give it plenty of room and a site where breezes blow freely, or it will grow lanky and mildewed. And finally, divide clumps often, first thing in spring or early in fall, or they will spread, mintlike, into a tangled mat of weak shoots. Since roots travel just under the soil surface, division is easy, but one must toss out the spent centre of a clump and retain only the lively, three-to-five-shoot segments from the edges as new plants. Set these firmly and a little deeper than before in the best earth you can manage, in sun or partial shade. Thus treated, bergamot will be the jewel of the midsummer garden and its leaves will make many a cup of fragrant tea.

Baby's-Breath
(*Gypsophila paniculata*)

"See-through flowers," Vita Sackville-West calls gypsophila, another flower that, like coral bells, is noted for "lightness and transparency." Everyone who has ever given or received a gift of cut flowers knows baby's-breath as that delicate, tiny-flowered filler that enhances a bouquet of showier things. But if our visitors' reactions are typical, few are aware that baby's-breath is an easily cultivated hardy perennial that can do the same in a flowerbed. I can think of few places where a mist of baby's-breath would be amiss. Growing to 3 feet tall and as wide across, clouds of countless pearly blooms threaded on a weblike framework of thin, wiry stems hover lightly in a border in front of stout clumps of delphiniums and rose loosestrife or among heavy-headed day lilies, bright-coloured lilies and bergamot – to name a few of gypsophila's contemporaries. That said, gypsophila – from *gypsos* (gypsum or lime) and *philos* (friendly) – has not just a preference but a definite need for sweet earth. Other requirements are an open sunny site and soil that drains swiftly. Drought does not menace baby's-breath, but standing water is fatal. If your garden qualifies, give some thought to the plant's initial placement, because once its anchoring taproot has burrowed deeply, you will not shift gypsophila without doing it serious damage.

Although I have raised gypsophila from seed, I do not recommend this method. Chances are, you will end up with single-flowered baby's-breath, ethereal to the vanishing point. Even seed of *paniculata* 'Double White' grows "only 50 percent doubles," according to Stokes' catalogue. Far more satisfying are grafted double cultivars, such as 'Bristol Fairy' and 'Snowflake,' from a nursery. And the

Perfectly formed to entice foraging hummingbirds, bergamot flowers may be pink, lavender or mauve, but none are as showy as the cultivar 'Cambridge Scarlet,' FACING PAGE. *Bergamot leaves add a scent of citrus and spice to home-grown herbal teas. Effective anywhere in a sunny garden are misty mounds of baby's-breath,* ABOVE, *which lighten other flowers such as lilies, lythrums and delphiniums. Baby's-breath also forms a useful screen for vanishing bulbs and Oriental poppies, and even one clump provides valuable material for bouquets. Once planted, this taprooted perennial resents disturbance.*

111

small, soft pink double blooms of 'Rosy Veil' are exquisite, especially when jewelled with dew. This one stands only 18 inches tall, but needs a yard of free space around it. Set about 18 inches back of front in a border, it billows out naturally to the edge. A clutch of daffodils can be planted around gypsophila (but not too close) for early colour. The bulbs do not interfere with its growth, and in no time, baby's-breath will draw a beaded curtain over the fading bulb leaves.

If it takes to your garden, gypsophila returns every year with little attention, taking several seasons to fill out to full potential. As it grows, however, a clump should be supported with two or three yard-tall stakes pounded a foot into the ground and wound around with strong string. This corseting sends the otherwise lax stems straight up and allows the great panicles of flowers to assume a nicely rounded form on top. If you want gypsophila to cover the bare places left by spring bulbs or vanishing Oriental poppies, a few strategically placed twiggy branches will guide the stems where they are needed.

Gypsophila paniculata has an important place in the midsummer garden, but *G. repens*, either pink or white and fairly easy to raise from seed, is a lax, 8-inch trailer that foams over border edges or down rock garden slopes in May and June. Crocuses bloom through it for April colour.

Purple Loosestrife
(*Lythrum* spp)

The setting sun backlighting loosestrife's swaying, purple-rose spires creates one of those brilliant garden scenes to store in memory for grey winter days. Loosestrife, not the invasive *Lythrum salicaria* but lythrum cultivars – plant breeders in Morden, Manitoba, have given us 'Morden Gleam,' 'Morden Rose' and 'Morden Pink' – ought to be high on the list of easy-care, self-supporting and enduring perennials for midsummer colour. If your garden is damp and partly shaded, you've found your plant. In definitely soggy gardens, or in any that include a stream or pond, lythrum can be planted generously with hostas and astilbes for company and with Siberian irises for earlier colour. Above willowlike foliage, rosy wands spire 4 to 6 feet and need no support. At its best, as I have seen in other gardens, loosestrife grows to a yard-wide girth and may be crowded with 50 or more spikes and side branches, all thickly set with starry florets. I only wish it would grow more enthusiastically for us, but alas, this denizen of damp places seems to resent our sandy soil and sunny site no matter how much manure or compost we entice it with.

Nursery plants, either potted or dormant clumps, are the simplest way to introduce lythrum and the only way to avail yourself of the improved hybrids. Once planted, they should be left alone ever after to fatten in peace. Like peonies and gas plants, loosestrife will live in one place for many years but can be divided in early spring if necessary. Maintenance means only cutting down the stalks in late fall – the persistent foliage turns halfheartedly red in September – and applying an annual moisture-holding mulch where the soil is prone to dry too quickly.

Monkshood
(*Aconitum* spp)

Several monkshoods, members of the family Ranunculaceae and therefore related, surprisingly enough, to common field buttercups, are fine companions to the loosestrife, thriving in the same moist soil and light shade and not unlike them in height and habit. But a caution: all parts of all aconites are extremely poisonous. "Without question, there is no worse or more speedie venom in the world," wrote 16th-century herbalist John Gerard. But, he went on to say, aconite's tall spikes of dusky blue or violet hooded flowers are "so beautifull, that a man would thinke they were of some excellent vertue."

Monkshoods provide pleasing colour for the back of a border. Among the most decorative is the

two-toned sport of *Aconitum napellus*, a Himalayan mountain dweller whose 6-foot wands of blue and white hooded flowers create a favourite midsummer picture, with bergamot and baby's-breath for company. The 6-foot *A. autumnale* colours coldly blue in October, although sometimes if fall is cool and short, it makes no show here at all. Shorter at 4 feet and flowering for almost a month as June turns to July, slate blue *A. henryi* competes with day lilies for root room beside the steps of many local farmhouses. A piece of the plant salvaged from a long-abandoned garden nearby is now four stout clumps through the middle of a border where it makes a background for soft yellow lilies.

Occasionally, a few hybrid monkshoods crop up on nursery benches. One with showy deep violet flowers came to our garden as a single shoot, but I found it so pretty and useful as a shadowy contrast that I couldn't resist dividing it down to the last stem and spreading it around the garden with pink phlox, bergamot or lilies, a striking combination for company.

Although all aconites grow slowly from seed, a clump pried from the ground in spring with a spading fork practically falls apart into separate divisions. Stems end in little knobby tubers that can be further eased apart by hand. Divisions establish readily in a new location. Well-enriched, moisture-holding earth supports this thirsty perennial best, in sun or partial shade. If starved, overcrowded or dry at the roots, aconites lose their lower leaves and grow stunted and yellowish. Although a mulch is a help, it is no substitute for humusy soil from the start.

Astilbe
(*Astilbe* spp)

Plants that live in moist shade seem to deal in especially lovely leaves. Ferns, hostas, Solomon's seal and sweet woodruff come to mind. Astilbes, too, fan out lush, fresh-looking greenery, in this case, compound pointed leaves sharply toothed along their edges. In some cultivars,

Some perennials do best in soils that are usually moist. Purple loosestrife, a North American native, grows tall and lush in damp places, FACING PAGE, LEFT. Lythrum salicaria *is invasive, but cultivars of other species are more restrained. Monkshood,* FACING PAGE, CENTRE, *will lose its lower leaves if starved, overcrowded or dry. Astilbes,* ABOVE, *are at home beside a stream or lily pond; moisture and fertility ensure that they, too, reach their loveliest potential.*

both leaves and stems look as if they have been washed with a water-colour brush dipped in crimson. And for many midsummer weeks, astilbes also yield feathery flower panicles, like the plumage of some exotic bird, tinted rose, salmon, crimson or white.

Most astilbe cultivars—a good nursery may have six or eight—grow from 18 to 24 inches tall, but some top 3 feet. While the tallest astilbes are conspicuous accents when planted singly, the rest are more effective in groups of three or more, the plants spaced 18 inches apart. Given that one plant fattens into a multicoloured clump in a year or two, it is easy enough to work up a stock of this elegant perennial by spring division. Otherwise, however, they can be left in place for many years.

Although shade is usually suggested for astilbes, at Larkwhistle they grow in full sun in an 18-inch-deep bed of loam, manure and peat moss—lime is not on their diet. Since our astilbe bed borders a concrete lily pool, it is no hardship to empty a

bucket of water over the astilbes from time to time. Moisture and soil fertility are essential for this plant, especially if shade is lacking.

Yarrows
(*Achillea* spp)

Better in sun is the genus *Achillea*, which is high on my list of decorative, easy-care perennials, although some of the invasive sorts such as the 'Cerise Queen' cultivar of the common roadside yarrow, *A. millefolium*, and *Achillea* 'The Pearl' are best left out of small gardens. Several bring both silver and gold to the garden. Big brother of the clan is *A. filipendulina*, better known for its cultivars 'Coronation Gold,' 'Parker's Variety' and 'Gold Plate.' These 4-foot plants are ornamental from tip to toe, from the time the elegant aromatic foliage, like silver fern fronds, emerges in spring until the last of many flat heads of yellow have mellowed to autumnal brown. The taller yarrows are mid-border plants—given their bulk, one may be enough—where

they shine effectively with *Salvia superba* or Shasta daisies.

Although 'Gold Plate' is a strong contender, my favourite yarrow is 'Moonshine,' a 2-foot garden-bred achillea that has traded the burnished tansy gold of the genus for clear, lemon yellow flowers above finely cut silver-white foliage.

Shorter still and just right for edging or rockery is 8-inch woolly yarrow (*Achillea tomentosa* or *A. t. aurea*), a Lilliputian version of the first two. This hardy little creeper from high places in Europe and Russia has densely furred grey leaves below flat, mustard-yellow flower heads. It thrives in dry, gravelly ground but must have full sun for health. A mat of woolly yarrow is composed of many separate plantlets, each with its own roots, the whole strung together by shallow underground stems. To propagate it, you can easily detach individual crowns with clippers and trowel, or an entire mat may be lifted and eased apart. After a season or two, a single starter plant can be conjured into a dozen to border a bed or carpet a patch of ground. For another crop of colour in the same place, I push tiny bulbs of wild crocuses through the mat.

With the exception of hybrids such as 'Moonshine,' which must be purchased or propagated asexually, yarrows are easily grown from seed sown indoors or out in spring. Set seedlings in their permanent place when they are a couple of inches high. We have used part of a vegetable garden bed as an achillea nursery, where the plants grew 8 to 10 inches apart for a season and then went to the flowerbeds the following spring. All will flower the year after sowing, while purchased plants will flower the first year. Drought-resistant and self-supporting, all yarrows thrive in full sun and warm, well-drained soil.

Midsummer Daisies

The vast family of daisies, known to botanists as Compositae – the typical flower is a composite of many tiny individual florets packed into a central buttonlike disk surrounded by showy ray petals – is said to be among the most advanced of plant groups. Everyone knows the simple ox-eye-daisy, prototype of the lot, that each June decorates roadsides, meadows and vacant city lots with countless white and gold flowers, but wild composites also include hawkweed, wild asters, teasels, dandelions, thistles of many kinds and sundry other outlaws and garden interlopers. However, the garden is the proper home for at least a dozen perennial daisies (I use the word generically for any and all composites). Although daisies bloom every month of the growing season save the earliest, July and August are their months to shine.

Larger versions of the ubiquitous roadside wildflowers, Shasta daisies (*Chrysanthemum superbum*) grow dark green, tongue-shaped foliage in basal clumps, from which flower stems rise from 1 to 3 feet, depending on the cultivar. Three or four plants set about 15 inches apart in decent earth – Shastas are sensitive to dryness – highlight a stretch of blue delphiniums or red bergamot

with classic white flowers in a border. Showier than the singles (those with one row of ray petals around a golden centre) are quilled and fluffy double shastas.

Shasta daisies have one fault: they are not as hardy or as enduring as other perennials, and a severe or soggy winter of freeze and thaw is apt to kill them. Because older clumps are more vulnerable, many gardeners make a point of splitting shastas every other spring or so. Nothing could be easier, since clumps tend to fall into distinct rooted divisions as you lift them. Toss out the woody centres, and replant three-crowned chunks, firmly and slightly deeper than they were growing, in freshly fertilized soil.

A little earlier than Shastas come golden marguerites, *Anthemis tinctoria*, 2-foot lacy mounds of aromatic greenery covered with 2-inch intense yellow daisies. Quick and easy from seed at the start – a March sowing indoors will yield flowers that summer – anthemis seedlings pop up here and there in the garden ever

Drought-resistant yarrows such as 'Gold Plate,' FACING PAGE, *are ideal easy-care perennials for hot, sunny sites. Their silver foliage lasts the season through, while the typically flat flower heads decorate a garden for nearly two months. Also at home in the sun are brightly coloured gaillardias,* ABOVE, *and other midsummer daisies. If the parent plants disappear, check for seedlings growing nearby.*

after. Just as well, because this chamomile relative seldom lives more than three seasons. On dryish sunny banks where grass grows with difficulty, golden marguerites can be left to seed and reseed as a tallish ground cover.

Coreopsis (*Coreopsis* spp), rough-and-tumble yellow-flowered perennials, which can provide similar ground cover, are still better suited, I find, to naturalizing in hot, half-wild places than grouping in borders. Although some experts say that coreopsis endures for years, clumps in our garden crushed under snow all winter sometimes melt to a mess of soggy leaves by spring, never to rise again. Consequently, I do not count on this one for consistent colour but relegate it to out-of-the-way sunny corners where it can seed at will. Recently bred dwarf coreopsis such as 'Baby Gold,' 'Sunray' and 'Gold Fink' are more apt to last. They are preferable, in any case, because they do not need props and stakes to keep them upright. Warm, well-drained soil, not overly endowed with organic matter, suits the Spartan tastes of coreopsis best.

Much the same is true of gaillardias (*Gaillardia grandiflora*), hot-coloured, red and yellow flowers that refuse to live more than several seasons in our snowy northern garden. One summer, a gardening friend gave us a clutch of extra seedling gaillardias, which we set a foot apart in the vegetable garden. The leafy tufts sailed through winter unharmed, flowered well through July and into August and then (all but a few) disappeared the next winter. Good results seem to come from treating gaillardias as biennials, but this is altogether more effort than I am willing to expend on these gaudy daisies. If they stay, fine; if not, adios.

Bellflowers
(*Campanula* spp)

Campanulas may be ground-hugging dwarfs or the garden's tallest herbaceous plants. Although their flowers, always some variation on the simple bell shape, are not large or opulent, they generally come in such quantity as to make a solid splash of colour, typically, soft lavender-blue or white. Larkwhistle includes 10 or 12 different bellflowers within its boundaries, and several others grow along roadsides or hang from crevices in the massive mossy rocks that line the nearby Georgian Bay shore. I have edited the following list with a typical garden in mind, one that might contain a small rockery and a bed or border of hardy plants.

Both *Campanula garganica* and *C. muralis* – the latter is sometimes smothered under the alias *C. portenschlagiana* – belong to safe nooks in a rock garden or elsewhere among small unthreatening plants. *Garganica*, all of 4 inches tall, is a little galaxy of starry blue flowers over a foot-wide mat of tiny triangular leaves. *Muralis*, meaning "of the wall," looks best threading its stringy shoots along the crevices of a dry-built stone wall, where its pendant, glossy purple bells can swing freely. If planted on level ground, its flowers trail in the dust.

Back in the open border, Carpathian harebells (*Campanula carpatica*) are all aflutter with shallow, up-turned bells, cloudy blue or white, that make an effective floor for wine-red lilies growing through them. Indispensable for front-of-the-border colour in midsummer, 10-inch *carpatica* is easy to grow and wildly floriferous in decent, well-drained loam that has been mixed with organic matter. A true herbaceous perennial, it can be divided in early spring, if necessary, just as the new crop of leaves is showing above ground. Lift a clump, and cut it into wedges with a sharp knife; or, if you want one small piece to give away or to plant elsewhere, slice gingerly into a clump without lifting it and trowel out only the severed bit. 'Blue Chips' and 'White Chips' are garden-bred carpaticas, shorter than their parent at 6 inches. Another form, *C. c. turbinata*, is like *carpatica* but more compact. Seedlings of this species have appeared voluntarily in the sand-filled gaps between the flat stones that pave our front porch, where they flower in all shades of lavender-blue from dark to light. One self-sown campanula that positioned itself just to one side of our entrance

has been dubbed by a visitor "the doorbell flower."

Toward the middle of a border, peach-leaved bellflowers, *Campanula persicifolia*, send up 2-foot stems crowded with flared bells, like carpaticas, only side-swinging and either china blue or white. The thin leaves stay close to the ground. This bellflower shines in partial shade or sun but flowers much longer if rooted in earth that stays nicely moist.

At 6 feet, *Campanula lactiflora*, the milky bellflower, is an imposing giant that can stand toward the back of a flowerbed with delphiniums or aconites, where its great pyramid of bloom – a myriad of small, tubular soft blue bells, which are flared at the mouth and hung near the ends of branching stems – can rise behind bergamot or lilies. In our garden, visitors are always drawn to a lone specimen of *lactiflora* that stands out boldly at the front of a shady bed. Moist, fertile earth keeps it flourishing. Needing the same staking treatment as delphiniums to keep it upright, this species (and all

bellflowers) can be raised from specks of seed by patient gardeners or bought as starter plants. *Lactiflora* is, however, far too heavy and deeply anchored to lift and divide. Let it stay put as long as it is thriving, and avail yourself of seedlings that are sure to appear if you need new plants. If too many appear, consider snipping off the faded flower heads before they spill their crop of seeds.

Last summer was the first time we saw the long, purple-satin tubular bells of *Campanula latifolia macrantha* swinging near the tops of 5-foot branched stems. Requiring the same cool site and nourishing loam as the foregoing, this showy bellflower would be a fine substitute for biennial Canterbury bells (*C. medium*) if it wore more colours than one.

Balloon Flowers
(*Platycodon grandiflorum*)

Close kin to bellflowers, balloon flowers contribute what Sackville-West calls "an effective splash of truly imperial purple . . . in the July-August border," where I like to see them neighboured by lilies and baby's-breath and perhaps backed by pink rugosa roses, if space allows.

Their buds have given balloon flowers their common name. Before opening, each is a little inflated five-sided sack, "like a tiny lantern," says Sackville-West, "so tightly closed as though its seams had been stitched together, with the further charm that you can pop it like a fuchsia, if you are so childishly minded. This, I need hardly say, is not good for the eventual flower." The eventual flowers, on 2-foot stems, are five-lobed, deep lavender and veined with inky blue. There is also a white sort and a double variety with one flower nesting neatly inside another.

A neighbour of ours has naturalized platycodons all down a rocky slope by collecting seeds from his strongest-coloured or most fully double flowers and flinging them over the hillside. "Whatever grows, grows" is his garden philosophy. But balloon flowers are more pictorial

There is a bellflower for every corner of the garden since campanulas range from the lowliest dwarf alpines, such as Campanula portenschlagiana, FACING PAGE, *to 6-foot giants. For general border use, especially in partial shade, the elegant peach-leaved bellflower* C. persicifolia, ABOVE, *either white or blue, is one of the best.*

117

generous with its crop of cupped yellow blooms above attractive green leaves marked with maroon. A no-care mid-border perennial, *fruticosa* clumps quickly into a weed-suppressing mat of closely packed rosettes that can be divided in spring or fall. Chances are, however, that you will need to curb this mover rather than increase it. I have seen *fruticosa* used both as a tallish ground cover and as a herbaceous hedge. In a flowerbed, it combines well with scarlet Maltese cross and day lilies of any hue. Easily cultivated, all evening primroses crave sun and warm ground but do not need much in the way of fertile soil. Seed will grow them, but starter plants are a shortcut to first-season flowers.

Maltese Cross
(*Lychnis chalcedonica*)

Lychnis means lamp in Greek, a name that suits the flaming flowers of *Lychnis chalcedonica*. Native to northern Russia and Siberia, this decorative perennial—a natural with tall evening primroses, if you like the hot contrast of red and yellow—tops 2½-foot stems of pleasant greenery with flat heads of clustered, vivid scarlet flowers, their four petals arranged in the shape of a Maltese cross. Flourishing in any fertile soil, this brilliant thing is completely hardy and loves the sun. It is non-invasive and can be left to grow in peace as long as it is doing well. If an older clump begins to wane, there will likely be replacement seedlings nearby.

Sea Holly
(*Eryngium* spp)

Our garden grows its share of oddities: other-worldly onions; strange Turkish mulleins as white and woolly as sheep; a sinister-looking 8-foot giant cow parsnip; and viciously armed, tall silver thistles that always remind me of mediaeval, mace-wielding knights in armour. As odd as any—indeed, as one writer put it, they "do not have the aspect of true flowers" at all—are sea hollies, species of *Eryngium* that seem more mineral than vegetable. Growing to 2½ feet, *Eryngium amethystinum*'s well-

when planted in groups of three to five with a foot between each. Deep, moist, humusy earth grows them best, in sunshine or light shade. Not difficult to raise from seed but quicker from nursery plants, this slowpoke perennial flowers tentatively in its second year and takes a few seasons to clump up. A few twiggy branches pushed into the earth around balloon flowers keep their slender stems from falling over. A note: Since this is one of the last perennials to show through the earth in spring, it is the better part of wisdom to mark the location of each clump with a label so as not to snap the unseen shoots during rounds of spring cleaning or cultivation. Once established, this "sumptuous alien from China and Manchuria" will return for many years if left in peace.

Evening Primroses
(*Oenothera* spp)

The genus *Oenothera* consists of about 80 species native to North and South America. In spite of their common name, they are not primroses at all, but many do bloom in the evening. Others, known as sundrops, bloom by day.

Here and there along our border edges, the Missouri primrose (*Oenothera missourensis*) trails over a shoulder of limestone. Lax 8-inch stems end in a cluster of longish, red-spotted green buds that open successively into showy, round, clear yellow flowers which are a full 4 inches across. "They are a truly beautiful, hardy plant," says Ippolito Pizzetti in *Flowers: A Guide for Your Garden*, "excellent for rock gardens, for pockets in drywalls, for use as a ground cover or for planting along the edges of paths." If only the flowers lasted more than a day each and the plants were more compact, the Missouri primrose would be one of the better midsummer edgers. As it is, I like it as an interesting incident next to a drift of Carpathian harebells or dianthus.

Most decorative of all is *Oenothera fruticosa*, a 2½-foot evening primrose branched, glinting stems, clothed in white-veined heart-shaped leaves, mature from a mercury sheen to silvery blue as an abundant crop of pseudoflowers appears. Tiny and inconspicuous, these are arranged in thimble-shaped cones surrounded by rather outrageous ruffs of glossy, spiny blue bracts. En masse, this sea holly becomes a misty cloud, a fine setting for ruby or rose lilies or gladioli of any hue. Grown with satiny white musk mallow (*Malva moschata*), our sea holly makes a soft-toned picture that lasts for weeks in good shape.

The 2-foot alpine sea holly (*Eryngium alpinum*), stunning in a well-grown clump, encircles its larger (but fewer) flower cones with an elegant double fringe of bracts so ghostly blue and spiny that they have inspired the name "elves' bones." The branching inflorescences of all sea hollies cut wonderfully well for summer bouquets, and they dry quickly, if hung in an airy, shaded place, for a winter arrangement.

All eryngiums, botanically related to dill, angelica and other members of the family Umbelliferae, grow best in sandy well-drained earth that need not be overly fertile. In cold wet clay, they tend to rot away. As well, they

The shape of its florets, FACING PAGE, *has given scarlet lychnis—the Greek root word means lamp—the common name Maltese cross. Clumps of scarlet lychnis enhance white, soft yellow or orange lilies and sky blue delphiniums. Strangely beautiful, the ghostly metallic blue bracts of alpine sea holly surround a cone of inconspicuous true flowers,* LEFT. *Cut early, this and other sea hollies dry reasonably well for winter bouquets.*

need an open, sunny position, and once established, they should not be disturbed or divided. New plants are best raised from your own seed, collected as soon as it is ripe and sown while still fresh. Like other umbelliferous plants, sea holly seed loses its spark quickly. Probably a few baby sea hollies will appear near the mother plant, and these can be set out elsewhere if needed.

Golden Knapweed
(*Centaurea macrocephala*)

Another rather unusual perennial, this hardy kin to blue annual cornflowers grows a lush clump of rough-textured, oblong leaves and shoots up strong 4-foot stems, each topped by perfectly round, light brown buds that rustle like strawflowers if you tousle them. Buds do not actually open, but rather, flowers emerge from them; first a few yellow threads poke out, and soon a fluffy golden cornflower, very attractive to butterflies, sits jauntily on top. After the flowers have faded, the little brown globes become perfect packages for maturing seeds. "A really magnificent plant," says one perennial expert, which "can produce up to 40 erect stems, each bearing a globose inflorescence 4 inches in diameter. The rich yellow colour makes a remarkable contrast with the brown calyx."

Sun and fertile earth grow this

bulky but self-supporting perennial best. Start with seeds or nursery plants, but once they are established, leave golden knapweed alone to clump up without division or casual shifting from place to place. Your reward will surely be a grander show each year.

Hardy Geraniums
(*Geranium* spp)

Geraniums are a confusing lot. The annual bedding plants most gardeners know as geraniums are more properly called pelargoniums. True perennial geraniums (also called cranesbills because of their long, beaklike seedpods) are, unlike the flashy pelargoniums, subtle plants that are far less well known or appreciated. The genus *Geranium* contains about 250 species ranging all through the north temperate zone, but only a handful are suitable for garden use. Others, including our pretty native herb Robert (*Geranium robertianum*), are either overzealous spreaders best enjoyed in the wild or dowdy weeds.

Our introduction to hardy geraniums began with *Geranium sanguineum*, a useful perennial that grows into nicely rounded, foot-high mounds of elegant lobed leaves over a tangled network of wiry, reddish stems. From midsummer onward, a succession of simple round blossoms, like little magenta saucers, decorates the plants. Pretty toward the front of flowerbeds, this hardy geranium can also be massed as a ground cover or allowed to naturalize at will down a difficult-to-plant slope or in half-wild places. The pleasant foliage stays freshly green until fall and then colours in harmony with the autumnal scene. A little rooted slip of the beautiful white-flowering *G. sanguineum album* taken from another garden is now three thriving clumps growing in the deep fertile earth of our "quiet garden." "One of the treasures of the garden," Louise B. Wilder calls this plant, which is laden with glistening blossoms for weeks.

Geranium endressii is like *sanguineum* in height and habit, but its flowers are pure rose pink veined with red. Blooming over a remarkably long period, this species is just right for massing as a ground cover, either

in sun or partial shade, where it helps to crowd out weeds. I have noticed that *endressii*, which is said to do best in a damp climate such as that of the Pacific Northwest, wilts badly and stops flowering during a spell of drought; humus-rich earth, mulch and a few deep drinks, however, will help. The cultivar 'Wargrave Pink' is a darker rose.

At 2 feet high, *Geranium grandiflorum* is a taller species for mid-border. Cupped flowers, a deep but clouded blue, are veined with maroon. Suitable for sun or light shade, this hardy Russian native and its cultivar 'Johnson's Blue' recommend themselves for low-maintenance gardens on account of their fine and lasting greenery and their generous crop of blue.

A protected corner of a rock garden or somewhere along the edge of a flowerbed well away from strong-growing neighbours is the place for *Geranium* 'Ballerina,' a neat 6-inch perennial generously endowed with soft rose flowers conspicuously veined and centred with maroon. I would like more of this pretty plant, but I cannot summon the courage to lift and split our lone specimen for fear of losing it entirely. All hardy geraniums have long, ranging roots that do not divide well; small slips stolen from the outside of a clump, however, may have a few incipient roots attached, and these bits can be treated as cuttings or simply planted

out and kept moist until they take.

Seed is the surest route to geranium species in the garden, although you may have to search several catalogues to find them. Thompson and Morgan is one source. But however you get them, cranesbills are easily grown, thriving in any decent garden loam in any place, in sun or partial shade.

Potentilla
(*Potentilla* spp)

Kin of geums, potentillas (or cinquefoils) are most familiar as exceedingly hardy, low (to 3 feet) shrubs. Several are native, others foreign or garden-bred. Their tangled, arching stems are set with round five-petalled flowers, which are like small single roses. Commonly yellow, they also crop up dressed in white or washed-out orange. Several shrubby cinquefoils are compact and restrained enough to mix with herbaceous plants. Especially pretty here is the 2½-foot *Potentilla fruticosa farreri*, whose soft, buttery blossoms

appear in time to make a picture with creamy and deeper yellow irises behind an edging of golden thyme and a few flakes of blue flax. They continue into midsummer to accompany lilies, yarrows and the like. Golden potentillas are also useful as tall, permanent ground covers in dryish, sunny places.

Far more exotic, however, is the 'Gibson's Scarlet' cultivar of an unfamiliar herbaceous cinquefoil, *Potentilla atrosanguinea*, originally from the Himalayas. Visitors invariably take this beauty for some overgrown strawberry if they see only the attractive, five-leaved fans of glossy green leaves mounding to a foot high near the front of a border. Even when the lovely blood-red cupped blossoms are in evidence, few identify the plant as a potentilla. Everybody, on the other hand, wants it. So far, we have had to respond with a firm "No," because we are reluctant to tamper with our few established clumps for fear of doing them damage.

"Leave well enough alone" is one of

Several easy perennials are not as well known as they should be. Golden knapweed, FACING PAGE, LEFT, *tops self-supporting 4-foot stems with fluffy globes that reappear every summer for many years with little or no attention. Looking like overgrown strawberries and botanically related to them are shrubby potentillas such as 'Gibson's Scarlet,'* FACING PAGE, CENTRE. *Hardy geraniums are very different from the tender annual bedding plants that inaccurately go by that name. Opening a succession of magenta saucers above a mound of persistent greenery,* Geranium sanguineum, ABOVE, *is a useful perennial for naturalizing in partial shade or along the edge of a border.*

our garden mottoes. The corollary, of course, is "Try, try again"; if a plant is not thriving where it sits, try a little more shade or sun, richer earth or drier. Let's hope that more nurseries become aware of this decorative plant and the tawny and yellow semidouble 'William Rollisson,' which grows lovelier every year in manured soil moist enough to satisfy the plant's large appetite. We have found, as one expert suggests, that the shrubby potentillas are more tolerant of dry conditions than the herbaceous ones, which need cool, moderately moist soil.

Hollyhocks
(*Alcea rosea*)

At the very back of most of our flower borders, tall swaying hollyhocks fly their colours from July onward, often into September. Flared, funnel-shaped flowers are shaded from pink to scarlet and deepest crimson, from pale yellow to apricot, peach and plum-purple.

Visitors often ask us for a few hollyhock seedpods because, it seems, this erstwhile favourite has been ousted from most catalogues by flashier newcomers. And seeds, preferably sown outdoors where they are to flower, are the best route to hollyhocks in the garden. Even though young plants move fairly well, the earth occasionally falls away from the thonglike roots, and they are set back. Besides, seeding *in situ* saves the work of transplanting. Left to seed, hollyhocks will spring up everywhere and surprise you by flowering in colours unlike those of the parent plants.

Hollyhocks would likely be more popular if they did not succumb so easily to rust, a fungal disease whose nasty orange spots can quickly render a clump leafless. One possible remedy is garden sulphur sprayed or dusted on the leaves. Breezes blowing freely around the plants also help keep rust at a minimum. Another solution is to plant hollyhocks at the very back of a border, where their stems will be hidden by the growth of peonies, gas plants, baptisias or aconites in front. And since young plants are apt to be healthier, we remove badly infected older clumps

and leave new seedlings to carry on.

Although I have seen them flourishing in dry gravelly ground, hollyhocks respond to the rich earth of the perennial border, where they often reach 10 feet. "Hollyhocks are among the most pictorial of plants," says Louise B. Wilder in *My Garden*, her first book, published in 1916 and still a treasure trove of information and inspiration, "and it is very difficult to find anything else to take their place." Wilder suggests setting tall white hollyhocks behind the flat heads of 3-foot yellow yarrow with baby's-breath nearby, a picture we have planted at Larkwhistle with good effect. For many years, I preferred the fat doubles but now find them congested and graceless next to the simple singles, perhaps because of the comment that doubles look "like those toilet paper decorations on wedding cars" — enough to put one off any flower.

Mulleins
(*Verbascum* spp)

Certain plants are unaccountably absent from North American gardens. Mulleins, for instance, hardly ever make an appearance, even though several are beauties. Perhaps their two-season habit discourages gardeners. Like foxgloves, to which they are related, mulleins are biennials that grow leafy rosettes one season, send up flowering stalks the

Although they are actually biennial rather than perennial, hollyhocks, FACING PAGE, are such picturesque plants that they are valuable additions to a perennial garden, where they make their own way around with far-flung seeds. Also biennial (that is, it produces a rosette of leaves the first year from seed, flowers the second) is Greek mullein, ABOVE, which lights up a garden like a candelabrum. Mullein can tower to 6 feet but is nevertheless best displayed with no other plants in front of it.

next and then, after maturing a crop of seeds, disappear. Or perhaps the mania for dwarf plants has led to mullein's exclusion. True, most of them are imposing giants, but since their growth is all upward and the plants are slender and self-supporting, mulleins can be grown in gardens too small for sprawling delphiniums or top-heavy dahlias.

Almost anyone who has travelled country roads has seen the conspicuous grey-flannel rosettes of common mullein (*Verbascum thapsus*), whose downy spires are sparsely set with five-lobed yellow blossoms. If this species is a trifle weedy for flowerbeds — I do know one gardener who lets a few interloping rosettes stay if they are not in the way — two European species are among the most striking plants of midsummer. Like other mulleins, these suit the many common names that connect them with light: candlewick plant, hag's taper, torches and the German *konigskerze*, or king's candles.

Like a candelabrum when in full bloom, *Verbascum olympicum* is a branching Greek relative of our single-stalked native mullein. Here is a truly Olympian 6-footer to shine at the very back of a flowerbed or to be naturalized in a wild garden or in the corners of a vegetable patch. The first year from seed, wide woolly rosettes develop. The next season, the spot is alight with yellow blossoms from July until September.

Left to seed, Greek mullein finds its own way around the garden. If it is needed in a specific place, seedling mulleins can be shifted when they are still fairly small. Later on, you will not get the hefty plants out of the ground without root damage and wilting leaves.

Few plants at Larkwhistle draw as much comment or as many requests for seeds as the Turkish mullein, *Verbascum bombyciferum*. Known in one catalogue as 'Arctic Summer,' as 'Silver Spire' in another, this is a species so thickly coated with downy wool, both leaf and stalk, as to be entirely silver-white. In the dry sandy soil of a raised iris bed, Turkish mulleins grew beautifully into head-high wands studded with clear yellow flowers. Thinking to encourage the plants to greater heights, we moved a few seedlings into a new bed prepared with manure, peat moss and clay loam. The move was a mistake. The rosettes pined, dwindled and died from overfeeding and dampness. Clearly, it is sand, sun and drought for Turkish mullein, no doubt a denizen of deserts back home.

A first step with mulleins is to find the seeds. Start the pepper-fine seeds indoors, six or eight to a 4-inch pot, thinning eventually to the single sturdiest seedling. After a month or so, when the plants fill the pots, set them in the garden where they are to flower. I like to situate mulleins where their silver first-year rosettes will show to best advantage. Turkish mullein must live in full sun, but the Greek will flower in light shade if it must. Leave them to seed; even the flower stalks have an interesting outline, and the seeds are a favourite winter forage for chickadees. Mulleins will thus linger in and around the beds perennially, sharing space with the other inhabitants of the midsummer garden.

With careful selection and placement of perennials, a garden need not lapse into the midsummer doldrums once the June display is past. Hollyhocks, FACING PAGE, *contribute a strong vertical element reminiscent of childhood gardens and simpler times. At Larkwhistle,* LEFT, *lilies, delphiniums, roses and clematis carry the garden beautifully into July.*

Until the Frost
Late colour from long-distance flowers

Many perennials such as day lilies, FOREGROUND, *and heliopsis,* BACK-GROUND, *are large, robust plants suitable for spacious beds or borders or even for half-wild, soggy corners of a garden. These plants, many of which continue to bloom after the first fall frost, are relatively easy to tend and undemanding, so that the late-summer garden rewards its owner with time to rest before fall chores begin.*

"This August is the month when, if ever, the gardener may claim a well-earned rest," says Louise B. Wilder in *My Garden* (1916). Of course, she admits that insects "may have arrived in staggering hordes, moles may be tunnelling imperturbably beneath one's most precious plants, or the garden may be drying up in the fierce clutches of relentless drought." All would be cause for action. But ordinarily, with seeding, transplanting and staking accomplished and weeds more or less in check, the lazy, hazy days of August and early September bring a lull in flower garden activity before the full fall schedule of dividing perennials, rearranging parts of the garden picture, improving soil fertility, planting bulbs, cleaning up, composting and tucking the garden in for winter. For me, the first fall frost, which usually occurs here around the end of September, rings the back-to-work bell after a late-summer hiatus. The flowers in this chapter are those that colourfully carry the garden through this relatively effortless time. Some continue to bloom even after the first frost.

Phlox
(*Phlox paniculata*)

Gardeners who aim to keep their flowerbeds showing colour until fall have many late-summer perennials from which to choose, including the dependable *Phlox paniculata*, a North American native that has traded its original dim magenta for hybrid shades of pink, crimson, purple, white or scarlet. Phlox are "perhaps the very best of hardy plants," says Wilder, "seeming to embody all the qualities desirable in a plant — hardiness, upright carriage, fine foliage, beautiful and various colours, fragrance."

The finest phlox I know grows unattended in the moist black earth of a neighbour's lightly shaded streamside garden. Lush and healthy after many years, the plants are decorated every August with cones of penny-round lilac flowers on 4-foot stems well furnished with dark green foliage. Lovely, I thought when I first saw the stand; just what our August garden needs. But when I trans-

planted several generous divisions to a sunny, sandy bed at Larkwhistle, the effect was lost. The foliage grew yellowish and dropped off the lower part of the stems, while the flowers appeared small and insipid. It was altogether an uninspiring effort but confirmation of an opinion I had read that phlox needs rich soil.

I set about providing the plants with full-course fertility, enough to satisfy a hearty appetite and a thirst to match. This meant digging the topsoil from an area 2½ feet by 5 feet, a space sufficiently large to accommodate five clumps, and then completely removing two or three

wheelbarrow loads of subsoil, before shovelling in the same amount of well-decayed manure and mixing it with the returned topsoil. A little tramping to settle the soil, and I was ready to try again. The phlox, of course, sank eager roots into the fat, nourishing mix and grew to full potential. Now we count on phlox for solid blocks of colour toward the back of flowerbeds in late summer.

Noninvasive and completely hardy into the coldest regions, phlox can be planted in spring or fall. Start with either named nursery plants or pieces from fellow gardeners. Seeds take forever, and you are never sure what colour they will yield. Self-sown seedlings are also variable in colour and should be removed or treated as weeds. Most of our phlox has come from other gardens. My favourite is a lovely mauve-pink, large-flowered variety that arrived four years ago as a lone shoot with a few roots. Split time and again, it is now six hefty clumps that make one of August's best pictures, with lingering lythrums, late aconites, spires of white cimicifuga or *Artemisia lactiflora* and a background of white and mauve perennial sweet peas trained up a trellis.

To divide phlox into three- or four-shoot wedges, cut down between the shoots with a strong, sharp knife and keep cutting to sever the woody roots. If a hot, dry spell hits, spring-split phlox must have plenty of water until they put out vital new roots. Some experts suggest lifting, dividing and resetting phlox in newly enriched ground every three years or so, an easy task with primroses or coral bells but a daunting one with heavyweight phlox. If plants are flowering well, I am all for laissez-faire. As an alternative division, I sometimes thin the annually increasing shoots to 8 or 10 of the strongest in early spring and then mulch the clumps with leaves laid over compost and/or manure to hold moisture and boost fertility. Lots of water, particularly during budding and blooming, is a must.

"My phlox always get covered with mildew and look awful," one city gardener told me, a comment echoed by many others. In regions of high summer humidity and wherever the free flow of air is blocked (as it is in city gardens overshadowed with buildings and trees), mildew can coat phlox foliage with a sickly white fuzz. It is most apt to develop on phlox grown on the dry side. Japanese researchers have found that a solution of one-quarter ounce of ordinary baking soda (sodium bicarbonate) in a gallon of water controls powdery mildew on certain plants, and it is worth a try on phlox. A chemical spray is a sure cure, but if mildew appeared at Larkwhistle, I would forgo phlox on principle before resorting to fungicide. After cultivating both food and flowers or-

ganically for more than a decade, I feel that no crop, let alone a drift of summer colour, is worth coaxing with chemicals.

Day Lilies
(*Hemerocallis* spp)

"Beautiful for a day" is the translation of the apt Greek genus name for day lilies. But despite fleeting flowers that last only a day apiece, day lilies recommend themselves to gardeners looking for trouble-free summer colour. Completely hardy and apparently immune to insects and diseases, day lilies sprout a sheaf of decorative long-lasting leaves, reed-narrow and arching, below many-hued funnel-shaped flowers that keep on coming – one after another, day by day – for weeks. If early, midseason and late-blooming sorts are planted, there will be day lilies from June until almost September.

Tough in the extreme, day lilies – either the early, soft yellow, fragrant "lemon lilies," *Hemerocallis flava*, or the robust Indian red *H. aurantiaca* – often survive in old, untended country gardens alongside faithful flag irises, wildly suckering lilacs and crowded poet's narcissus. In many locales, they have escaped the confines of gardens and decorate roadsides and ditches like any native.

Indeed, it is their unsophisticated background that led one writer to

Among the tall, dependable plants for the late season are phlox, FACING PAGE, and day lilies, ABOVE. Both are self-supporting, extremely hardy and available in several colours. Phlox are also fragrant. Good air circulation, organically enriched soil and adequate water all help to prevent mildew, which can bother phlox grown in dry, airless sites. Attractive arching foliage and an extended blooming season recommend day lilies for prominent places in perennial borders, where they associate well with later true lilies and lingering scarlet lychnis.

the old rusty species.

Although I have started them from seed, a fairly easy process that yields second-season flowers from a spring sowing, I prefer to select specific colours of named cultivars from a nursery or catalogue to fit the picture. But division is also possible, either from one's own stock or a friend's garden. Day lilies can be split with ease in early spring, just as new shoots show through the ground. To divide: Lift a clump — much more easily said than done — and cut carefully between the shoots and down through the roots with a sharp knife. More than once, I have shifted day lilies in full flower to vacant spots in the borders, a task that requires careful digging and an extra hand or two to lift the heavy clumps into a wheelbarrow. Firm planting and lots of water ensure that the plants survive the untimely move. Except for propagation, however, division is neither necessary nor desirable; like peonies, gas plants, and baby's-breath, hemerocallis improve with age and should be left alone as long as they are flowering well.

Hosta
(*Hosta* spp)

Close kin to hemerocallis, hostas (formerly called *Funkia*) are cultivated in much the same way except that they have a decided preference for shadowy places, especially in hot, dry gardens. They sprout some of the garden's loveliest leaves — broadly heart-shaped, attractively veined and puckered, wavy-edged and coloured shades of green, grey or slate blue, often streaked or banded with white or cream. The cultivar 'Frances Williams' earns top marks with hosta society members for her seersuckered bluish leaves decorated with a wide band of creamy yellow. In general, hosta flowers are not flamboyant, but the little lavender or white bells swinging from slender stems (up to 18 inches long) make a pleasant show where the plants are grown in generous groups. The plantain lily, *Hosta plantaginea*, with its wands of fragrant white flowers above broad lettuce-green leaves is a likely prospect for such an

call day lilies the "Cinderella of herbaceous perennials." Once relegated to no-account garden corners, they have recently stepped into the limelight dressed in a new array of colours — peach and pink, soft purple, bold reds and oranges and shades of yellow, copper and russet; some are zoned with a darker colour or are prettily crimped along the petal edges. But for all the changes worked by hybridists, the plant retains its sturdy constitution and still adapts to sun or partial shade, hot gardens or cold and almost any soil short of dust-dry, with a definite preference for well-manured earth that retains a modicum of moisture over a dry summer. A mulch of old manure, straw, compost or leaves keeps up fertility and reduces maintenance to near zero; it is not even necessary to cut away foliage in fall. During winter, let it lie where it falls (unless you are bothered by slugs), and new shoots will push through the tangle come spring.

Perfect for the middle sections of perennial beds, day lilies associate well with later-blooming true (that is, bulbous) lilies. The curious orange of old-fashioned tiger lilies is just right with all but purple cultivars, and wands of tall blue aconite could complete the picture nicely.

Day lilies are also at home beside a stream or pond — but not standing in water — in the company of astilbes, Siberian irises, lythrums, hostas and moisture-loving ferns. Excellent for massing as a tall, weed-smothering ground cover, they can fringe a band of shrubs or be naturalized in half-wild spaces with tall mulleins, gloriosa daisies (*Rudbeckia* spp), heliopsis and other self-sufficient plants. More formally, they stand as specimens in city gardens, along the walkway to a front door or on either side of entrance steps, where their arching, light green leaves are as decorative as the here-today-gone-tomorrow flowers. Day lily varieties abound, but I can put in a good word for 'Hyperion,' a vigorous older cultivar that is tall, lemon yellow and fragrant. Hybrid day lilies, too, are not as invasive as

assemblage, and with damp soil, it is even comfortable in the sun.

Neat and clumping in habit, hostas are formal plants for massing on 15-inch centres in conspicuous places where one wants easy, persistent cover. Or they can be set singly, as focal accents, along a walkway or at regular intervals in a shaded border. At Larkwhistle, a grand silver-leaved hosta, *Hosta sieboldiana*, grows with almost tropical luxuriance in moist, fertile earth beside a homemade water lily pool, where it softens the pool's sharp concrete edge. Wherever you place hostas, consider planting bluebells (the common *Scilla sibirica*) and snowdrops around them for a show of colour weeks before the late-rising hostas unfurl.

To increase a favourite hosta, lift a well-anchored clump out of the ground with a strong shovel – I have snapped several spading forks while struggling to pry up both hostas and day lilies – and slice cleanly down between shoots and roots with a sharp knife. Wedges supplied with three or four shoots make an im-

mediate effect, but even a single-crowned piece will expand to full size in a season or two. Like all leafy plants, hostas respond with lush, healthy growth if nitrogen-rich manure, leaf mould or compost is stirred into the ground before planting or is laid down as a top dressing – or both; it is scarcely possible to overfeed them.

Helenium
(*Helenium autumnale*)

Before I grew heleniums – the misnamed sneezeweed, or, more pleasantly, Helen's flower – I had seen them growing only once, but wonderfully well, in a friend's clay-bound, sometimes soggy garden. Raised from spring-sown seed, the strain 'Mound Mixture' (from Park Seeds) bloomed the second season, revealing abundant, 2-inch daisy flowers with ray petals flaring smartly downward from a dark central disk. I was especially taken by the colour range – clear yellow, maroon, shades of orange and, nicest of all, one with

At Larkwhistle, Hosta sieboldiana, FACING PAGE, *grows with almost tropical luxuriance in the moist earth beside a homemade concrete water lily pool. Either in the garden or in a bouquet, yellow, bronze or red heleniums,* ABOVE, *are good company for early chrysanthemums.*

131

petals streaked yellow and rust red, intense at first but mellowing to overall coppery hues.

Heleniums soon grow into 3- or 4-foot-tall clumps of distinct and easily detached rosettes, each with its own roots. A slip of each colour from our friend's garden was our start with a perennial that provides almost six weeks of late-summer colour. And this bug-proof, self-supporting plant is not hard to grow in sun or very light shade, as long as its need for humusy moist earth is met. In our dry sandy garden, we plant heleniums in well-manured soil and mulch them over summer. Even so, we are prepared to soak them deeply at the first sign of wilting.

When weaker growth and fewer flowers indicate that the plants are crowded or undernourished (perhaps after four or five years), the time has come to split a clump (as with aconites, page 112) and start over with lively three-crowned divisions. Turn more humus into the ground before setting the divisions 16 to 20 inches apart. Gardeners who like to concentrate on native plants should know that the named helenium cultivars are derived from *Helenium autumnale*, a species found wild from Quebec to the southern states and from British Columbia to Arizona. Hardy to minus 10 degrees F, they need no protection in most areas, but a 6-inch layer of straw or evergreen boughs will see plants through winters that are intensely cold. First-rate perennials, heleniums deserve space in more gardens.

Heliopsis
(*Heliopsis* spp)

Heliopsis, sometimes called false or orange sunflower, is another North American native composite that, like helenium, thrives best in moist earth and full sun—a combination that can be tricky to arrange in many gardens unless one turns plenty of humus into the ground, lays down a summer mulch and turns on the hose when necessary. In our sandy garden, this thirsty plant is the first to wilt during a spell of dry weather, but it perks up quickly when watered.

A robust, almost coarse perennial, heliopsis is perhaps better suited to country gardens than to trim city spaces. It can grapple for root room with strong-growing day lilies, lythrums, Siberian irises and the like or be left to its own devices in damp, half-tamed corners, where its strong 4-foot stems, clothed top to bottom with heart-shaped leaves, support 3-inch, single or fluffy double daisies tinted sunflower-yellow. Each spring, more shoots emerge from gradually widening clumps until a plant may be 4 feet across and rather too leafy for its crop of flowers.

Like many composites, heliopsis grows quickly from seed and may flower the first summer from an early start. Better than the original species, *Heliopsis scabra*, are the varieties 'Goldgreenheart,' 'Incomparabilis' and others that are less robust than their parent—an advantage in this case. All bloom for almost a month and can be left in place for many years.

Perennial Sunflowers
(*Helianthus* spp)

Many vegetable gardens grow a stand of the tall, heavy-headed annual sunflowers *Helianthus annuus*, whose black-shelled seeds are the best of snack foods and yield a fine cooking oil as well. I hesitate, however, to recommend the less familiar perennial sunflowers, many of which are North American natives. Gangling giants that can grow out of bounds and be altogether more trouble than they are worth, they are perhaps better suited to wild or naturalistic gardens, even soggy places. Like the related heliopsis, perennial helianthus, which are always yellow, can effectively brighten forgotten corners of farm gardens, where their flopping ways above ground and the aggressive underground wandering of some species will not threaten other plants. Our own lesson came years ago, when we set a small, innocent-looking shoot of an unidentified helianthus in a perennial bed. It was only with the

utmost diligence that, seasons later, we finally succeeded in extracting the last scrap of its wildly running rootstock.

But among these vegetable invaders — the prolific Jerusalem artichoke is another greedy sunflower — are more restrained species, notably *Helianthus multiflorus*. Growing about 5 feet tall, it is as compact and controlled as a sunflower gets. With its dark green foliage below many round flowers, shaded yellow to orange depending upon the cultivar, *multiflorus* makes a fine background for white phlox and lingers long enough to flower alongside lavender-coloured hardy asters.

Black-Eyed Susans
(*Rudbeckia* spp)

Yellow daisy-type flowers abound in the North American wilds. In addition to a host of native sunflowers, sneezeweeds, small yellow asters, coreopsis and the weedy ranks of dandelions, sow thistles and goat's beard, there are perky black-eyed Susans (*Rudbeckia hirta*), which decorate meadows, roadsides and open woods from the Prairies to the Atlantic. Suitable for naturalizing in half-wild corners of large gardens, these self-seeding native plants bloom too sparingly to earn space in a perennial bed.

More lavish and floriferous are gloriosa daisies, big yellow hybrid rudbeckias often zoned with chocolate-brown or Indian red. Truly glorious in a mass but short-lived — virtually annuals at Larkwhistle — gloriosa daisies nevertheless often reappear year after year from their own hardy seeds. Even 'Goldilocks' and 'Marmalade,' recently developed compact cultivars said by one seed catalogue to be long-lived, seldom survive the first winter in our garden, although they cover themselves with showy yellow daisies during the first summer after early indoor seeding. During that initial year, however, they are tough; I have lifted clumps of 'Goldilocks' in full flower from a nursery bed and shifted them to vacant places in flowerbeds where they continued blooming blithely without any apparent setback.

In many nearby farm gardens, golden glow, a fluffy, double-flowered sport of *Rudbeckia laciniata*, grows unattended, but the 6-foot perennial is so lanky and weak-kneed that wind and rain always bring it down. And it's invasive to boot. Although it is useful for screening unsightly outbuildings or filling difficult corners with sprays of mustard-yellow bloom in early autumn, gardeners looking for good

Late-summer daisies contribute warm tones of gold, yellow and bronze to the garden. Only in damp, fertile ground will heliopsis, FACING PAGE, LEFT, reach its full flowering potential. It is better suited to large borders or country gardens than to confined city spaces, as is the perennial sunflower, FACING PAGE, CENTRE, which is too aggressive and bulky to be admitted into mixed borders. Another of the robust daisies, Rudbeckia 'Goldsturm,' ABOVE, covers itself with a cascade of grand black-eyed Susans that last a long time either in the garden or in a vase.

border plants should give golden glow a miss.

Best of the black-eyed Susans for flowerbeds are *Rudbeckia fulgida* and its more compact cultivar, 'Goldsturm,' 2-to-3-foot mounding plants whose nondescript greenery is all but hidden under a blanket of 3-inch, yellow dark-eyed daisies. Even a single plant makes a fine drift of colour.

Autumn sun is the apt moniker for another native rudbeckia, *Rudbeckia nitida* — 3 to 12 feet tall depending on soil and site — that displays a crop of lemon yellow daisies with ray petals flared down around greenish central disks. This one needs staking, but 'Goldquelle,' a double zinnia-like sport, supports its 4-foot stems without props.

Vigorous branching plants, rudbeckias need plenty of elbowroom and associate well with 'Gold Plate' yarrow, white phlox, globe thistles, heliopsis and the taller ornamental grasses. Where there is space enough, 'Goldsturm' is extraordinarily effective in a garden bed adjacent to the cream and green striped grass *Miscanthus sinensis* 'Variegatus.' All rudbeckias grow quickly from seed and may yield first-summer flowers from an April sowing indoors. Most self-sow. Lots of sun and decent loam are all they need to thrive.

Purple Coneflower
(*Echinacea purpurea*)

Botanically connected to the rudbeckias are the strange but showy purple coneflowers, whose fully expanded blossoms have narrow, gracefully twisted mauve petals that flare downward around central cones bristling with little spiked, orange-tipped seeds-in-the-making. Since the crown-shaped buds develop slowly into full-blown flowers, each lasts an exceptionally long time, a fact that compensates for their meagre numbers. Here, 8 or 10 coneflowers is considered a good crop from an established clump.

Growing as tall as 4 feet, echinacea clumps seldom survive division, so it is best to leave them alone once they are settled. Started from seed indoors in spring, they yield a few

flowers the first season, then return as stronger clumps with more blooms the next and the next. But then, just when you are counting on coneflowers for yet another summer, a hard winter may take the older clumps. The observant gardener will likely find young, self-sown coneflowers near the wilted parent. Look for ground-level tufts of dark green pointed leaves, deeply veined and attached to short stalks. If they are well placed, leave seedlings where they are to fatten up and flower. If not, carefully shift them to better quarters.

Like heleniums and other late summer composites, echinacea thrives best in humus-rich (hence, moist) earth, in full sun in cooler gardens but tucked out of the midday glare in hot sites. Long respected as a medicinal herb — echinacea roots are said to make a powerful antibiotic tincture — this perennial forms part of a quietly effective garden picture against a background of other decorative medicinals, such as hoary southernwood (*Artemisia abrotanum*), with blue-green rue bushes shining metallically in front. The coneflower's subdued colouring seems to call for this sort of neutral association; echinacea is lost in a jumble of bright blooms.

Sea Lavender
(*Limonium* spp)

Annual statices in all their many colours are among the most familiar dried flowers for winter bouquets. But in the late-summer flower garden, a perennial relative, *Limonium latifolium*, does what baby's-breath does in July, that is, lightens more substantial things such as phlox, coneflowers and heleniums.

From a ground-level tuft of smooth and elongated leaves, this perennial sends up branching foot-high stems set with a myriad of tiny lavender flowers — little amethyst gems when the dew collects on them. Misty and delicate in effect, these blooms dry well for winter bouquets that can also include yarrow heads, poppy seed-pods, dried globe thistles and sea holly. More effective in the garden in groups of three or more, with individual plants set about 16 inches apart, sea lavender plants need only full sun and nourishing, light loam and are best set at the front of flowerbeds where they can be seen in their entirety.

Gooseneck Flower
(*Lysimachia clethroides*)

Although the gooseneck flower has lived at Larkwhistle for only two seasons, it has already proved to be one of our finest late-summer perennials—problem-free, self-supporting and elegant in bloom. I wonder why it crops up so seldom in nurseries or gardens. It grows 3½ to 4 feet tall, its sturdy stems set with narrow, dusty green leaves, ending in gracefully drooping, elongated tapers. With its small, starry white flowers that continue to open in succession for almost a month, the gooseneck flower looks in profile like the head and neck of a swan or goose. Since faded flowers drop off cleanly, the plant appears fresh all through its flowering season.

A Japanese native and kin of the June-blooming yellow loosestrife, the gooseneck flower has clumped up very quickly in the moist, fertile earth (equal parts loam, manure and peat moss) of our "quiet garden." A two-shoot starter plant has increased to more than a dozen stems in two seasons—a rate that may spell invasive. No matter, because I know any number of gardeners who would appreciate a chunk of this hard-to-find perennial.

Useful for mixed borders, for wild gardens that never get too dry or along the margins of streams or ponds, the gooseneck flower needs no care once it settles in. But mark the spot where it grows, because it is one of the last plants to show through the ground in spring. If you forget its location, you're apt to break off hidden shoots during early cultivation and cleanup. Spring bulbs, daffodils especially, planted around clumps of lysimachia bring early colour to the same spot.

Black Snakeroot
(*Cimicifuga racemosa*)

Fred and Mary Ann McGourty, who cultivate an astonishing 700 species and cultivars of hardy perennials at Hillside Garden in Connecticut, count black snakeroot among their top 10 selections—high praise indeed. Well grown in moist, humusy soil in sun or partial shade, snakeroot, a denizen of moist woodlands from Ontario to Georgia, is a robust but graceful 6-footer decorated for almost a month with branched, tapered plumes of pearly buds and fluffy white blooms above

At all stages of development of the purple coneflower, FACING PAGE, *there is a striking contrast between its rosy ray petals and its bristling orange cone. Also eye-catching is black snakeroot,* LEFT, *whose pearly buds gradually open as the skyrocket spires mature. It attains its most decorative heights only in well-nourished loam, which also suits the gooseneck flower,* ABOVE. *The flower's profile indicates the reason for its unusual name.*

135

fanning, compound dark green foliage.

An effective and enduring element at the back of borders, snakeroot "retains a great deal of architectural character," says one writer, even after its flowers have faded. Because it is such a tall, slender thing, three plants grouped together make more impact than a single specimen. Cimicifuga is well placed behind medium-height ferns and is fine with rose loosestrife, day lilies, pink phlox or crimson astilbe. Where hosta and Siberian irises do well, snakeroot is sure to thrive. In definitely damp places, consider grouping the native cardinal flower (*Lobelia cardinalis*, nursery-bought, never collected in the wild) in front of snakeroot for a brilliant show of intense crimson and ivory.

Cimicifuga can be divided carefully or raised, albeit slowly, from fresh seeds. A better plan, however, is to set potted nursery plants a full 2 feet apart in the best soil you can manage, and leave them to clump up undisturbed. Like peonies, gas plants, baby's-breath, baptisias and hostas, bugbane does not take kindly to casual shifting about, unnecessary splitting or other well-intentioned meddling on a gardener's part.

Obedient Plant
(*Physostegia virginiana*)

An easy—a little too easy, some might say—but neglected late-summer perennial, the obedient plant (also known as false dragonhead) shoots up 4-foot, self-supporting square stems densely clothed with glossy, deep green oblong leaves that make even flowerless clumps presentable all season long. By mid-August, an abundant crop of 8-inch symmetrical spires of pretty white- or purple-lipped flowers, like small snapdragon blossoms, appear. If you have nothing else to do, you can reposition the individual flowers, which are attached to their stems by the botanical equivalent of a ball-and-socket joint; however you turn them, left or right, up or down, the flowers stay put, a trait that has suggested the common name, obedient plant.

If only its roots were as amenable. A mint relative, physostegia has but one fault: its outward-creeping rootstock expands, mintlike, rather too quickly for the comfort of less aggressive things nearby. The plant's wandering ways need not deter you from growing it, however. Any shoots that move out of bounds can simply be sliced away and dug out. Like mint, the obedient plant thrives in moist loam, in sun or partial shade, and will run beautifully wild along the banks of a stream or pond.

Artemisia
(*Artemisia* spp)

Most garden artemisias are aromatic silver-leaved herbs valued for their persistent, finely cut foliage, which serves as a soft-toned filler in beds of bright flowers. Some species are flowerless, while some send up sprawling wands of dowdy yellow-green buttons. Among the best for the northern perennial garden are:
•*Artemisia* 'Silver Mound,' whose feathery, foot-high symmetrical hummocks of thread-fine, silver-blue leaves make an excellent edging where the plants have room to

spread out in full sun and perfectly drained soil;

•*Artemisia absinthium* 'Lambrook Silver,' an improved wormwood that fills a space 3 feet tall and wide with delicately incised, silver-white foliage. Pruning in spring and again in midsummer keeps this exuberant perennial shapely;

•*Artemisia abrotanum*, or southernwood, a robust, hoary-leaved 5-foot herb that shines all season long toward the back of a flowerbed, where it is especially pleasing with foreground clumps of *Achillea* 'Moonshine,' *Salvia superba* and purple coneflowers. Prune as for 'Lambrook Silver';

•*Artemisia ludoviciana* 'Silver King,' a showy but extremely invasive bit of garden silverware that should be grown either where it can be contained or where there is room for its rapid spread. Gardeners who plant this 2½-foot herb in sandy soil may come to regret it;

•*Artemisia lactiflora*, an exception to the artemisia's rule of silver leaves and no-account flowers. This tall, handsome plant is also known as almond- or hawthorn-scented mug-

wort. A hardy Chinese native, it has slightly arching but self-supporting 6-foot-tall stems that are dressed top to toe with dark green lobed leaves, and its feathery, branching panicles are packed with small but abundant milk-white (hence *lacti-flora*) flowers. After several seasons, a single plant makes a striking, tall accent behind dark red or pink phlox, with day lilies or helenium of any hue or all on its own against a backdrop of evergreens or shrubs. Fertile, moist loam ensures robust growth and keeps foliage from turning yellow. Otherwise, the "milky mugwort," as I translate the Latin, grows itself. Cut this perennial back in late fall, or you will have a mess of smashed stems to cope with come spring. And if you need another plant or two, slice away divisions from the outer edges of an established clump in spring without lifting the parent plant.

Globe Thistles
(*Echinops ritro*)

Visitors to Larkwhistle find globe thistles either weird and wonderful

Globe thistles, FACING PAGE, *top their bold architectural foliage with perfectly round flower heads. This robust 5-foot perennial is good company for pink and white phlox or for any of the late-summer daisies. Also weird and wonderful, the obedient plant,* LEFT, *has the vegetable equivalent of a ball-and-socket joint that holds each floret to the stalk. This quirk allows the gardener to reposition individual flowers, and they "obediently" stay put.*

or weedy; but whether they feel pleasure or puzzlement, most notice this strange yet striking perennial. Bright colours are not the attraction of this daisy relative but, rather, bold architectural foliage and perfectly round flower heads. Hoary grey-green leaves, indented and spiny like overgrown silver holly, arch out from stout 4-foot stems topped with steel blue, spiky spheres that change very little whether in their bud, flowering or seed phase. Cut while in bud and

hung in an airy, shaded place to dry, globe thistles hold their round shape for winter bouquets. Cut later, they are apt to shatter while drying.

Fine companions for phlox or heleniums, globe thistles take to any well-drained sunny site, provided their roots find enough moisture to support their robust growth. Groups of three, each plant set 2 feet from the next, form an arresting feature toward the centre of an island bed behind black-eyed Susans, showy

stonecrop, any of the yellow yarrows or mounds of hardy geraniums showing the last of their pink or white saucers.

Fairly quick from seed at the start, *Echinops ritro*, or its improved form 'Taplow Blue,' sometimes crops up in nurseries. However you start it, your original plants will likely spawn stripling thistles from their own hardy seeds. In very fertile, damp ground, echinops grow lush and sappy and may need some support.

Digging and dividing globe thistles is as unnecessary as it is difficult, but to share this perennial with appreciative gardening friends, one can detach a rooted shoot or two from the outside of a clump with a small spade in spring. Wrenching the whole plant out of the ground might well wrench one's back in the process.

Showy Stonecrop
(*Sedum spectabile*)

If I could grow just a dozen perennials, *Sedum spectabile* would be among them. Neither spectacular nor flamboyantly coloured, the showy stonecrop is nevertheless a hardworking and dependable plant that maintains (with not a bit of attention) a neat and steady show of succulent grey-green foliage the season through, all the while masking fading bulb leaves or screening transient Oriental poppies behind. Its late and enduring flowering is decidedly welcome and serves to keep a border lively during the season of frosts, farewells and general seediness. The 2½-foot showy stonecrop, grande dame of a genus of succulents that includes a number of smaller species useful for edgings or sunny rock gardens, thrives unattended in any soil short of soggy, either in full sun or shaded for a few hours a day.

Late August sees the dome of broccoli-like buds begin to shade from pale green to mauve-pink as the massed, starry flowers open, drawing hungry honeybees and passing butterflies. The flower heads deepen in colour during September and finally mellow to rusty brown in harmony with the shades of fall. Frost leaves this tough plant unscathed, however. Upright, self-supporting and symmetrical in its growth, showy stonecrop is a calm and orderly presence among perennials that are prone to sprawl or topple.

Fine as a specimen plant, this perennial is even more effective in groups of three, five or more, set toward the middle of a mixed border. Nursery plants—these will likely be the cultivars 'Brilliant,' 'Autumn Joy' or 'Meteor'—or plants from a neighbour's garden are the best way

to introduce the showy stonecrop. In spring, established clumps can be split down to the last shoot if necessary. Growing plants can also be moved any time, if one digs them carefully with a ball of earth intact around their roots and waters newly set clumps copiously to settle them in.

Chrysanthemums
(*Chrysanthemum* spp)

A plot of land about 5 feet wide by 8 or 10 feet long, situated in full sun to encourage flowers in short-season gardens, is an ample canvas for a full fall picture that could include a few chrysanthemums, heleniums and clumps of *Sedum spectabile*. Into the soil, turn copious amounts of fine-textured organic matter, especially decayed manure, the fall before a springtime planting of chrysanthemum divisions, secured from a nursery or a gardening friend. Mulch will maintain moisture, but water the chrysanthemums frequently and well during dry spells, perhaps feeding them with fish emulsion in the process to keep them moving.

Even the shortest "mums" need 18 inches of elbowroom between them. All flower more abundantly if the growing tips are pinched back once or twice before July 1, something I have yet to do in more than a decade of growing them. Finally, in cold gardens, a covering of evergreen boughs ensures that "mums" survive winters where snow comes and goes, revealing and concealing the last traces of the fall garden.

Chrysanthemums, FACING PAGE, FOREGROUND, *and the hardy aster 'Harrington's Pink' need frequent division to keep them vigorous. They draw the perennial season to a close, along with the showy stonecrop,* ABOVE, *which has kept its corner of the garden furnished with succulent silver-green foliage all season. When the broccoli-like buds break into September flowers, bees and butterflies stop by for a sip of nectar; the flower garden is not just for people.*

139

Carrying On
Fall work and perennial maintenance

The end of the flowering season is the time to explore the roots of the perennial garden. Many of its inhabitants, such as globe thistles, FACING PAGE, proliferate underground in a manner that makes them ideal candidates for multiplication by division, a procedure done not only to increase a gardener's stock of prized plants but also to check the spread of certain aggressive flowers and to rejuvenate those that are dwindling from age or overcrowding.

I always look forward to fall. Throughout the summer, I have been plotting changes I wish to make in the perennial beds; I make note of places or plants that would benefit from a generous helping of humus and watch over burgeoning seedlings in the nursery, which can soon take their place among the old-timers. My aim is to send the flower garden into winter nicely trimmed, weed-free, well fertilized and in such good order that when the snow curtain lifts the next April, I can relax and enjoy the unfolding show. Besides, in spring, with crocuses blooming soon after the snow melts, bulb noses showing and perennials sprouting sheaves of new greenery, I am reluctant to be digging around and disturbing all of this eager new beginning.

Traditionally, May is the month for putting in the garden, and the fall weeks are for cleanup, composting and soil improvement. This pattern may be appropriate for the vegetable plot, but in the perennial garden, early fall—from mid-September until the end of October—is an excellent time to make or remake a bed, to plant or transplant, to divide crowded clumps or to rearrange the garden picture. Cooler weather makes for pleasant outdoor work, and frequent rain showers entice newly set or divided perennials into anchoring themselves before the snows. "Do the work in the spring," writes Richardson Wright in his *Practical Book of Outdoor Flowers*, "and your plants will be expending so much energy in getting established that they cannot flower effectively; do the work in autumn, and you gain six months, because when spring comes again, [they] are already established."

Bed Renewal

A perennial planting inevitably needs periodic overhauling. Every fall, my partner and I settle on certain parts of the flower garden for renovation. We may choose sections that have become shabby, dull or disorganized, corners that have grown overcrowded or places where heavy feeders reveal by weak growth and fewer flowers that they have depleted the soil. Garden renova-

tion entails several tasks:
- setting fresh young plants in areas where perennials have dwindled;
- dividing any crowded clumps;
- rearranging plants that are obviously pining or those that mar the picture;
- evicting altogether any invasive troublemakers;
- thinning borders to give the plants that remain room to fill out and flourish.

As Wright notes, "Upon how well and how completely the fall work is done will depend much of the border's success the following year."

Like sod breaking at the start, border renovation can be hard work. The prospect of disturbing an established planting, even one that has grown into a tangled mess, is daunting, I know. If spring bulbs are hiding under herbaceous plants, one winces at the thought of slicing into them.

First, be realistic. Rather than tearing into an entire bed, tackle only as much space as you feel you can complete in a day or two at the most. Time and energy permitting, you can then move to another section. I find a 10-foot length of a 10-foot-wide border plenty to cope with at a go; or I may decide to revamp the planting along the edge of a 30-foot stretch of border. Before you dig in, take note of perennials that are robust and flourishing and plan to let them be. There is nothing to gain from digging and dividing Siberian irises or day

lilies that are flowering well. In addition, peonies, gas plants, baby's-breath, balloon flowers, false indigo, loosestrife and hostas all resent well-intentioned meddling. If they are well placed and thriving, take heed of the implied "do not disturb" sign.

Now, with a shovel or a spading fork—this gardener's preferred tool—pry out of the soil all other plants in the area, and set them somewhere in the shade, if possible. Protect roots from drying with a cover of damp burlap bags or a tarpaulin. Next, digging gingerly, lift out clumps of daffodils, other spring bulbs or lilies. Organized gardeners will have marked the location of bulbs before the foliage disappears in summer. I always plan to but never do. However, because we tend to interplant spring bulbs among perennials such as peonies, phlox, heleniums and day lilies, I have a fair notion of where they are. But only fair—a few skewered bulbs are probably inevitable during fall delving.

With an area emptied of perennials and bulbs, dig it over to extract weeds. You have a second chance now to catch bothersome perennial weeds and also to improve the earth by turning under a generous layer of organic matter (see chapter 2). If humus is in short supply, dig it in only where you plan to set bulky, heavy-feeding perennials or spot-enrich. Rake the soil fine and smooth, and you are ready to recompose.

Renovating a flowerbed presents an opportunity to remedy some of its unsatisfactory features, and as one writer notes, "these are commonly not a few." Do not feel obliged to put back everything you have taken out. No sense keeping plants you do not admire, those that covet more than their share of space or any that stubbornly refuse your hospitality. Before I start to replant, I check our home nursery for suitable things—some strong young seed-raised columbines that would be perfect toward the border's edge or a chunk of day lily that arrived in the mail last spring and has since grown large enough to be a mid-border accent. I also survey other sections of the garden for perennials I can steal and relocate without leaving holes in the

floral tapestry. During reorganization, the notes made earlier in the season – when flaws were more visible – prove invaluable.

Bulb Planting

With necessary renovations under way, the time has come to add spring bulbs to parts of the garden that need pepping up. After over a decade of flower gardening, our fall bulb orders have shrunk considerably. The dozens of crocus corms tucked in years ago now provide a generous overflow of new bulbs for other places. A clutch of pricey crown imperial bulbs has sprouted enough offsets to furnish several more groups. Most bulbs – tulips are a notable exception – give gratifying returns. And like clumping perennials, most need periodic lifting, dividing and replanting. There is no strict schedule for this work; rather, the bulbs themselves let you know by weaker growth or paucity that they have outgrown their present quarters or have exhausted the soil. If, for instance, you notice in spring that daffodil blooms are smaller and sparser than usual or, later, that lilies are not growing as tall and are showing fewer flowers, the time is

In the fall, overcrowded clumps of daffodils or lilies, FACING PAGE, *can be pried out of the ground and split apart to extend or renew a planting. Tulips, too, are thinned, sorted and planted in fall,* ABOVE. *At Larkwhistle, tulip bulbs are arranged in a bed by a dry-built stone wall so that next spring, they will bloom along with basket-of-gold and creeping baby's-breath, which will spill over the wall.*

wise to wait until all of their green leaf juices have flowed back into the bulbs before disturbing them. Here, October is lily-splitting time. Big lily or fritillaria bulbs always go in singly (details about siting bulbs, planting depths and distances apart are given in chapters 3, 4 and 7). With bulbs safely underground, a gardener need only cultivate patience. It will be half a year before the first snowdrops lead off a parade of blossoms that let you know it is spring again.

Division

With bulbs planted, another essential part of border renovation is dividing overgrown, sparse-flowering clumps. Not all perennials are divisible. Hollyhocks split poorly but spawn more than enough seedlings to carry on; nor have I ever divided delphiniums (although I have heard of it). Columbines resent division, and it is better to raise fresh plants from seed occasionally in any case.

With those plants that do lend themselves to multiplication by division, rejuvenation is the goal. First, dig up an entire clump, and shake out some of the earth, the better to see where it splits naturally into separate crowns. Some plants tend to untangle themselves; coral bells, shasta daisies, peach-leaved bellflowers, aconites, heleniums, tall evening primroses and other loosely knit perennials often fall into distinct segments that can be further pulled and pried apart by hand. To divide more tightly woven clumps of phlox, hostas, day lilies, yarrows or loosestrife, use a sharp, hefty knife to slice down between shoots and right through the roots. Or you can sever some ties with pruning shears before prying the sections apart using two hand forks. Some gardeners simply plunge a sharp spade into a clump and slice it into bits, but this strikes me as cruel and unusual punishment. I wouldn't blame any plant so treated for sulking.

Resist what someone has called "the fallacy of the big clump." Two-to-four-shoot divisions supplied with lively roots always outpace and prove more satisfactory than larger chunks. Also, being the most recently formed, divisions from the outside edges of

ripe in fall to renovate the plantings. Division is the method.

Bulbs are among the easiest (and most satisfying) plants to split. Even if many of them are tightly clustered, each bulb is an obvious unit that snaps away from the rest with a gentle tug. Bulbs increase at different rates. A single daffodil may take 10 years to proliferate into a crowded clump of 20 or more small bulbs. Some vigorous lilies, especially if they are planted a bit too close in fertile soil at the start, may be straining for space in as little as four years. Crocuses, snowdrops and glory-of-the-snow soon reach the clotted stage but seem to flower freely despite growing practically on top of each other. In our garden, a pesky chipmunk usually thins and relocates crocus corms—help we would just as soon do without.

To divide bulbs, first pry clumps out of the earth. To keep from slicing into bulbs or skewering them on the fork tines, dig well back from the cluster. Bump the joined bulbs a few times in a wheelbarrow to shake away most of the soil. Now pull bulbs apart by hand, and sort them into larger and smaller sizes—you may have room to replant only the fattest. Before replacing bulbs, enrich the area again with organic matter, as you would for any perennial.

Daffodils and crown imperials can be lifted for division anytime after their foliage has yellowed and withered, but because it is in their nature to send out new roots early in fall, they should be replanted before the end of September. Summer-blooming lilies are the latest bulbs to ripen; it is an older clump will re-establish and grow more readily than the spent woody centre. A large clump may yield 10 to 20 divisions, some clearly better than others, as well as a pile of severed shoots, broken roots and other debris. Be firm, and select only as many divisions as you need from among the best, resisting the impulse to keep every last shoot. The compost heap will take care of the rest.

But if you are dividing something special or unusual, why not pot up the extras and arrange a Thanksgiving perennial trade-off with gardening friends or organize the horticultural equivalent of a yard sale.

Replant divisions, firmly and pronto, in the loose, humusy soil you have just prepared. Fine-textured organic matter spurs recently split plants to extend new roots and get a firm hold before freezeup. Water the new divisions immediately after replanting.

Although early fall is a fine time to divide many perennials, others are on a different schedule. Primroses are best split in June, several weeks after they have finished flowering. July or early August is the time to pull crowded iris clumps apart for overhauling. In addition, any perennial that comes into bloom after the middle of August is best left in place until early spring. Among these are heleniums, hardy asters, chrysanthemums, *Artemisia lactiflora* and perennial sunflowers.

I know several gardeners who are forever playing "musical plants," shifting perennials from place to place every season or so and then wondering why their harried flowers seldom bloom to expectation. Most hardy plants are deliberate growers that take time to extend anchoring and sustaining roots before they show their true colours. In fact, it may be that only the helenium clumps want dividing one year, coral bells the next and the phlox are fine for yet another season. Depending on soil, climate and their own nature, plants increase at rates ranging from snail-paced to rampant. By attending to a few clumps every spring and several more in fall, a gardener may

Division is the swiftest way to increase or renew perennials such as hardy asters, FACING PAGE. *After a clump is pried out of the ground with a spading fork, a sturdy knife or pruning shears may be needed to sever the necessary ties so that the plant can be pulled apart into three- or four-shoot segments. Not all perennials need frequent division, however. Large-leaved hostas,* LEFT, *can stay put for many years, while peonies are among the perennials that, like false indigo and gas plant, settle in for decades. In contrast, the spread of yellow evening primroses may require checking every few years.*

never be faced with the formidable task of renovating an entire bed or even one whole section.

New Designs

Unless, that is, you want to change the picture. Given the complexity of a perennial planting, it is scarcely possible to get it right the first time. Once a bed or border has been in place for four or five years, an observant gardener will probably be eager to overhaul it, adding and subtracting plants in the process. Few garden tasks are quite so satisfying, I find, as plunging into a tangled perennial bed, pulling the works apart (carefully) and shuffling things around in a fashion I hope will improve the picture. If this work is done in fall, as it usually is here, I can retire the garden for the season with a keen sense of anticipation. What will spring bring? How will the changes pan out?

In the process of renovation, it is always helpful to recall some of the principles of perennial design discussed in the first chapter:

•Include several perennials for each phase of the flowering season to ensure continuous colour from spring to fall.

•Distribute early, midseason and late-blooming plants fairly evenly throughout a border so that it shows some colour here and there along its length at any given time.

•For continuity and to carry the eye along, repeat certain prominent plants, particularly those with decorative, long-lasting leaves, at intervals throughout a planting. Perennials suited to forming this stabilizing backbone in a border of more wayward or ephemeral things include peonies, loosestrife, cushion euphorbias, day lilies, Siberian irises, the taller yarrows, hardy geraniums and clumps of lilies, phlox or heleniums.

•A perennial planting that is neatly, but not necessarily evenly, edged always has its best foot forward; a tidy edge can compensate for a fair bit of "controlled untidiness" behind it, to borrow a phrase from Vita Sackville-West. In sunny sites, alter-nating plants of dianthus, coral bells and Carpathian harebells creates neat foliage mounds and a long-blooming ribbon of pink, red, lavender-blue and white. In partial shade, replace the dianthus with hostas for an elegant, leafy border. Again in sun, a solid line of *Sedum kamtschaticum* presents a neat low front of succulent greenery and weeks of bright yellow starry flowers followed by conspicuous dark red seedpods. This is my favourite dwarf sedum. Many other fine edging plants are discussed in chapters 3 through 7.

•For pleasantly varied contours, contrast bushy, rounded perennials with more erect, vertical spires.

•Set most perennials in groups of three or more.

•Trust your own colour sense.

•Do not feel you need to stay strictly with perennials. Gaps can be left for a swath of snapdragons or salvias or a bouquet of long-flowering marigolds. At Larkwhistle, brilliant orange California poppies and frothy sweet alyssums, both annuals, rou-

tinely crop up from their own hardy seeds at the base of edging rocks. Where space allows, put in shrubs or flowering trees to add height and stability. The herbaceous borders of days past have given way in most gardens to more natural blends of hardy perennials (herbaceous and shrubby) interspersed with bulbs and annuals for variety and colour.

Into Winter

A consistent snow cover is by far the best winter protection for perennials, most of which are safe in ground that freezes hard in December and stays that way until spring. But in many places, winter temperatures move erratically between deep-freeze and balmy, and perennials are robbed of their needed rest, moved to untimely growth and then stopped cold in their tracks – sometimes heaved out of the earth altogether. Who can blame some for taking their leave? Wherever fickle winters are the rule, an 8-inch mulch of straw or leaves laid around the crowns of plants – but not on top of them – during November will ensure the comfort and safety of any species not completely ironclad. The goal is not to keep these hardy plants warm over winter but, rather, to insulate the earth, as snow would do, against a repeated freeze-and-thaw cycle – in fact, to keep them from becoming warm too soon. In very cold areas, low-growing, evergreen perennials such as dianthus, heather, sun roses or hardy candytuft are best protected with several layers of evergreen boughs. Christmas tree branches are handy in early January. The boughs are left in place until spring seems fairly settled. Otherwise, the foliage of these winter-coddled ones is apt to be seared and desiccated by cold spring winds.

Fortunately, Larkwhistle receives a heavy snow cover perfect for perennial protection. After the climbing roses have been loosened from their supports, bent to the ground and covered with a protective mound of earth, the last flower-garden task at Larkwhistle is to cut the leafy stalks of herbaceous perennials back to ground level. Some garden writers recommend leaving

the top growth in place over winter to trap the snow. This is, no doubt, a good plan wherever snowfall is spare and unpredictable, but stalks left standing here flatten after a few winter storms, and picking away the smashed, soggy remnants of last year's perennials in spring is tricky, time-consuming work, especially in borders clotted with sprouting bulbs.

Some gardeners, I know, like to look out at a snow-filled garden punctuated with dried mullein stalks, crackling seedpods and the tan heads of yarrow and tall fall sedum. Certainly, lingering goldfinches and winter-resident chickadees appreciate the homegrown feeders. But for my part, I would rather see the flower garden go into winter spruced up, trimmed and orderly, a clear canvas for next spring's unfolding perennial picture.

Every season, I am gratified once more by the garden's energy and abundance, by the plants' pluck and stamina in the face of adversity, by the lovely flower tints and their exquisite modelling, by the sheer variety that even a single garden bed can encompass. Louise B. Wilder, my favourite garden writer, provides a sound approach: "Love your garden, and work in it, and let it give you what it surely will of sweetness [and] health . . . and let no one feel that the benefit is all on the side of the garden, for truly you will receive more than you give."

The garden design may be improved in fall, when plants can be removed, divided and replanted in positions that suit one's overall scheme. At Larkwhistle, FACING PAGE, *bold foliage plants such as peonies and hostas are carefully placed where season-long greenery is needed, and harmoniously coloured plants are grouped for pictorial effect. Protected by the winter snow, the new garden picture will not begin to reveal itself until the first spring flowers emerge,* ABOVE, *heralding another season of floral colour and abundance.*

Sources

Flower seeds can be imported into either the United States or Canada without difficulty, but the importation of living plants and plant materials requires special arrangements in some cases. These are detailed under the headings below. Please pay for catalogues in the currency of the appropriate country. Where a catalogue is marked "refundable," its price will be subtracted from the cost of the first order.

Seeds (Canada)

Alberta Nurseries & Seeds Ltd.
Box 20
Bowden, Alberta
T0M 0K0
Flower seeds and some plants. Catalogue free to Canada, $2 foreign.

Butchart Gardens
Box 4010, Station A
Victoria, British Columbia
V8X 3X4
A small selection of old-fashioned perennials. Catalogue $1, refundable.

Dominion Seed House
Georgetown, Ontario
L7G 4A2
Vegetable and flower seeds, some perennials. Catalogue free. Canadian orders only.

Stokes Seeds Ltd.
1436 Stokes Building
St. Catharines, Ontario
L2R 6R6
Seeds of vegetables, herbs and flowers, including perennials. Catalogue free.

Seeds (U.S.)

W. Atlee Burpee Co.
300 Park Avenue
Warminster, Pennsylvania 18974
Vegetable and flower seeds, including some perennials. Catalogue free. No Canadian orders.

Far North Gardens
16785 Harrison
Livonia, Michigan 48154
Seeds for an extensive list of primroses; other "rare flower seed." Catalogue $2 to U.S. and Canada.

Dr. Joseph C. Halinar
2334 Crooked Finger Road
Scotts Mills, Oregon 97375
Specialist in lilies and day lilies from seed. Price list free to U.S.; send an International Postal Reply coupon from Canada.

Maver Nurseries
Route 2, Box 265B
Asheville, North Carolina 28805
A good selection of flowering perennial seeds. Price list $2.

McLaughlin's Seeds
Buttercup's Acre
Box 550
Mead, Washington
99021-0550
Seeds of vegetables, herbs and flowers, including perennials. Catalogue $1.

George W. Park Seed Co., Inc.
Box 31
Greenwood, South Carolina
29647-0001
Seeds of vegetables, herbs and flowers, including perennials. Catalogue free.

Select Seeds
81 Stickney Hill Road
Union, Connecticut 06076
Seeds of flowering perennials. Price list $1.

Stokes Seeds Ltd.
1436 Stokes Building
Buffalo, New York 14240
Seeds of vegetables, herbs and flowers, including perennials. Catalogue free.

Thompson & Morgan, Inc.
Box 1308
Jackson, New Jersey 08527
An excellent selection of seeds, including flowering perennials. Catalogue free. Represented in Canada by C.A. Cruickshank Ltd., listed below.

Seeds (England)

Chiltern Seeds
Bortree Stile, Ulverston
Cumbria LA12 7PB
England
All kinds of seeds, with an excellent selection of perennial flowers. Catalogue $2.

Plants (Canada)

In order to import plant materials from Canada, Americans must ensure that their purchases are accompanied by two items: an invoice showing the quantity and value of the plants and a document from Agriculture Canada stating that the plants are free from diseases and insects. Canadian nurseries who accept U.S. orders routinely comply with these requests.

Nurseries that will not accept foreign orders are listed as such.

Aubin Nurseries Ltd.
Box 1089
Carman, Manitoba
R0G 0J0
Hardy ornamentals. Catalogue free.

Beaverlodge Nursery Ltd.
Box 127
Beaverlodge, Alberta
T0H 0C0
Hardy ornamentals. Catalogue free. Canadian orders only.

Cedar Creek Farm
RR 4
Rockwood, Ontario
N0B 2K0
Specialists in peonies (formerly Gilbert's Peony Gardens). Catalogue $1. Canadian orders only.

Corn Hill Nursery Ltd.
RR 5
Petitcodiac, New Brunswick
E0A 2H0
Specialists in apples, but some perennial flowers too. Catalogue $2, refundable. Canadian orders only.

C.A. Cruickshank Ltd.
1015 Mount Pleasant Road
Toronto, Ontario
M4P 2M1
Specialists in flowering bulbs, other flowering perennials. Three catalogues (spring, midseason and fall) $2.

Farleigh Lake Gardens
Box 128
Penticton, British Columbia
V2A 6J9
Perennial flowers and herbs. Price list free; sent to British Columbia, Alberta and Saskatchewan addresses only.

Ferncliff Gardens
SS 1
Mission, British Columbia
V2V 5V6
Irises and peonies. Catalogue free. Canadian orders only.

Gardenimport, Inc.
Box 760
Thornhill, Ontario
L3T 4A5
Flowering bulbs and perennial flowers. Catalogue $2 for two years (4 catalogues).

Honeywood Lilies and Nursery
Box 63
Parkside, Saskatchewan
S0J 2A0
Summer list of perennial flowers is free; fall lily catalogue $2.

Hopestead Gardens
RR 4
6605 Hopedale Road
Sardis, British Columbia
V0X 1V0
Hardy perennial flowers. Price list free.

Hortico, Inc.
RR 1
Waterdown, Ontario
L0R 2H0
Ground covers, perennial flowers, ferns. Price list free.

McFayden Seed Co. Ltd.
Box 1800
Brandon, Manitoba
R7A 6N4
Best known for seeds, but also some hardy perennial flower plants. Catalogue free.

McMath's Daffodils
6340 Francis Road
Richmond, British Columbia
V7C 1K5
Daffodils and narcissi. Price list free. Canadian orders only.

McMillen's Iris Garden
RR 1
Norwich, Ontario
N0J 1P0
Canada's largest source of irises. Also day lilies. Catalogue $1.

Morden Nurseries Ltd.
Box 1270
Morden, Manitoba
R0G 1J0
Mostly food plants, but also a selection of perennial flowers, including those developed at Agriculture Canada's Morden research station. Catalogue free.

Sears-McConnell Nurseries
RR 1
Port Burwell, Ontario
N0J 1T0
Perennial flowers as well as other plants. Catalogue free, available also from Sears outlets.

Sheppard's Bulb Farm
6707 Bradner Road
RR 1
Mt. Lehman, British Columbia
V0X 1V0
Daffodils and narcissi. Price list free. Canadian orders only.

Stirling Perennials
RR 1
Morpeth, Ontario
N0P 1X0
Hardy perennial flowers. Catalogue $1.

T & T Seeds Limited
Box 1710
Winnipeg, Manitoba
R3C 3P6
Specialists in vegetable and flower seeds, but also a selection of hardy perennial flowers. Catalogue $1.

Plants (U.S.)

In order to import plant materials from the United States, Canadians must obtain a "permit to import" from the Permit Office, Plant Health Division, Agriculture Canada, Ottawa, Ontario K1A 0C6. Obtain one form for each nursery. Nurseries which will not accept foreign orders are listed as such.

American Daylily & Perennials
Box 7008
The Woodlands, Texas 77387
Specialists in day lilies. Catalogue $3 to the U.S. or Canada.

Bluestone Perennials Inc.

7211 Middle Ridge Road
Madison, Ohio 44057
Specialists in flowering perennials.
Catalogue free. No Canadian orders.

Cooley's Gardens
11553 Silverton Road N.E.
Box 126
Silverton, Oregon 97381
Irises. Catalogue $2 to U.S. or
Canada.

Daffodil Mart
Route 3, Box 794
Gloucester, Virginia 23061
An extensive list of narcissi.
Catalogue $1, to U.S. only.

Four Seasons Nursery
2207 East Oakland Avenue
Bloomington, Illinois 61701
All kinds of plants, including hardy
perennial flowers. Catalogue free.
Seeds only to Canada.

Klehm Nursery
Route 5, Box 197
South Barrington, Illinois 60010
Peonies, day lilies, hostas, irises.
Canadians must pay a $15 handling
charge. Catalogue $2.

Milaeger's Gardens
4838 Douglas Avenue
Racine, Wisconsin 53402
Flowering perennials as well as other
plants. Catalogue $1. No Canadian
orders.

Mohn's Inc.
Box 2301
Atascadero, California 93423
Perennial poppies; some seeds.
Catalogue free. Seeds only to
Canada.

Prairie Nursery
Box 365-A
Westfield, Wisconsin 53964
Prairie plants, including wild lilies,
grasses, irises. Catalogue $1 to U.S.
and Canada.

John Scheepers, Inc.
63 Wall Street
New York, New York 10005
Flowering bulbs. Three dollars for 3
catalogues and 2 pamphlets, to U.S.
or Canada.

3625 Quinaby Road, N.E.
Salem, Oregon 97303
Irises. Catalogue $2, refundable, to
U.S.; $3 to Canada. Minimum order
of $75 to Canada.

K. Van Bourgondien & Sons
Box A
Babylon, New York 11702
Various plants, including hostas and
day lilies. Catalogue free to U.S. and
Canada.

Vandenberg Bulbs
3 Black Meadow Road
Chester, New York 10918
Perennial flowers and bulbs.
Catalogue $2. No Canadian orders.

Van Engelen Inc.
307 Maple Street
Litchfield, Connecticut 06759
Flowering bulbs. Catalogue free. No
Canadian orders.

Andre Viette Farm & Nursery
Route 1, Box 16
Fishersville, Virginia 22939
Day lilies. Catalogue $1.50. No
Canadian orders.

Wayside Gardens
Hodges, South Carolina 29695
All kinds of plants as well as
flowering perennials, bulbs.
Catalogue free. No Canadian orders.

White Flower Farm
Litchfield, Connecticut 06759
Specialists in flowering perennials,
bulbs. Spring and fall issues of
catalogue $5 to U.S.; $10 to Canada.

Gilbert H. Wild & Son, Inc.
HA-187 Joplin Street
Sarcoxie, Missouri 64862
Peonies and day lilies. Catalogue $2,
refundable, to U.S.; $3 to Canada.

Yerba Buena Nursery
19500 Skyline Boulevard
Woodside, California 94062
Flowers native to California; also
many ferns. Catalogue free. No
Canadian orders.

Glossary

Acidic – Refers to soils or other materials that have a **pH** lower than 7. The best garden soil for most perennials is slightly acidic, with a pH of about 6.5. Soil can be made more acidic with sulphur compounds or peat moss.

Alkaline – Refers to soils or other materials that have a **pH** higher than 7. Certain drought-loving perennials prefer a slightly alkaline or sweet soil. Soil can be made more alkaline with the addition of wood ashes or ground limestone.

Annual – A plant that grows from seed to maturity within one year. Many flowering annuals are sold as **bedding plants**, which are planted in spring and die in fall.

Basal Cluster – A group of leaves that grow close together at the base of a stem.

Beard – A bushy outgrowth, especially notable on the **falls** of some irises.

Bed – An area of open soil that can be viewed from all sides, usually planted with flowers or vegetables.

Bedding Plant – A plant used for temporary display. Most bedding plants are **annuals** purchased for more or less constant flowering during one growing year.

Biennial – A plant that produces flowers and seeds in the second growing season after seed germination. Many biennials form a rosette or **basal cluster** of leaves the first year. The following year, the flower stalk appears. Common flower garden biennials include foxgloves, sweet Williams and Canterbury bells.

Border – An area of open soil alongside another landscape feature such as a fence, wall, driveway or patio. The border usually features decorative plants that may be viewable from one side only.

Bract – A modified leaf at the base of a flower cluster or forming part of the flower itself. Bracts may be so brightly coloured that they suggest petals rather than leaves.

Bulb – A plant storage organ, usually underground, with fleshy scales that are swollen modified leaves enclosing an embryo flower. Tulips and alliums have bulbs.

Composite – Describes a flower or member of the daisy family Compositae, the largest and most advanced family of flowering plants. Typically, composite flowers have strap-shaped ray **florets** surrounding a central bloom of tubular disk florets.

Compost – Organic material such as garden and kitchen refuse piled in such a way that air and moisture break the materials down into a homogeneous substance that can be used as a garden soil additive.

Corm – A plant storage organ formed from the thickened base of the stem. The original corm dries up during the growing season and is replaced by a new one above it. Crocuses have corms.

Corona – An outgrowth above the **perianth** of a flower, most conspicuous on daffodils, where it forms what is also called the cup (if small) or trumpet (if long). **Synonymous with crown**.

Cotyledon – A seedling leaf, usually the first to appear when a seed germinates. In most flowers, two cotyledons will appear, although some, such as lilies, produce only one.

Crown – In botany, usually refers to the upper part of a rootstock from which the foliage and stems grow and to which they die back in fall, as is the case with delphiniums, lupins and peonies. Synonymous with **corona**. Also refers to the upper branching part of a tree.

Cultivar – A man-made plant variation, as opposed to one that has occurred naturally (and is known as a **variety**). Cultivars, from the term "cultivated variety," are indicated by single quotes; as for instance, the daffodil 'Fortissimo.' A cultivar may or may not breed true from seed, depending upon whether or not it is a **hybrid**.

Cutting – A portion of living leaf, stem or root that is used to produce a new plant.

Division – The easiest way to increase clump-forming plants, by cutting or pulling the roots apart and replanting the new sections elsewhere.

Dormant – Describes a resting state of plants, usually during winter in temperate areas, when visible activity ceases. **Herbaceous** plants may die down to the soil level to recommence growth in spring after a period of winter dormancy.

Double – A flower with more than the usual number of petals displayed by the wild species. In fully double specimens, the entire flower may be a mass of petals, while semidouble flowers have more petals than the original species but retain the appearance of an open centre. A double flower may be indicated by the species or subspecies name *flore-pleno* or the abbreviation *fl. pl.*

Evergreen – Describes plants that keep their leaves all winter. Unlike deciduous plants or **herbaceous** perennials, these plants do not become dormant in winter and so may be more susceptible to winter injury.

Falls – The outer ring of pendulous, petal-like **perianth** segments of some irises (as opposed to the upright segments, or **standards**).

Family – In botanical terms, the largest grouping of plants that is commonly listed. In terms of garden flowers, the most common family is the Compositae, the daisy family. Other popular flower families include Liliaceae, the lily family, and Rosaceae, the rose family. Families, which are made up of one or more genera, are indicated by capitalized names, usually with the suffix "aceae."

Floret – A small flower, especially if it is one component of a many-flowered inflorescence, or head, such as that of a **composite**.

Genus – (Plural: genera). A plant family is composed of one or more genera, each of which is, in turn, composed of one or more species. The plant family Liliaceae, for instance, houses the genus *Lilium*, to which the lily belongs, as well as *Fritillaria*, to which the crown imperial belongs. Genus names are capitalized and written in italics and frequently end with the letters "a," "us" or "um."

Hardy – A relative term that indicates a plant's ability to survive outdoors all year in a given climate. What is hardy in Whitehorse may vary considerably from what is hardy in Victoria, the important limitation generally being the lowest winter temperature that the plant will withstand.

Herbaceous – Describes a plant with soft upper growth rather than woody growth (in which case the plant is a **shrub**). Herbaceous plants may be **annual**, **biennial** or **perennial**.

Hybrid – A crossbred cultivar that is not likely to breed true from seed. Methods of vegetative propagation, however, such as division or cuttings, will produce identical copies of a hybrid parent. Hybrids are sometimes indicated by the letter "×" in the Latin names of plants. For instance, *Erica × veitchii* is a cross between *E. arborea* and *E. lusitanica*.

Layering – A propagation process in which shoots, still attached to the mother plant, are laid on top of or just under the soil surface so that rooting occurs. It may be necessary to wound the portion of shoot in contact with the soil and to hold it in place with a stone or piece of wire. Once rooted, the layered section can then be severed from the mother plant and moved elsewhere.

Loam – A soil that contains a good balance of clay, sand and humus, or decayed organic matter.

Manure – Livestock manures, purchased or obtained from farmers or other sources, are among the best of soil amendments, providing both organic matter and nutrients. All fresh manures should be composted at least a year before use.

Manure Tea – A liquid fertilizer made by dissolving or soaking a quantity of manure in a larger volume of water. The mixture is allowed to steep overnight or longer and is used to water any plants, especially nutrient-hungry species such as primroses, delphiniums and foliage plants.

Mulch – A layer of material laid over the soil for any of a number of reasons: to add nutrients to the soil, help prevent weed growth, protect plant roots in winter or raise soil temperatures (in the case of plastic mulches).

Neutral – Refers to soils or other materials that have a **pH** of 7. Higher ratings are considered **alkaline**, lower ones **acidic**. Most plants grow well in neutral or slightly acidic soil.

Organic – In describing agriculture or horticulture, the term refers to systems in which no chemical **pesticides** or fertilizers are used. Instead, natural plant-derived or mineral substances are used for killing pests, fertilizing the soil and getting rid of fungus and other diseases. Organic methods also include passive techniques such as the removal of damaged plant parts and the acceptance of a certain number of pests and diseases in the garden.

Panicle – Often used to describe any flowering part of a plant that is branched in a complex way. Correctly used, it means a stem on which alternating or opposite branches (or **racemes**) carry the actual flowers.

Perennial – A plant whose life is at least three growing seasons long but that may live many more. Most flower garden perennials are **herbaceous**, although shrubs and trees are also perennial plants.

Perianth – The outer parts of a flower that enclose the reproductive organs.

Pesticide – A term that includes a variety of substances, usually synthetic, used to kill an assortment of "pests" including insects, fungi, bacteria and weeds. Herbicides, fungicides and the now less used term insecticides are all types of pesticide.

pH – Meaning "potential hydrogen," the term refers to a logarithmic scale for measuring relative **acidity** or **alkalinity**. A pH of 7 is **neutral**, while values below 7 are increasingly acidic and values between 7 and 14 are increasingly alkaline. A good general garden soil has a pH between 6.5 and 7. The pH can be measured with litmus paper – acid turns the paper blue; alkaline substances, pink – or with a soil test.

Pinching – Removal of the growing tip of a plant to slow growth and encourage branching.

Raceme – An elongated, unbranched flower spike on which each flower has its own stalk. The youngest flowers are nearest the apex.

Rhizome – An underground or surface stem, usually horizontal, which produces new roots continuously and new shoots at intervals from the parent plant. Irises have fleshy rhizomes, which make division of the plant easy. Rhizomes can be distinguished from true roots by the fact that they have nodes as well as scalelike leaves or buds.

Shrub – As opposed to a **herbaceous** plant, a shrub has stems that are mainly woody, or fruticose.

Single – Describes flowers with the normal number of petals for the species, as opposed to **double** or semidouble flowers. All wild roses and single rose **cultivars** have just five petals.

Species – The smallest unit of classification within which a plant has distinguishing characteristics that consistently breed true. When written, the italicized species name always follows the genus, although in lowercase only. Thus *meleagris*, the species name of a certain type of plant of the genus *Fritillaria*, has the full name *Fritillaria meleagris*.

Sport – The botanical term for a plant mutation.

Standard – Part of a flower, most notable in the iris, where the standard consists of the three upright petals, in contrast to the pendulous or horizontal **falls**.

Tender – Refers to plants that are liable to suffer injury or death in cold climates; the opposite of **hardy**. Tender **perennials** must be brought indoors over winter in the north or otherwise carefully protected.

Variety – Often used as a general term to denote any type of plant. Correctly used, it indicates a variation in a wild species sufficiently distinct to be given a name of its own. The variety name is denoted after the **species** name, also in italics. The Roman hyacinth, *Hyacinthus orientalis albulus*, is a variation of the species *Hyacinthus orientalis*.

Index

Photo Credits

p.4 John Scanlan
p.6 John Scanlan

p.8 John Scanlan
p.10 John Scanlan

p.12-24 John Scanlan
p.25-29 illustrations by Marta
    Scythes

p.30-39 John Scanlan

p.40 John Scanlan
p.42 (top) John Scanlan;
    (bottom) Walter Chandoha
p.43-48 John Scanlan
p.49 Walter Chandoha

p.50-53 John Scanlan
p.54 (top) Walter Chandoha;
    (bottom) John Scanlan
p.55-61 John Scanlan
p.62 Derek Fell
p.63-65 John Scanlan

p.66 Walter Chandoha
p.68-70 John Scanlan
p.71 Charles Marden Fitch
p.72 L.L.T. Rhodes/Earth Scenes
p.73 John Scanlan
p.74 (left) John Scanlan;
    (right) Charles Marden Fitch
p.75 John Scanlan
p.76 Derek Fell
p.78-79 John Scanlan
p.80 Derek Fell
p.81 Karen D. Rooney/Valan Photos
p.82-83 John Scanlan

p.84-86 John Scanlan
p.87 Derek Fell
p.88 (top left) Derek Fell;
    (bottom right) Turid Forsyth
p.89-91 John Scanlan
p.92 Farrell Grehan/Photo Researchers
    Inc.
p.93 Derek Fell
p.94 Angelina Lax/Photo Researchers
    Inc.
p.95 John Scanlan
p.96 (top left) John Scanlan;
    (bottom right) Derek Fell
p.97 John Scanlan
p.98 Turid Forsyth
p.99 Derek Fell
p.100 Charles Marden Fitch
p.101-102 John Scanlan

p.104 John Scanlan
p.106 Derek Fell
p.107-111 John Scanlan

p.112 (top left) Adrian and Turid Forsyth;
    (bottom right) Val Wilkinson/
    Valan Photos
p.113 John Scanlan
p.114 Walter Chandoha
p.115 Turid Forsyth
p.116 John Scanlan
p.117 Derek Fell
p.118-119 John Scanlan
p.120 (top left) Derek Fell;
    (bottom right) John Scanlan
p.121 Derek Fell
p.122 Turid Forsyth
p.123 John Scanlan
p.124 Turid Forsyth
p.125 John Scanlan

p.126 John Scanlan
p.128 Walter Chandoha
p.129-131 John Scanlan
p.132 (top left) Derek Fell;
    (bottom right) Lincoln Nutting/
    Photo Researchers Inc.
p.133 Derek Fell
p.134 Walter Chandoha
p.135 Derek Fell
p.136 Turid Forsyth
p.137 John Gerlack/Earth Scenes
p.138 John Scanlan
p.139 Jennifer Bennett

p.140 Turid Forsyth
p.142-144 John Scanlan
p.145 Walter Chandoha
p.146-147 John Scanlan